A TROUBLED FEAST

A TROUBLED FEAST
American Society Since 1945

Updated Edition

WILLIAM E. LEUCHTENBURG
UNIVERSITY OF NORTH CAROLINA AT CHAPEL HILL

 LITTLE, BROWN AND COMPANY
Boston   Toronto

Library of Congress Cataloging in Publication Data

Leuchtenburg, William Edward, 1922–
  A troubled feast.

  Includes index.
  1. United States — Civilization — 1945–
I. Title.
E169.12.L46   1983   973.92   82-13991
ISBN 0-316-52188-4

Library of Congress Catalog Card No. 82-13991

ISBN 0-316-52188-4

9 8 7 6 5 4 3 2 1

VB

Published simultaneously in Canada
by Little, Brown & Company (Canada) Limited.

Printed in the United States of America

With the exception of pages 265–291, the text of this book originally appeared as Chapters 7 and 8 in *The Unfinished Century* (Boston: Little, Brown, 1973), William E. Leuchtenburg, General Editor. Pages 1–279 also appeared as *A Troubled Feast, Revised Edition* (Boston: Little, Brown, 1979), by William E. Leuchtenburg.

CREDITS AND ACKNOWLEDGMENTS

Part opening and closing photographs:

  Pages 2–3: Elliott Erwitt, Magnum
  Page 124: United Press International
  Pages 128–129: Wide World Photos
  Page 293: Peter Southwick from Stock, Boston

Permission to use excerpts from works by the following authors is gratefully acknowledged:

  W. H. AUDEN. Quotation on page 186 from "Whitsunday in Kirchstetten" from *Collected Poems* by W. H. Auden, edited by Edward Mendelson. Copyright © 1962 by W. H. Auden. Reprinted by permission of Random House, Inc. and Faber and Faber Ltd.

Credits and acknowledgments continue on page 294.

For Dot

Preface

Early in the spring of 1973, Little, Brown published *The Unfinished Century*, a multi-author account of twentieth-century America, under my editorship. Six of the eight extended essays in that volume were contributed by Richard M. Abrams, University of California, Berkeley; Stanley Coben, University of California, Los Angeles; Robert H. Ferrell, Indiana University; Otis L. Graham, Jr., University of California, Santa Barbara; David F. Trask, State University of New York, Stony Brook; and Samuel F. Wells, Jr., University of North Carolina, Chapel Hill. I wrote the two final essays, on the domestic history of the United States from the opening of the modern era in 1945 through the reelection of Richard Nixon in November 1972.

A Troubled Feast includes these two essays and, in addition, a coda on developments since the 1972 election. It seeks to fill a large gap in courses in the history of the United States by providing the first account of the national experience from 1945 to the present day.

The essence of this book is suggested by its title. The "troubled" aspects may well be the more familiar—the frightful assassinations of public men, the malignant effects of two Asian wars, the endemic violence, the persistence of social ills. Acknowledgment of the reality of the "feast"—that is, the widespread affluence made possible by the prodigious expansion of the economy—has often been more grudging. Yet in these years millions were lifted out of poverty, millions more into the ranks of the middle class. And it was the abundance that shaped many of the contours of American society in the nearly three decades since 1945, especially the consumer culture in its multifarious ramifications, and that exerted a decisive influence upon not only the troubles of this era but the too little noticed advances.

It is a pleasure to thank those who have assisted me in writing this book. I owe a very large debt to my co-authors in *The Unfinished Century*, who made numerous suggestions for improving the manuscript, and to the editors at Little, Brown, notably Charles H. Christensen, Jane E. Aaron, and Patricia Herbst, who labored tirelessly to get both books to press. John Chambers, an exceptionally resourceful and indefatigable associate on more than one enterprise, proved indispensable in locating and photocopying materials. My son Christopher Leuchtenburg rendered much appreciated aid in proofreading, and James Collins performed a number of chores in the final stages. I am grateful most of all to the one to whom this volume is dedicated, my sister Dorothy Ford, who at a time when she was carrying on a courageous battle against a serious illness cheerfully volunteered her help, and who has sustained me in this endeavor as she has in so many others throughout her life.

This second revision of *A Troubled Feast* carries the narrative from the second year of the Carter administration into the second year of the Reagan administration. I am indebted to Madelyn Leopold for supervising the production of this book.

W.E.L.

Contents

Maps, Charts, and Tables

A TROUBLED FEAST

Consumer Culture
and Cold War

In the summer of 1945 United States troop ships, carrying thousands of homeward-bound GI's from farflung battle fronts, steamed past the Statue of Liberty and up the Hudson River to be nudged into their berths on the New York waterfront. Aboard vessels like the majestic *Queen Mary*, jubilant soldiers and sailors howled with delight when they discerned the familiar tracery of the Manhattan skyline, and in the river fireboats sent geysers of water into the air as a signal of welcome. For some, the future seemed bright with promise. New York gave the triumphant commander, Dwight Eisenhower, arms raised above his head in a victory salute, a more tumultuous reception than had greeted Charles Lindbergh after his solo flight across the Atlantic in 1927, and the whole town of Farmersville,

Texas (pop. 2,206), turned out in 98-degree heat to hail the bashful
Lieutenant Audie Murphy, the infantry's most-decorated combat
officer. But others were advised painfully of the nation's shortcomings. The window of a gas station in McFarland, California,
greeted returning servicemen with a crudely lettered sign: "Colored
Trade Not Solisited at Fountain," and in other west coast towns
Japanese-American veterans, who had fought with conspicuous
bravery in Italy, were assaulted, denied jobs, often unable to recover
property which had been seized during the period of mass evacuation
and internment. Congressional Medal of Honor winner Charles
"Commando" Kelly came back to a Pittsburgh slum that lacked both
plumbing and lights, a grim reminder of how recently the scourge of
the Great Depression had ended.

As the veterans and their families tried to take the measure of the
future, they riveted their attention on the interwar years, little real-
izing that much of that recollection would be irrelevant to the postwar world. Often their questions went back to the 1920's, and they
wondered whether the country would regress to an era like that of
Harding and Coolidge, which had followed the first world war. Of
much greater immediacy were the issues surrounding the age of
Franklin D. Roosevelt. There were widespread forebodings that hard
times would soon return, for many doubted that the economy would
be able to absorb the 10 million war workers and the 12 million men
in the armed services. The experience of the 1930's also determined
post-1945 political alignments. Some hoped that the aggrandizement
of the presidency and the government intervention associated with
the New Deal would be halted; others looked forward to an extension
of liberal legislation or even a radical reordering of social institutions.
For years to come political debate would continue to revolve around
the quarrels of 1935, and the lineaments of the Roosevelt coalition
could still be seen in election returns in the 1970's.

Yet, however persistent, traditions of the Great Depression proved
less pertinent to the quarter-century following the war's end than
two other developments, the force of which was only dimly perceived in 1945 — the diffusion of affluence and the consumer culture
and the impact of the cold war in the shadow of the nuclear bomb.

Of all the influences on postwar America, none exceeded that
exerted by dramatic economic changes. Buoyed by consumer spending and bloated military budgets, the economy expanded in so explosive a fashion that the sociologist Seymour Martin Lipset could
claim, "The fundamental problems of the industrial revolution have
been solved." When the Harvard economist John Kenneth Galbraith

It's over! In New York's Times Square on V-J Day a sailor exploits the mood of celebration at the ending of World War II and the birth of the postwar era. The photograph is the work of Alfred Eisenstaedt, who came to the United States from Hitler Germany in 1935 and the following year pioneered the candid camera technique for the new magazine *Life*.

published *The Affluent Society* in 1958, he gave a name to a phenomenon that had been captivating writers on the United States for more than a decade. Never in the long annals of mankind had so many people in any nation enjoyed so high a level of prosperity, even though the impoverished continued to be numbered in the millions.

In the flush times of the postwar era, every standard by which Americans had measured material progress fell. Through the grim years of the Depression the country had yearned to reach once more the high plateau of 1929. But in 1956, the income of the average American was more than 50 percent greater than in 1929, even when allowance was made for increases in prices and taxes. By 1960, per capita income was 35 percent higher than in the war boom year of 1945. "The remarkable capacity of the United States economy in 1960," concluded the economic historian Harold G. Vatter, "represents the crossing of a great divide in the history of humanity."

This economic performance made possible the elaboration and diffusion of the consumer culture. With the nation at close to full employment, millions were freed from the anxieties about subsistence that had engrossed them in the 1930's, and manufacturers and advertising agencies encouraged the sovereign consumer to indulge his preoccupation with marginal differentiation of products. Much as life in medieval society centered around the religious observances of a cathedral town, postwar America became absorbed in the acquisition of goods and evolved a variety of institutions —from suburban supermarkets to gourmet food stores—that ministered to the shopper. Moreover, the consumer culture penetrated far beyond the shopping mall. Foreign countries that had earlier borrowed such American innovations as the assembly line and the skyscraper erected "Beba Coca Cola" signs, listened to Muzak, bought Colonel Sanders' Kentucky Fried Chicken, and became accustomed to wheeling carts laden with Campbell's soup and Quaker Oats through the aisles of the *supermarche* or *supermercado* or *supermarked*. Within the United States the consumer culture left its imprint on styles of travel and on modern art, on popular music and on presidential elections, even on the cold war.

America's role as the preeminent great power molded the United States in these years no less than did affluence and the consumer culture. In the midst of prosperity, there was always awareness of a dreadful apparition at the feast—the threat of nuclear holocaust. Secretary of War Henry Stimson predicted in 1945 that the Promethean feat of unlocking the secret of the atom would have "more effect on human affairs than the theory of Copernicus and the law of gravity," and some took pride in this latest of American technological achievements. But for many more the knowledge of Hiroshima meant that victory in World War II was, *Time* observed, "as charged with sorrow and doubt as with joy and gratitude." Man had bitten the

The cold war intrudes on the consumer society in Alan Dunn's
cartoon from a 1947 issue of *The
New Yorker*. While the periodical poked fun at cold war
America, its advertisements
were offering alluring images
of the consumer culture.

"Oh, dear, I'd really be enjoying all this if it weren't for Russia."
Drawing by Alan Dunn; © 1947, 1975. The New Yorker Magazine, Inc.

forbidden fruit, had found "the ultimate stuff of the universe," and
was troubled by his own temerity.

The post-Hiroshima generation felt a special awareness of im-
permanence and premonition of doom. Infants imbibed Strontium
90 with their morning milk, and pupils hunched under their desks
as air raid sirens wailed during drills. Years later students at San
Francisco State reported that nuclear bombs had exploded in their
dreams, and young children expressed Doomsday anxieties. In the
1960's the "post-Hiroshima" people would make a jukebox favorite
of P. F. Sloan's unsettling "Eve of Destruction":

> Don't you understand what I'm try'n' to say?
> Can't you feel the fear that I'm feelin' today?
> If the button is pushed there's no running away.

There'll be no one to save with the world in a grave.
Take a look around you boy,
It's bound to scare you boy. . . .

Yet, curiously, the cold war, for all its hideous menace, would serve to foster more benign developments — prosperity, social advances, and, most unexpectedly, the movement for greater equality. Although the "military-industrial complex" raised justifiable alarm, armaments expenditures provided the biggest impetus for the boom in the 1950's that lifted many above the poverty line. Economists spoke of the "Soviet effect," meaning the way in which compulsive American countermoves to Russian actions came to justify everything from increased spending on research and development to the construction of the St. Lawrence seaway to the breakthrough in federal aid to education. Most important, at a time when the United States vied with Soviet Russia for the allegiance of the peoples of Africa and Asia, American racial and religious mores came under close scrutiny.

Despite the rumblings of change during the Great Depression and in World War II, the United States in 1945 remained a country dominated by WASPs. Jews confronted covert discrimination in the professions and, when they sought to buy homes, blatant rejection through restrictive covenants in which Gentile home owners contracted to sell only to their own kind. Radio showed the man of color how the white world preferred him — the faithful, obedient servant of the Lone Ranger's Tonto and the Green Hornet's Kato, or a jovial retainer like Jack Benny's Rochester. In the South, Negroes rode in the back of the bus, most were disfranchised, and none went to school with whites. Apartheid prevailed in much of the North too. Even Topeka in John Brown's Kansas segregated schoolchildren by race. The greatest democracy on earth recruited a Jim Crow army, and as late as 1945 in the downtown section of the nation's capital Negroes could not stay at a hotel, eat at a drugstore lunch counter, or attend a movie.

These patterns of prejudice proved an intolerable burden for the United States in international affairs. World War II brought America face to face with the inconsistency between fighting a war for democracy against Hitler's master race state and condoning discrimination at home. During the war *Fortune* pointed out that "a fracas in Detroit has an echo in Aden," and in what Richard Dalfiume has called "the forgotten years" of the Negro revolution Gunnar Myrdal made the country aware of "the American dilemma." In the cold war era Washington would take pains to highlight racial advances. After the Supreme Court handed down a desegregation decision, the Voice of America broadcast the news in thirty-four languages all day and night and through the following day. The iron curtain countries in turn exploited evidence of persisting racial discrimination in the land of their cold war rival. When a United Nations committee voiced disapproval of the Russian invasion of Hungary, a Budapest newspaper invited the committee "to make a study trip up the Arkansas River." Signs of "a new world acoming" were increasingly evident even in 1945. That year Bess Myerson became the first Jewish Miss America, and Branch Rickey of the Brooklyn Dodgers signed up the sensational black shortstop of the Kansas City Monarchs, Jackie Robinson.

The cold war and the consumer culture also defined the parameters of American politics. Both sustained a politics of the center. Though the rivalry with Soviet Russia provided an occasion for ideologues of the Right who wanted to launch a crusade to exterminate the heretics, the peril of nuclear devastation motivated most of the Right to advocate a less extreme course. At the same time the actions of the U.S.S.R. in Poland, in Berlin, and in Hungary diminished the appeal of the fatherland of socialism to all but a small fringe on the Left. The cold war drove a wedge through the liberal movement, with one wing organized by the avowedly noncommunist Americans for Democratic Action in 1947 and a more leftist sector mobilized under Henry Wallace. Beginning in 1950, liberal influence was diminished by a frustrating limited war that spawned phenomena like McCarthyism and focused attention not on present needs but on bygone encounters with alleged subversives. Assertion of the superior claim of the national interest in the cold war militated against demands for costly social welfare legislation and subdued the ardor of the union movement. The consumer culture generated a politics of inflation that plagued the Democrats in the aftermath of World War II and during the Korean conflict. In 1946 the Republicans would win their only emphatic victory in congressional elections over a period of four decades in a contest affected by the irritation of housewives about the price of hamburger. More significantly, rising income and the enticements of the consumer culture kindled a sense of contentment that encouraged a politics of moderation.

Both of the first postwar Presidents, Harry Truman and Dwight Eisenhower, operated within the boundaries fixed by the consumer culture and the cold war. If in his first term Truman was disconcerted by ill-humored consumers, in his second term he was troubled by the imperatives of the cold war. In the 1948 election

Truman narrowly missed defeat because of the challenge from a
third party born of the cold war, and in 1952 the strains of limited
war would terminate the Democrats' twenty-year reign. The circumstances under which he functioned explain in part why Truman
was associated with, in Samuel Grafton's words, a "new centrism"
—"a strange combination of conservatism without animus and liberalism without glow." From necessity and conviction his successor,
General Eisenhower, did not stray far from the middle of the road.
"Never has a popular figure who dominated so completely the national political scene affected so negligibly the essential historic
processes of his time," observed the historian Norman Graebner.
Yet Eisenhower appeared to suit millions of Americans, for he was
credited with thawing the cold war and with a piping prosperity
that brought the consumer culture to fruition. His opponents readily adapted to the temperate environment. In 1956, Adlai Stevenson
said, "I agree that it is time for catching our breath; I agree that
moderation is the spirit of the times." Four years later, John F.
Kennedy concentrated his presidential campaign on suburban shopping centers, and when Norman Mailer decided to support him, he
entitled his essay, "Superman Comes to the Supermarket."

In this "post-industrial society," Americans turned away from
public issues to take up more personal matters—fitting together the
pieces of marriages sundered by the war, nest-building, nurturing
the psyche, enjoying the fruits of prosperity after the grinding years
of the Depression. At a time when Leonard Bernstein was scoring
a musical based on *Candide,* they heeded Voltaire's advice to cultivate their own gardens. Though critics found this society depress-
ingly homogenized, there was more diversity and creativity than
they conceded, in art and in the theater, in popular culture and in the
university, even in life styles. As early as 1948, with the publication
of Dr. Alfred C. Kinsey's *Sexual Behavior in the Human Male,* the
nation was made keenly aware of divergent standards of behavior.
Furthermore, reformers could point to a number of accomplishments—Truman's Fair Deal, Eisenhower's acceptance of a good part
of the New Deal, the dedicated leadership of Adlai Stevenson, and,
most particularly, the passive resistance movement of Martin Luther
King and the pathbreaking decisions of the Supreme Court under
the new Chief Justice, Earl Warren. But, overall, it was not a period
hospitable to agitation for fundamental change. Having known more
than fifteen years of crisis in depression and war, the nation rejected
the politics of intensity much as it had in the 1920's. By the close of

the Eisenhower era, Adlai Stevenson was stating that "for the first time in history the engine of social progress has run out of the fuel of discontent," and Walter Lippmann commented, "We talk about ourselves these days as if we were a completed society, one which has no further great business to transact."

The Man from Missouri

The death of Franklin D. Roosevelt on April 12, 1945, catapulted into the White House a man of very different background and temperament. In contrast to Roosevelt's patrician upbringing as the young squire of Hyde Park destined for Groton and Harvard, Harry

The first postwar President, Harry S. Truman, is caught with a characteristic grin. He attracted admirers by his openness and geniality as well as by his courage. In 1948 he made the transcontinental train part of American political folklore in his cross-country campaign against the Republicans.

United Press International

Truman's youth was spent in a small Missouri town where his father was a mule swapper. Shriner, Moose, Elk, Lion, Eagle, deacon of the Second Baptist Church, Truman traveled in circles far removed from FDR's *haut monde.* Roosevelt first won national attention as a foe of Tammany Hall. Truman—World War I artillery captain, consumer culture failure as haberdasher, courthouse politician—made his way under the tutelage of the notorious Kansas City boss Tom Pendergast. In 1934, Pendergast decided to send Truman to the United States Senate, where he became an obscure back-bencher. Even after he had won respect as the head of a watchdog committee in World War II and was elected Vice-President in 1944, he remained outside the main councils of government, and not until after he assumed the presidency was he briefed about the atomic bomb. To this man fell the awesome responsibility of persuading the country, and the world, that he could cope with the demands of the office that FDR had held for more than twelve years.

Truman brought to this task a mixed assortment of talents, sentiments, and personal qualities. None doubted his grit. He made bold decisions quickly and executed them briskly. However, he also was generally unreflective, sometimes cocky and brash. Determined to carry on the New Deal tradition, he sent Congress a twenty-one-point program that included liberal reforms just four days after the Japanese surrender. Yet he lacked the grand vision necessary to inspire a nation, and he appointed to office lackluster plodders who suffered by comparison with the New Deal luminaries. "It is more important to have a connection with Battery D, 129th Field Artillery, than with Felix Frankfurter," remarked one commentator. To FDR loyalists Truman never measured up. Each time he acted they would ask, "What would Roosevelt have done if he were alive?" (At the outset of his tenure, Truman himself consulted his predecessor's widow, observed Joseph and Stewart Alsop, "as he might have consulted a medium.") As late as January 1947, Fiorello La Guardia, the former New York mayor, said of Roosevelt: "How we miss him. Hardly a domestic problem or an international situation today but what we say 'Oh, if F.D.R. were only here.'"

Throughout his presidency, Truman lived in Roosevelt's shadow, but those who compared him to Roosevelt often did him less than justice. Truman benefited from the legacy the New Deal left him— an ideology of sorts, a legislative agenda, a corps of experienced administrators, an expansive view of the executive office, an effective electoral coalition of low-income voters in the great cities. But

FDR's admirers sometimes forgot that their leader had been fought to a standstill by the conservatives in Congress in recent years. Truman inherited the same opponents and had to work in an atmosphere that was not conducive to reform. His main assignment was to adapt the liberalism of the Great Depression to an age of economic growth and to make way for the newer emphases of the consumer culture, the cold war, and the civil rights revolution. In carrying out this task, he often met with setbacks. Still, a poll of historians would subsequently put him in the "near great" category of Presidents, for reasons best stated by Elmer Davis: "There are two Trumans—the White House Truman and the courthouse Truman. He does the big things right, and the little things wrong."

Hardly more than four months after Truman took office, the war ended, and the new President confronted the first of the "big things"—reconversion from a war to a peace economy. The job had been bungled after World War I, and many thought it would be again. Since the New Deal, government had become more humane, and measures like the GI Bill of Rights spared veterans the travail of the aftermath to 1918. But there was a more pertinent worry—that the economy, denied the artificial stimulus of war, would rapidly return to the massive unemployment of the Great Depression. Within a week after V-J Day, the Springfield Arsenal fired every employee, and across the country a million workers drew their final paychecks. Abruptly, contracts worth $35 billion were canceled. The mobilization director foresaw 8 million jobless by spring. However, the economy swiftly absorbed the millions of returning servicemen, and in a remarkably short time the reconversion had been achieved, although not until 1950 did real GNP reach its wartime high. This accomplishment owed a good deal to the fact that the American consumer came out of the war with a bulging wallet and a frustrated yen for goods that had too long been unavailable.

Yet this same consumer demand threatened to undermine these feats by creating a runaway inflation, and when Truman attempted to limit price rises, he precipitated a keen debate over the role of government in the postwar world. Businessmen, after more than a decade of regulation, wanted to lift the wartime controls, and they won backing from consumers weary of ration coupons and shortages. On the other hand, New Deal liberals saw need of more intervention from Washington and feared that a premature ending of controls would injure unorganized groups.

As the debate raged, every interest sought to protect itself, but the press focused the greatest attention on action by labor unions. In April 1945, when Truman took office, strikes devoured 1.5 million man-days; in September, 4 million; by February 1946, 23 million. Unions, smarting under the cut in take-home pay resulting from the ending of war industry overtime, insisted that wage increases were necessary to maintain real income. Their critics countered that wage boosts were driving prices up. Each group—business, labor, farm—demanded that the President clamp a bit on the others while giving it free rein.

Truman now confronted a problem that Roosevelt had not had to take on in the New Deal years. The historian Barton J. Bernstein has written, "Whereas the politics of depression generally allowed the Roosevelt Administration, by bestowing benefits, to court interest groups and contribute to an economic upturn, the politics of inflation required a responsible government like Truman's to curb wages, prices, and profits and to deny the growing expectations of rival groups." Roosevelt had faced this difficulty in World War II, but he could appeal to patriotism for sacrifices in the common cause. With V-J Day, these compunctions ended, and Truman was put in the unhappy position of trying to restrain not only businessmen, most of whom were in the Republican camp, but the farmer and labor elements in his own Democratic coalition. The President's troubles reached a climax in May 1946 when he asked Congress for authority to draft rail strikers into the army. Nothing came of this, but while failing to appease conservatives, his action served to hasten the defection of liberals and unionists from the administration. A CIO conference denounced Truman as the country's "No. 1 Strikebreaker."

By the time the first postwar elections were held in November 1946, Truman had been victimized by the politics of the pressure group state. When Congress in the summer of 1946 refused to grant him adequate price control powers, he found himself in a tiger's cage equipped with a cap pistol. Housewives blamed him when there was no meat on the butcher's counter and again when it appeared but at astronomical prices. A New York *Daily News* headline read:

PRICES SOAR, BUYERS SORE
STEERS JUMP OVER THE MOON.

During the campaign, Republicans derided "Horsemeat Harry" and jeered, "To err is Truman," and in Massachusetts Joe Martin, destined to become Speaker of the House, promised consumers that he would "take the meddling hands of political despots out of the kitchens of America." On election day, the GOP won decisive control of the House, as well as a narrow margin in the Senate. Democrats like J. William Fulbright of Arkansas recommended that Truman, having lost a vote of confidence, resign from office immediately and give way to a Republican. Henceforth, Truman referred to him as "Senator Halfbright."

The Eightieth Congress, that much disparaged progeny of the 1946 election, pushed aside Truman's recommendations for new social legislation and set out to repeal the New Deal. Since 1938 a bipartisan conservative coalition had blocked liberal endeavors. Now its ranks were swelled by Republican newcomers such as Joseph R. McCarthy of Wisconsin in the Senate and Richard M. Nixon of California in the House. The Eightieth Congress voted a "soak-the-poor" tax proposal, cut funds for rural electrification and crop storage, and enacted a displaced persons measure discriminating against Catholics and Jews. Under Robert Taft, the brilliant but often parochial captain of the Senate Republicans, Congress adopted a law, over Truman's veto, that made the first serious modification of the 1935 Wagner Act, the law that had put the weight of government behind efforts at unionization. The Taft-Hartley Act prohibited secondary boycotts, jurisdictional walkouts, and the closed shop; it increased the legal responsibility of unions and authorized the President to seek injunctions to delay strikes for eighty days. The cold war made its presence felt in the requirement that union officials file affidavits that they were not Communist Party officials or affiliated with any subversive organization. Hardly the "slave labor law" union leaders branded it, the statute did impede organizing drives for new recruits. In the same year, the Eightieth Congress approved the Twenty-second Amendment (ratified in 1951), which limited the President to two terms, "a belated act of vengeance" against FDR's Long Presidency.

Truman grappled with the Eightieth Congress not just over the legacy of the New Deal but about a new concern that had not found a place on Roosevelt's "must" list—civil rights for the Negro. In December 1946, following an outcry over vicious racial murders in the South, he appointed a President's Committee on Civil Rights, which on October 29, 1947, issued a magisterial report, "To Secure These Rights." On February 2, 1948, Truman sent a message to Congress calling for the implementation of the committee's precepts through measures such as a Fair Employment Practices Act. These propositions failed to win substantial Republican support, and southern Democrats were outraged. "Not since the first gun was fired on Fort Sumter, resulting as it did in the greatest fratricidal strife in the history of the world, has any message of any President of these glorious United States . . . resulted in the driving of a schism in the ranks of our people, as did President Truman's so-called civil rights message," protested Representative William M. Colmer of Mississippi. "No President, either Democrat or Republican, has ever seen fit heretofore to make such recommendations."

The controversy over the President's civil rights message appeared to remove any lingering doubt that Truman would go down to defeat in the 1948 elections. Truman's contingent of liberal advisers headed by Clark Clifford stressed the importance of appealing to black voters and claimed that the President could do this without risk because the South, "safely Democratic," could be "safely ignored." But it soon became clear that politicians in the Deep South were bitterly disaffected. Scared by the prospect of a rupture in Democratic ranks, the administration sought to moderate its stand on civil rights. At the nominating convention in Philadelphia, however, a liberal element organized by Americans for Democratic Action and supported by urban bosses upset these plans. Under the leadership of the young mayor of Minneapolis, Hubert H. Humphrey, they drove through a strong civil rights plank. Waving the battle flag of the Confederacy, Mississippi and Alabama delegates marched out in protest. Three days later a convention of States Rights Democrats, meeting in Birmingham, chose Governor J. Strom Thurmond of South Carolina as the presidential nominee of the bolting "Dixiecrats." Truman's hold on the "Solid South" was in peril.

While the civil rights dispute was cutting off a segment of the Democratic Party's right wing, the cold war was threatening to split off the left wing of the Democrats. In September 1946, Truman had fired his secretary of commerce, Henry A. Wallace, widely regarded as the main legatee of the Roosevelt tradition and more recently a critic of the administration's "get-tough-with-Russia" policy, in so inept a manner that *Time* accused the President of "a clumsy lie." At the end of 1947, Wallace announced he was taking leave of the Democrats. "There is no real fight between a Truman and a Republican," Wallace said. "Both stand for a policy which opens the door to war in our lifetime and makes war certain for our children." Seven months later, his supporters formed the Progressive Party and selected him their standard-bearer. Wallace's campaign of opposition to the cold war and advocacy of social reform, featuring rousing rallies at which singers like Paul Robeson and Pete Seeger performed, appealed especially to the big-city voters who believed that Truman was betraying FDR's ideals. Early polls showed that Wallace had put in jeopardy Truman's chances of holding the large bloc of states in which the big-city vote was pivotal. Given the defection of both wings of the Democrats, the Republican nominee, New York's Governor Thomas E. Dewey, was so certain of victory that he leaked his Cabinet choices to reporters. And the reporters, the columnists, the experts, "everyone," knew that Dewey would win in a canter.

Everyone but Truman and his liberal advisers. The Clifford circle argued that the President could beat Dewey by stressing his adherence to the New Deal tradition and by concentrating his campaign on the metropolitan areas that had given Roosevelt success. Truman agreed. He took off on a transcontinental give-'em-hell-Harry jaunt in which he blasted the do-nothing, good-for-nothing Eightieth Congress and told farmers and workers they would be ingrates if they did not vote Democratic. "If you send another Republican Congress to Washington," he would tell his audience, "you're a bigger bunch of suckers than I think you are." And the crowd would yell back, "Pour it on, Harry!" Dewey, in deliberate contrast, ran a restrained campaign, "with the humorless calculation of a Certified Public Accountant in pursuit of the Holy Grail." Nonetheless, George Gallup, Elmo Roper, and the other pollsters all agreed that Dewey could not lose.

On election day, Truman scored the biggest upset victory in American history, rolling up 24.1 million votes (49.5 percent) to Dewey's 22 million (45.1 percent) and a more emphatic 303 to 189 in the Electoral College; Thurmond's 1.2 million total gained him 39 of Dixie's electoral votes, all but one of them from four Deep South states in which he captured the Democratic Party's symbol. As V. O. Key, Jr., has shown, Thurmond ran best in counties of high black concentration (and high black disfranchisement), the area that had been fire-eating secessionist in 1861 but had stayed loyal to the Democrats in 1928 when parts of the upper South bolted. Wallace, with the same popular tally as Thurmond, did not break into the electoral column. He was embarrassed by the Communist coterie in the party and by the Soviet coup in Czechoslovakia and was undercut by Truman's liberal deeds. The President's party scored well in other races, too. Elected to the Senate in 1948 for the first time were Democrats Humphrey of Minnesota, Estes Kefauver of Tennessee, and, by eighty-seven votes, "Landslide Lyndon" B.

Election of 1948

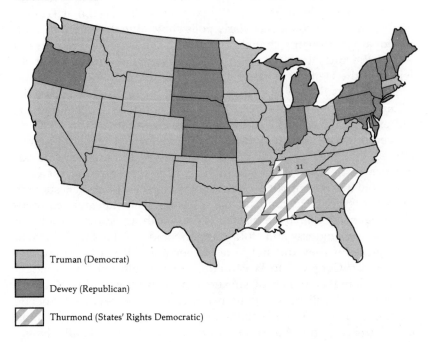

Truman (Democrat)

Dewey (Republican)

Thurmond (States' Rights Democratic)

Johnson of Texas; to the House from the St. Paul district came Eugene McCarthy; new governors included Adlai Stevenson in Illinois and Chester Bowles in Connecticut. Stunned by the surprising outcome, Gallup, said an election night reporter, looked "like an animal eating its young." In Chicago an elderly lady, disillusioned with the polls, was heard to tell her companion on a bus, "Now I don't know whether to believe even the Kinsey report."

The results were a tribute to Truman's spunk, but they demonstrated even more the tenacity of New Deal alignments. The 1948 contest was, in the terminology of the Survey Research Center at the University of Michigan, a "maintaining election" in which "the pattern of partisan attachments prevailing in the preceding period persists, and the majority party wins the Presidency." In a match marked by low turnout and sharp class cleavage, Truman won by mustering enough of the old Roosevelt following in Negro and labor precincts in industrial cities as well as by winning farmers angry at the performance of the Eightieth Congress. Truman ran particularly well, Richard Kirkendall has written, among those who "had recently joined a new, blue-collar middle class" and "were grateful to the Democrats for their prosperity and looked to them for the preservation of it." Although new preoccupations—the cold war and the civil rights revolution—had begun to make their way, memories of the Depression continued to dominate American politics.

President for the first time in his own right, Truman told the new Congress that "every segment of our population and every individual has a right to expect from his government a fair deal." To some observers, the Fair Deal seemed little more than a warmed-over version of the New Deal, with the same reliance on federal action to aid the identical elements who had benefited before, and Truman's tenure was categorized as "Roosevelt's Fifth Term." The Eighty-first Congress adopted more progressive legislation than any Congress since 1938, but, save for a rare exception like the legislation creating the National Science Foundation, the new acts were chiefly extensions of New Deal statutes—expansion of social security and minimum wage provisions, conservation and public power ventures, and a big low-cost housing and slum clearance program. The Fair Deal differed from the New Deal chiefly in the fact that it concerned itself with an economy of abundance rather than depression and that it embraced proposals the New Deal had not included or had given only minor attention. Among these were civil rights legislation, national health insurance, federal aid to education, and the "Brannan Plan" of Secretary of Agriculture Charles F. Brannan for a system of crop subsidies that would serve both the family farmer and the urban consumer. But on all these more novel Fair Deal measures, the President met defeat.

Truman's experience proved characteristic of this whole period, for in the quarter-century after 1938, Congress enacted almost no innovative legislation. It might amplify New Deal statutes, as by raising the minimum wage a few cents, but essentially it was living off the heritage of the 1930's. Occasionally a new principle would win limited approval—maximum employment in the badly gutted Employment Act of 1946, some modest civil rights legislation in the late 1950's—but that happened only rarely. Both conservatives and liberals were frustrated by this "politics of dead center." The strength of liberal Democrats, especially in the Senate, impeded most efforts by the right to repeal the New Deal. Neither could the liberals make headway against the pivotal bipartisan conservative coalition and the formidable obstacle course in Congress—malapportioned representation that overweighted rural areas opposed to spending for the urban masses, arbitrary committee chairmen, the filibuster, seniority rule, and the balky Rules Committee.

The stalemate owed something, too, to changes in the liberal persuasion. The revelation of human depravity at Belsen and Buchenwald, the mass deaths in Soviet Russia, the incineration of Dresden and Hiroshima, all shook faith in the onward march of progress. These events sensitized people to the complicity in evil of men of goodwill. The power of TVA's Norris Dam, wrote the poet Selden Rodman, stoked "the atomic ovens at Oak Ridge," and Buchenwald "lay in the beech forest where Goethe walked." Reformers found the old liberal texts less relevant than the "tough-minded" theology of moral ambiguity of Reinhold Niebuhr or the tortured novels and stories of Franz Kafka. Because collectivism in Soviet Russia had become associated with the barbarities of the secret police and because nationalization in Britain was not bringing a new Jerusalem, liberals became less certain that extending the power of the State was the answer to every social problem, but they were puzzled about where else to turn. The international situation also had a chastening effect, both because progressives shared a number of cold war assumptions and because the recognition that one hyped-up ideologue could blow the world to bits added to their distrust of thoroughgoing solutions. This set of influences helped persuade them to temper their criticism of the American system. Reflecting on the common sense of a people who understood the wisdom of pragmatic responses to problems, Daniel Boorstin, who in the 1930's had been a radical, lauded *The Genius of American Politics,* a politics of accommodation rather than doctrinal excess. Although still wistful for the era of Franklin Roosevelt, they became more appreciative of battlers like Harry Truman, whose struggle with Congress was waged against uneven odds but who managed nonetheless to chalk up small gains that expanded "the vital center."

Despite their uneasiness about unbridled governmental authority, liberals continued to believe in a potent presidency, and they admired the use Truman made of his executive powers, especially in civil rights. He was first to appoint a Negro to the federal bench, and he strengthened the civil rights division of the Department of Justice. His attorney general filed briefs *amici curiae* in support of endeavors by the National Association for the Advancement of Colored People to end segregation in the schools (an undertaking that would bear fruit after Truman left office) and to wipe out judicial enforcement of restrictive covenants, an action that led to a notable victory in the Supreme Court in 1948. Above all, he put the cold war to advantage by stepping up the pace of desegregation of the armed forces.

The executive office expanded significantly in the Truman years, even during the Eightieth Congress, in part as a consequence of the cold war. By January 1947 the President was sending Congress three separate messages—state of the union, budget, and economic report—the last of these as a result of the Employment Act of 1946, which also created a three-man Council of Economic Advisers charged with keeping a weather eye on the economy. Congress unified the armed forces under the newly established post of secretary of defense, set up an Atomic Energy Commission with civilian control, and, ironically, added to the President's authority over industrial relations by enacting the Taft-Hartley law. Truman took full advantage of these new grants of power and in addition reorganized some parts of the executive branch along lines suggested by a commission headed by Herbert Hoover. He stoutly resisted encroachments by Congress on his prerogatives and vetoed more bills than any two-term predecessor. "I mean to pass this office on to my successor unimpaired," Truman said.

Yet it was an assertion of presidential power that greatly eroded Truman's authority in his last years in office. By resolving to intervene in Korea in June 1950, he appropriated from Congress the right to declare war and in doing so opened up a hornets' nest. When North Korean and Red Chinese soldiers were killing young Americans in Asian rice paddies, those who warned of the Communist menace at home found a more attentive audience, and the news media shifted their focus from the White House to the klieg-lighted committee rooms on Capitol Hill. The accusation that the Truman administration, despite its willingness to fight in Korea, had been "soft on communism" served the Republicans as a bludgeon in the 1950 campaign. When the returns were in, the Democrats had sustained enough losses to end hopes for the passage of Fair Deal legislation, quite apart from the fact that the costs of the war served as a convenient excuse for not embarking on expensive new programs. Moreover, the war fueled an inflationary boom that irritated consumers. When Truman tried to halt a price rise in the critical steel sector by seizing the mills in the midst of a labor dispute, the Supreme Court, in the *Youngstown Sheet and Tube* case, invalidated his edict as presidential lawmaking, a decision that former FDR brain-truster Rexford G. Tugwell called "perhaps the most serious setback the presidency has ever suffered."

The "police action" in Korea provided the occasion, too, on April 11, 1951, for Truman's firing of General of the Army Douglas Mac-Arthur as supreme commander of United Nations forces. After the general, who opposed the strategy of limited war and claimed "there is no substitute for victory," politicked with Republican leaders in Congress, the President concluded that he could "no longer tolerate his insubordination." Liberals believed that Truman had made a necessary move in defense of the presidency against one whose flamboyant manner sometimes gave the impression that he fancied himself as a man on horseback. The liberal editor Freda Kirchwey wrote that the dismissal had "ended a very present threat of Bonapartism." However, the "Asiafirsters," who had long been convinced that the United States should force a showdown in the Far East, and those who would brook no compromise in the struggle with the Communist world were outraged. Senator McCarthy called the President a "son of a bitch" and blamed the deed on a White House cabal stoned on "bourbon and benzedrine." Communications to the executive office ran 20 to 1 against Truman, and from Cape Cod to California flags flew at half-mast. After a congressional hearing revealed that all three chiefs of staff disputed MacArthur's contention that it was preferable to have a wider conflict, the controversy simmered down. But it had cost the President valuable political capital and placed in greater danger his party's twenty-year tenure.

History has been kinder to Harry Truman than his contemporaries ever were. No aftermath of a great war is ever easy. In retrospect, though, it was acknowledged that this "highly successful Andrew Johnson," to use Clinton Rossiter's phrase, had kept the reform tradition intact and even strengthened it. Truman encountered many reverses, but he at least raised new public issues that two decades later would still form part of the agenda of Lyndon Johnson's Great Society. Yet Truman left office in ill repute, his legislative proposals stalemated, his administration embroiled in rancorous disputes, his country bogged down in a land war in Asia. The revelation that an applicant for a government loan had helped the wife of a loan examiner acquire a fur coat and that the President's military aide had accepted a deep-freeze unit enabled Republicans to talk about "the mess in Washington" and made household words of "mink coat" and "deep freeze," early artifacts of the effect of the consumer culture on politics. In the spring of 1952, Truman's popularity rating in the polls plunged to the all-time low of 26 percent. No longer did the President have the stature to unify the nation.

Truman would be the first twentieth-century President, unhappily not the last, to learn the cost of fighting a limited war.

The Cold War in America

The cold war and America's role as an imperial nation affected the country in a multitude of ways. The economy was stimulated, and warped, by munitions spending; political currents were rechanneled by the perception that the Democrats were the "war party"; Senator McCarthy exploited cold war anxieties about national security; and the peacetime draft became an accepted feature of American life. The civil rights movement enjoyed the not inconsiderable benefit of the argument that the United States, as the leader of the free world, could not tolerate the blot of racial discrimination on its escutcheon. The Point Four program of United States aid to underdeveloped nations gave literature a new kind of protagonist in *The Ugly American* of Eugene Burdick and William J. Lederer and *The Quiet American* of the British novelist Graham Greene. In 1950 the country whistled the number 3 hit, the "Third Man Theme." And when sports writers matched the U.S.A. bag of gold medals against the U.S.S.R. total, Olympic games served as surrogate battlefields.

The United States rapidly assumed a more imperial style, as befit a republic that was, in Robinson Jeffers' phrase, "heavily thickening into empire." Even the symbol of discharge from the armed services was modeled on a bas-relief from Trajan's Forum in Rome. "As far as the Free World was concerned," the British historian H. G. Nicholas later wrote of the United States, "her shoulders held the sky suspended." In the prewar era, "empire" often suggested little more than a concern about the Caribbean, but in his report on the Potsdam Conference, President Truman discussed the Kiel Canal and the Far East, the Danube and the Dardanelles. United States proconsuls took up their stations in occupied Germany and Japan, and to house the envoys of the world's greatest power appropriately, architects such as Edward Stone in the 1950's designed embassies like the magnificent edifice in New Delhi, a work that asserted the mission of a society of untold wealth.

The country's move away from isolationism was accompanied too by a more cosmopolitan sensibility. World War II had uprooted millions of Americans and brought them in intimate contact with the culture of alien societies—New Guinea, the Aleutians, Tunisia,

In *Echo*, a 1951 work, Jackson Pollock swirls black paint across raw canvas, in what one critic
described as "violently interwoven movement," to induce a sense of perpetual motion and
limitless possibilities, qualities that foreign critics judged typically American. "If Pollock
were a Frenchman," wrote Clement Greenberg after viewing the show in which *Echo*
appeared, "people would already be calling him '*maître.*' " Born on a ranch in Cody, Wyoming,
in 1912, Pollock died in an automobile crash at East Hampton, Long Island, in 1956.

Lombardy—and the postwar world bore the mark of this experience.
The representative theme of the American novel of the late 1940's
was the Young Man from the Provinces trying to adapt to Old World
ways; the spread of Zen Buddhism in the 1950's reflected, in part,
the acculturation of occupation forces in Japan; and a critic observed less "aggressive nativeness" in American poetry after the

war. When a reporter toured the country in 1947, he found that hundreds of people to whom he spoke agreed with the wife of a trolley repairman in a small Indiana town who said, "I believe that talk about Europe is in every household now."

As the capital of the art world moved from Paris to New York, American painters turned their backs on the "corn belt academy" of Thomas Hart Benton, Grant Wood, and John Steuart Curry, who had won favor during the Depression by exploring indigenous subjects. Like their counterparts among poets, notably W. S. Merwin and Richard Wilbur, artists such as Mark Rothko evinced more interest in themes from mythology having a universal significance. Benton's student, Jackson Pollock, who was deeply affected by the migration to the United States of European surrealists, protested: "The idea of an isolated American painting, so popular in this country during the thirties, seems absurd to me just as the idea of creating a purely American mathematics or physics would seem absurd." Benton himself realized that the struggle had been lost. "Wood, Curry, and I found the bottom knocked out from under us," he wrote. "In a day when the problems of America were mainly exterior, our interior images lost public significance."

The cold war had its most direct and far-reaching effect on America in the enormous increase in military spending and the rise of "the military-industrial complex." After V-J Day, the yearning to go back to peacetime pursuits was so intense that troops at Pacific bases rioted and thousands of GI's marched down the Champs Elysées crying, "We wanna go home." Within a year an army of 8 million had been reduced to 1.5 million. Some even hoped that the United States could return to the situation of the 1930's when the air corps flew less than a thousand planes and the American army, with fewer than 135,000 soldiers, including Philippine Scouts, ranked seventeenth in the world. However, with the onset of the cold war, as well as of the costs of occupation, defense expenditures in 1947 were already up to nearly $14 billion a year. Still, Truman was scolded for putting a ceiling on such spending of "only" one-third of the government's budget. With the outbreak of the Korean War, the country quickly pushed through the ceiling to $44 billion (67 percent) in 1952. Although the outlays diminished after a truce was negotiated in Korea, they continued at a high level.

The United States by the mid-1950's nurtured 40,000 "prime" defense contractors and hundreds of thousands of lesser ones. A company like AC Spark Plug, once innocent of military affairs, turned out the internal power system for the *Thor* missile, and concerns that made goods not usually thought of as martial hardware—cloth and shovels—came to regard the Department of Defense as an important customer. During the 1960's, half of the government's money would go to military purposes, and by 1970 the Department of Defense had greater assets than the nation's seventy-five largest industrial corporations, employed nearly as many people as the top thirty firms, and was spending more than did the entire national government before the Depression.

Many communities and even whole regions of the country depended on the boon of the weapons industry. California thrived on Lockheed, Seattle on the contracts let to Boeing; in Georgia the payroll of one aircraft factory amounted to half of the value of the state's cotton crop. The Pentagon found that if it decided to cancel a defense contract or close down an unneeded base, the plan was met with howls of indignation from the citizens of the community. Congressmen made their reputations by securing juicy military contracts as once they had by gaining appropriations for rivers and harbors. Henry Jackson from the state of Washington was known as the "Senator from Boeing," and Richard B. Russell and Carl Vinson teamed up to cram twenty military installations into Georgia. But none matched the South Carolinian who would become chairman of the House Armed Services Committee, Lucius Mendel Rivers. That ardent defender of the Pentagon and advocate of hot war saw to it that his district housed an army depot, an air force base, a marine corps training center, a coast guard mine-warfare operation, and a navy shipyard, supply center, and weapons station, as well as defense plants with hundreds of millions of dollars in contracts. His predecessor as chairman of the committee, Carl Vinson, warned him, "You put anything else down there in your district, Mendel, it's gonna sink."

Radical critics perceived these arrangements not as a response to the challenge to security posed by the Communist powers but rather as evidence of the sickness of the capitalist system. In an article in *Politics* in 1944, Walter Oakes had predicted that the United States would develop a "permanent war economy," because capitalists preferred military public works to the perils of mass unemployment, and in 1961 Fred J. Cook delineated the creation of the "Warfare State." Arthur Selwyn Miller expressed concern over "the Techno-Corporate State" and H. L. Nieburg about the "contract state," which he characterized as "a fundamentally new economic system which at once resembles traditional private enterprise and the

Hank Walker. © 1953 Time Inc.

The viceroy of the Warfare State. For the post of Secretary of Defense, President Eisenhower named Charles E. Wilson, the president of General Motors, an appointment that personified the military-industrial complex. So often did Wilson embarrass the administration with indiscreet statements that reporters said that he suffered from "hoof-in-mouth-disease."

corporate state of fascism." Such critics noted the nexus between military expenditures and prosperity. One analyst stated flatly: "So long as relations between the U.S.S.R. and the U.S. are bad, military electronics will be a good business"; he added that a sudden thaw "would hit the industry very hard." During the Korean War, the gross national product soared; after military spending was cut back abruptly, a recession ensued.

When President Eisenhower left the White House in January 1961 he unexpectedly lent his great prestige to the argument that the United States was imperiled by these new developments. In his farewell address, he warned of "the conjunction of an immense military establishment and a large arms industry," a new phenomenon whose "total influence is felt in every city." He cautioned, "We must guard against the acquisition of unwarranted influence by the military-industrial complex."

If there was reason enough for grave concern about the military-industrial complex, those who pictured the United States as a "warfare state" painted with too broad a brush. Even in 1969 during the Vietnam War, 91 percent of the GNP went to nonmilitary spending. The rearmament program owed more to anxiety about Russian warheads and hydrogen bombs than it did to the frailty of the capitalist economy. In 1950, the United States had one tank division, the U.S.S.R. thirty, and the Russian army had four times more soldiers than the American army. By 1949 the Soviet Union had the A-bomb, by 1953 the H-bomb, and in October 1961 it exploded a nuclear device almost three thousand times as powerful as the Hiroshima bomb. Under these circumstances, no American President could have maintained popular support if he did not endeavor to match the Russians. While many undoubtedly thrived on the arms race, swollen military budgets represented less the machinations of malevolent men than the obsessions of ideological conflict, the tragic incapacity of nation-states to develop institutions of accommodation, and the headlong pace of technology that made costly weapons systems obsolete before they left the factory. Unhappily, each escalation of the arms race served to raise the level of terror and to make genuine world security still less attainable.

The cold war also gave the United States a new, and for many unwelcome, departure—the permanent peacetime draft. The draft card would become a young American's proof of identity and even of manhood, the palpable evidence that he had advanced beyond puberty and, in New York at least, was aged enough to buy a can of beer. Adopted briefly in 1946, the draft expired a year later, only to be reintroduced again in 1948 after the Communist coup in Prague. At first controversial, selective service legislation became so accepted that in 1963 the Senate devoted only ten minutes of debate to it before voting to renew authorization. Lewis B. Hershey, the general who headed what was ostensibly a civilian operation, even represented the draft to be an essential step in acquiring a sense of nationality. "Outside the income tax," he observed, "there aren't many things to make the male citizen feel much responsibility to his government any more. Selective Service is one of them." In truth, the draft did serve as a nationalizing force, pulling young men out of towns across the land and fitting them in olive drab at camps from Dix to Ord, speeding the desegregation of American life by throwing together boys from Tennessee farms and Chicago's black ghetto.

The cold war had one of its most venomous influences on American society in a phenomenon named for the junior Senator from Wisconsin—McCarthyism. In fact, the alarm over Communist subversion preceded the 1950 Lincoln's birthday speech in Wheeling that first brought Joe McCarthy to prominence. What Robert Griffith has called "the anti-Communist persuasion," the mindless conviction that all social change is the result of alien radical conspiracies, had a history as old as the republic. In the twentieth century, a "Red Scare" had sent tremors through the country during the aftermath of World War I and again, though in a much more muted form, in the Depression. Well before McCarthy seized upon the Communist issue, it had served the purposes of foes of reform, particularly the Republicans. Ever since its establishment in 1938, the House Committee on Un-American Activities had been a sounding board for the imputation that the New Deal had taken a long step on the road to Moscow. In the postwar period the cold war added plausibility to the view that the United States faced a serious threat from subversives within the government who were in league with Communist powers and movements abroad. When the State Department announced in 1949 both that Soviet Russia had the "secret" of the A-bomb and that China had "fallen," Republicans charged that traitorous architects of America's Far Eastern policy were to blame.

Furthermore, a series of shocking disclosures gave at least a semblance of credibility to some of these charges. Concern mounted from 1945 when a huge cache of purloined diplomatic documents was discovered in the offices of the magazine *Amerasia* to the announcement early in 1950 that the British physicist Klaus Fuchs, who had worked at Los Alamos, had confessed passing information on the atomic bomb to the Russians. For their part in this conspiracy, two Americans, Julius and Ethel Rosenberg, would subsequently be executed. Arthur Miller's drama *The Crucible,* about the Salem "witches," was understood to be a parable for the persecution of the innocent in modern America, and unhappily "witch hunt" was an apt metaphor for much that took place in the 1940's and 1950's. But it is sometimes forgotten that while the witches in seventeenth-century New England are presumed to have been illusory, McCarthyism thrived on the fact that there were real Communist plotters in the United States, though their menace was fearfully exaggerated.

The most consequential episode began in August 1948 when Whittaker Chambers, *Time* magazine's senior editor, told the House Committee on Un-American Activities that Alger Hiss, the president of the Carnegie Endowment for International Peace and a former State Department official, had been a member of the Communist Party. Since the unprepossessing Chambers produced little to back up these charges, and since the committee had often served as a forum for false accusations, President Truman seemed right to dismiss the allegation, brought out by the California Congressman Richard Nixon, as a "red herring" designed to distract attention from the shortcomings of the Eightieth Congress. But on a December night a month after the 1948 elections, Chambers led investigators at his Maryland farm to a hollowed-out pumpkin from which he extracted microfilms of classified government documents. Chambers declared that they had been given to him by a spy ring of which Hiss had been a member. On January 25, 1950, after two trials, Hiss was sentenced to five years in prison for perjury, the statute of limitations on treason having run out. Hiss could hardly have served the purposes of anti-Communist Republicans better, for he had been a New Deal official, had served as director of special political affairs in the State Department, had helped arrange the San Francisco Conference which gave birth to the United Nations, and had been present at Yalta. Truman's "red herring" remark appeared to indicate that the administration was indifferent to subversion, and troubles were compounded when Secretary of State Dean Acheson said, "I do not intend to turn my back on Alger Hiss." Acheson's statement did him credit as a man (he would base his conduct, he explained, on Matthew 25:34 — he who turned his back on one in trouble turned his back on Him), but it was politically maladroit because it could easily be misconstrued and came at an awkward time. In December 1949, Chiang Kai-shek's Nationalists had fled to Formosa; in late January 1950, Hiss was convicted and Acheson made his ill-advised comment; on February 3, Klaus Fuchs was arrested. Thus was the stage set for McCarthy's arrival in Wheeling on February 12, 1950.

The Wisconsin Senator's address to the Republican Women's Club rocketed him from obscurity to notoriety. Elected to the Senate in 1946 as one of the "meat shortage boys," he had made little mark save as a bully who continually flouted Senate rules and showed no inhibitions about making vicious verbal assaults. When he came to West Virginia, he was a little-known Senator, and the speech

he gave on that occasion was a quiltwork of snatches taken from
Nixon and others. But McCarthy had a genius for publicity, a shrewd
understanding of the tactical advantages in talking not about
treachery but about traitors, and a ruthlessness that others lacked.
His exact words in Wheeling remain in dispute. He appears to have
said: "I have here in my hand a list of 205—a list of names that were
made known to the Secretary of State as being members of the
Communist Party and who nevertheless are still working and shaping policy in the State Department." By the time he had reached the
airport to change planes for his next speaking engagement, he was
besieged by reporters asking to see the list. There was no "list,"
but McCarthy was making headlines. Scarcely a month after the
Wheeling speech, *The Washington Post*'s Herbert Block, who signed
his political cartoons "Herblock," was searching for an expression
to capture the new phenomenon of defamation of character. In that
day's cartoon, on a drawing of a barrel of mud he lettered a word
hitherto unknown in the national lexicon—"McCarthyism."

For a period of nearly five years McCarthyism besmirched American politics, and the issue of subversion left its mark on the pulpit
and the Hollywood movie lot, the campus and the union hall. Critics
of redbaiting sometimes exaggerated the extent of its reach. Some
thought they were witnessing a parallel to the closing days of the
Weimar Republic, and the theater critic Brooks Atkinson even blamed
McCarthyism for a mediocre Broadway season. But there was genuine occasion for alarm, not only because the latterday Red Scare
did claim victims who were ousted from their positions, within government and without, but because McCarthyism created an atmosphere which suffocated serious consideration of critical public issues.

Truman tried to free himself of the albatross of the Communist
subversion issue, but with little success. In 1947 he established a
program to screen government employees for disloyalty, and in 1951
he augmented the authority of the Loyalty Review Board. The Justice
Department in 1948 secured an indictment of eleven top Communist
Party leaders for violating the Smith Act of 1940, which outlawed
conspiracies that advocated the violent overthrow of any government in the United States. In 1951, in the *Dennis* case, the Supreme
Court under Chief Justice Fred M. Vinson affirmed the convictions of
the Communists and upheld the constitutionality of the Smith Act,
although the law proscribed the mere advocacy of revolutionary
doctrines. The administration's actions horrified liberals but failed
to appease Congress, which enacted legislation sponsored by Senator

Pat McCarran requiring Communist organizations to register with
the attorney general and submit lists of their members, barring the
admission of Communists from abroad, and even providing for concentration camps in the event of war. Truman vetoed these measures
("In a free country, we punish men for the crimes they commit, but
never for the opinions they have"), but Congress passed each bill
over his veto. The overwhelming support for these proposals demonstrated that "McCarthyism" had a solid base in Congress, among
Democrats like McCarran as well as among the Wisconsin Senator's
more numerous followers in his own party.

Contemporary analysts diagnosed McCarthyism as a disease of
class mobility and the consumer culture. Seymour Martin Lipset
asserted that the Senator "directed his appeal to the status resentments occasioned by prosperity." Another sociologist, Daniel Bell,
explained that "the central idea of the status politics conception is
that groups that are advancing in wealth and social position are often
as anxious and politically feverish as groups that have become
déclassé." Hence, McCarthy's legions numbered both WASPs on
the decline, including "a thin stratum of soured patricians," and
social groups on the rise, ranging from Texas oil wildcatters to up-
wardly mobile ethnics eager to affirm their Americanism. Certain
"authoritarian personality" types, of the sort studied by T. W.
Adorno and Hannah Arendt, were believed to be especially prone to
exhibit these characteristics.

Subsequent investigation has raised doubt about these hypotheses
and has advanced new ones. It has been pointed out that affluence
and mobility were conditions of American society before McCarthy's
rise and after his decline and that anti-communism was more an
elite than a mass phenomenon. In particular, McCarthyism has been
seen as an expression of the frustrations of desperate middle west
and mountain state Republican officials, conservative and nationalist
in persuasion, who had seen certain victory snatched from them in
1948. Yet if the protagonists of McCarthyism came from the leadership, his following derived disproportionately from the less educated,
from manual workers and other lower socioeconomic groups, and
from Catholics identifying with an Irish coreligionist who stuck pins
in the establishment.

Although McCarthy was regarded as the lay cleric of a creed of
conformity, he won a good deal of his following precisely because he
flouted convention. Richard Rovere, who characterized him as "inner-
directed," "closer to the hipster than to the Organization Man,"
wrote: "He seemed to understand, as no other politician of his stature

The Grand Inquisitor, Joseph R. McCarthy, sows his doom. To the dismay of the army's chief counsel, Joseph Welch, the Wisconsin senator launches an unfair attack on a young attorney in Welch's law firm that drew a scathing rebuke from Welch and led millions of television viewers to recognize how unsavory were McCarthy's methods.

ever has, the perverse appeal of the bum, the mucker, the Dead End kid, the James Jones–Nelson Algren–Jack Kerouac hero to a nation uneasy in its growing order and stability and not altogether happy about the vast leveling process in which everyone appeared to be sliding, from one direction or another, into middle-class commonplaceness and respectability." McCarthy, Rovere added, "didn't want the world to think of him as respectable. He encouraged photographers to take pictures of him sleeping, disheveled, on an office couch, like a bum on a park bench, coming out of a shower with a towel wrapped around his torso like Rocky Marciano." A boxer in his college days at Marquette, McCarthy attracted a segment of his supporters because he seemed to be a "guts fighter." Some of Mc-Carthy's backers found his brutishness disturbing; others, as a New London, Connecticut, study learned, admired him because he was "not afraid to 'get tough.'"

McCarthy appealed to a deep-seated distrust of eastern seaboard patricians by his tirades against striped-pants diplomats and "State Department perverts." Those who had been "selling the Nation out," he asserted, were "the bright young men who are born with silver spoons in their mouth." McCarthy found a ready-made target for such abuse in Truman's secretary of state. Leslie Fiedler observed:

Acheson is the projection of all the hostilities of the Midwestern mind at bay: his waxed mustache, his mincing accent, his personal loyalty to a traitor who also belonged to the Harvard Club; one is never quite sure that he was not invented by a pro-McCarthy cartoonist.

With something like genius, McCarthy touched up the villain he had half-found, half-composed, adding the connotations of wealth and effete culture to treachery, and topping all off with the suggestion of homosexuality.

McCarthy intimidated opponents who had an exaggerated notion of his political power. In 1950, one of his aides doctored a photo-graph to make it appear that Senator Millard E. Tydings of Maryland was collaborating with the leader of the Communist Party, and Tyd-ings went down to defeat. Other Democrats trembled at the prospect that they might be next on Joe's list if they incurred his wrath. On the other hand, conservative Republicans like Taft concluded that McCarthy's fulminations against "Commiecrats" were giving the Republicans the same sort of advantage, as one of the Wisconsin Senator's lieutenants claimed, that the Democrats had enjoyed with the "Hoover apple." In 1952 Richard Nixon made uninhibited use of McCarthyite invective by denouncing "Adlai the appeaser" who "carries a Ph.D from Dean Acheson's cowardly college of Communist containment" and saying he would rather have a "khaki-clad Presi-dent than one clothed in State Department pinks." When the GOP triumphed in 1952, after a campaign of K_1C_2 (Korea, Com-munism, Corruption), McCarthy was credited with a share in the national victory as well as with eliminating critics such as Senator William Benton of Connecticut. In truth, concern about communism had little influence on the 1952 outcome, and as late as the summer of 1953 most of those polled disapproved of McCarthy. Even in 1954, when the Senator reached his all-time high of 50 percent support

HERBLOCK
©1954 THE WASHINGTON POST Co.

This "Herblock" drawing is one of many depicting McCarthy as an unshaven Neanderthal. Herbert Block, political cartoonist of *The Washington Post*, played no favorites in the cold war. He won his second Pulitzer prize in 1954 for his sketch on the occasion of Stalin's demise, in which Death says, "You were always a great friend of mine, Joseph."

"Have A Care, Sir"
From *Herblock's Here and Now* (Simon and Schuster, 1955).

(with 29 percent unfavorable), the proportion of Americans who stated they were worried about the Communist peril was under 1 percent.

Eisenhower drew some of his backing in 1952 from those who believed that only a man of his stature could curb the Wisconsin Senator, but the general actually abetted McCarthy. When Eisenhower came to Wisconsin in 1952, he even deleted from a speech a paragraph praising General George Catlett Marshall, Ike's mentor in the army, whom McCarthy had damned as part of "a conspiracy so immense and an infamy so black as to dwarf any such previous venture in the history of man." Eisenhower's victory propelled McCarthy for the first time to chairmanship of the Senate Committee on Government Operations, and "the Grand Inquisitor" used his new power to rampage through the foreign affairs agencies of the

Republican administration. But the President refused to grapple with him ("I will not get in the gutter with *that* guy," he confided), and Secretary of State John Foster Dulles not only abandoned his subordinates but sent a directive excluding books and works of art of "any Communists, fellow travellers, et cetera" from United States information centers abroad. Some books were actually burned, a grim suggestion of the Nazis' *Walpurgisnachten* and of Ray Bradbury's *Fahrenheit 451*. While Dulles' edict reached out to the creations of "et ceteras," Eisenhower issued an executive order expanding the category of ineligibility for federal employment from disloyalty to "security risk," and Republicans and Democrats carried on an unseemly debate over which administration had fired the greater number of its civil servants. In December 1953, the Atomic Energy Commission shocked the scientific community by withdrawing the security clearance of the "father of the atomic bomb," J. Robert Oppenheimer.

However, when McCarthy chose to assault the military establishment, he overstepped himself, for he reckoned neither on the nation's tender concern for the army in the cold war nor on the peering lenses of the new medium of television. The televised portions of the army-McCarthy hearings, which lasted from April 22 to June 17, 1954, gave many Americans their first close glimpse of McCarthy—his bullying, his rasping intrusions, his unshaven face like that of a Hollywood "heavy." If there was a single point in time when McCarthy's house tumbled down around him, it came when the army's sweet-natured counsel Joseph Welch, outraged by a wanton accusation against a young associate, cried out, "Until this moment, Senator, I think I never really gauged your cruelty or your recklessness. . . . If it were in my power to forgive you for your reckless cruelty, I would do so. I like to think I am a gentle man, but your forgiveness will have to come from someone other than me. . . . Have you no sense of decency, sir, at long last?"

Thereafter McCarthy went rapidly downhill, carrying this latter-day "Red Scare" with him. The Democratic victory in November deprived him of his chairmanship at the same time that some of his fellow Republicans had become miffed at his badmouthing of GOP colleagues. It was a bit much to say of Senator Ralph Flanders of Vermont, "Senile—I think they should get a man with a net and take him to a good quiet place," and even more offensive to call Senator Robert C. Hendrickson of New Jersey "a living miracle in that he is without question the only man who has lived so long with neither brains nor guts." On December 2, 1954, the Senate voted, 67 to 22 (with no negative Democratic votes and the Republicans dividing evenly), to "condemn" McCarthy for various affronts to the dignity of the Senate. Shortly afterward a professional lecturer in San Francisco removed the Communist menace from his offerings because it no longer sold. Three years later, McCarthy died at the age of forty-eight. In his place, the voters of Wisconsin chose a Democrat who had married into the eastern seaboard aristocracy and, still worse, held degrees from both Yale and Harvard.

As a self-advertised gladiator against communism, McCarthy proved to be a charlatan. He first gained the limelight by piecing together a set of fabrications and innuendos. When a Senate subcommittee investigated his charges, it concluded that McCarthy was waging "the most nefarious campaign of half-truths and untruth in the history of the Republic." Curiously, even when McCarthy achieved immense power as chairman of a Senate committee, he did nothing to rid the government of alleged subversives. "Like Gogol's Chichikov, McCarthy is a dealer in dead souls," observed Dwight Macdonald. "His targets are not actual, living breathing Communists but rather people who once were or may have been but were not but may be made to appear to have possibly once been Communists or sympathizers or at any rate suspiciously 'soft' on the question." The astonishing fact about McCarthy is that he never once exposed a Communist in high places; his biggest catch was a "pink dentist" in the signal corps. Ironically, his inflated reputation owed much to his enemies, who insisted that because of him a reign of terror gripped American campuses and portrayed him as the leader of an incipient totalitarian movement. But, as the political scientist Earl Latham has written, "the sick forebodings of some liberals of the time did not materialize," and McCarthy, a man with neither an ideology nor a serious purpose, showed no inclination to exploit cold war anxieties to become America's first Führer.

Affluent America

Because of both cold war expenditures and unfaltering consumer purchases, the depression fears of 1945 proved groundless. The American economy pulled through the postwar reconversion and in the 1950's took off into the wild blue yonder of skyhigh prosperity. By the middle of the decade, the country, with only 6 percent of the earth's people, was producing and consuming over one-third of the

Gross National Product in Constant Dollars, 1929-1960

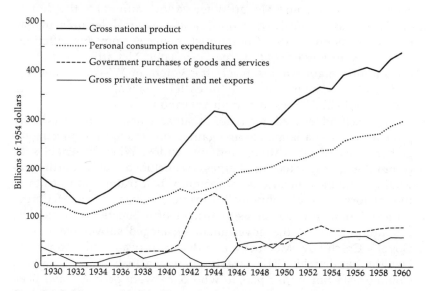

Source: Board of Governors of the Federal Reserve System, *Historical Supplement to Federal Reserve Chart Book*, 1961, p. 74.

world's goods and services. Economists were troubled that the average gain in gross national product (in dollars of the same purchasing power) ran only 2.9 percent in the 1950's, well below the 4.7 percent increment for the 1920's. Yet the economy still showed a rise in real GNP of 51 percent between 1949 and 1960. Since the standard of living in 1949 was already very high compared to that of other nations, the level in 1960 gave America an abundance that made concentration on the modest annual growth rate misleading. The real GNP increased from $206 billion in 1940 to above $500 billion in 1960, and the big leap of the 'sixties still lay ahead. The United States would close that decade with the world's first trillion-dollar economy (albeit measured in inflated money).

The cold war and the consumer culture contributed to this growth in several different ways. In the postwar period the United States moved into what W. W. Rostow called the "high mass-consumption" stage, and spending in the private sector played an important part in setting in motion a vigorous upswing in 1949. But it was the stimulus of the swollen military budget in the Korean conflict that accounted for the mightiest boom of the 1950's. By the third quarter of 1951 "national security expenditures" totaled more than all private domestic investment, and in just three years aluminum production doubled. The Pentagon provided the main market for new "glamour" industries like electronics, placed multi-billion-dollar orders with west coast aircraft plants, and financed experimentation in research and development. When military disbursements fell off after the Korean ceasefire, consumer purchases took up the slack, though output rose at only half the rate of the first part of the decade. Millions of suburban home owners took advantage of installment credit to purchase "consumer durables" and provided the motivation for the construction of imposing shopping centers. In the 1950's consumer use of electricity nearly tripled because of the evolution of household appliances, and advertising outlays more than doubled. The twin force of the cold war and the consumer culture, both dependent on a responsive government, emboldened corporations to adopt technological innovations like the computer and to step up investment at home and abroad.

The consumer culture thrived on a rapidly augmented home market. As the shrunken ambitions of the 1930's gave way to the great expectations of the postwar era, the two-child family came to seem inappropriate to the more expansive life style of the middle class, just as the confining coupé gave way to the station wagon. A Harvard senior who said his aim was six children explained that it was "a minimum production goal." Economists even suggested "that babies are viewed as a consumer durable good expected to yield a stream of psychic income through time." The burgeoning population, a source of grief in pre-industrial nations, guaranteed steadily growing demand, most immediately for diaper services and supermarket items like baby food.

The American people multiplied their numbers in these years at a pace that upset the predictions of population experts. The lowering horizons of the Great Depression had led demographers to forecast that in another generation the United States would enter a period of long-term decline. Even the spurt during World War II, which the Census Bureau soberly attributed in part to "occasional furloughs," was dismissed as a temporary phenomenon. But, to the chagrin of the prognosticators, the returning GI's (and their brides) proved intent on making up for lost time. In the 1940's, the population grew by 19 million, more than twice the increase in the previous decade, and the phenomenal gain of 29 million in the 1950's moved

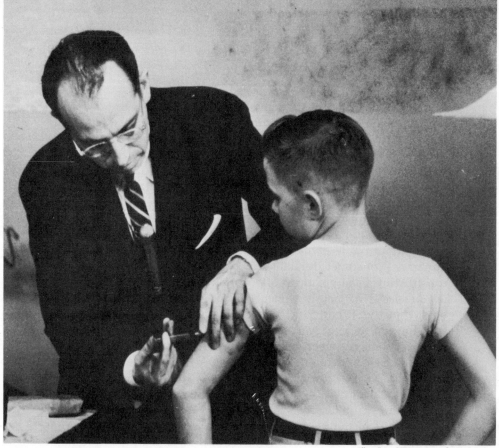

The benevolent needle. On March 28, 1953, Dr. Jonas Salk of the University of Pittsburgh announced the development of a vaccine for poliomyelitis (infantile paralysis), the dreaded crippler. Two years later, on April 13, 1955, Salk inoculated ten-year-old Randy Bazilausakas, the first person to receive the vaccine after its approval by the National Institutes of Health.

at the same pace as that of teeming India. "No decrease is in sight this century," announced a Census Bureau official in 1955. "We have come to consider it routine to report new all-time-high records."

Demographers ascribed the increments chiefly to the rising birth rate but also to decline in the death rate. Births, at below 19 per 1,000 people before the war, soared to above 25 in the mid-1950's, and only slowly fell thereafter. "It seems to me," wrote a British visitor in 1958, "that every other young house-wife I see is pregnant." To a lesser extent, the growth resulted from medical achievements (among others, streptomycin in 1945 and aureomycin in 1948) that lengthened lives, especially those of the young. A new-born child in 1900 could expect to live forty-six years; in 1940, sixty years; and by the early 1960's, seventy years, the biblical three score and ten.

The tides of population surged through the Southwest and the West, swelling the size of cities such as Houston, which became the nation's space capital, desert oases like Tucson, and, above all, the metropolises of California. By the time some got to Phoenix (which jumped from 65,000 in 1940 to 439,000 in 1960), others knew the way to San Jose (which tripled in the same period). Like forty-niners following the Oregon Trail, the Athletics, once the pride of Connie Mack's Philadelphia on the eastern littoral, stopped briefly in Kansas City, then pulled up stakes again and settled in Oakland. In 1958, the unthinkable happened. The Brooklyn Dodgers took French leave

Settlement and Population in the United States, 1940-1960

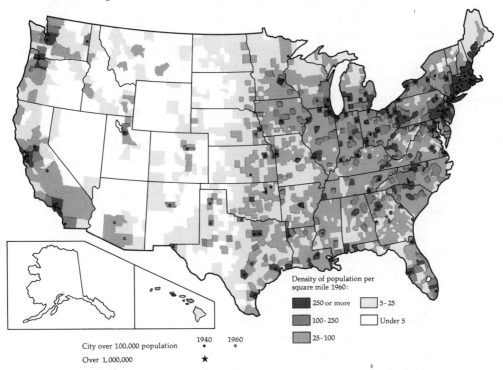

Density of population per square mile 1960:

250 or more • 5-25
100-250 • Under 5
25-100

City over 100,000 population — 1940 • 1960 ∘
Over 1,000,000 — ★

from Ebbets Field and moved to Los Angeles, and the New York Giants departed the antiquated Polo Grounds for windy Candlestick Park in San Francisco. Duke Snider, whose home runs had once bounced into Bedford Avenue, felt lost in the vastness of the Los Angeles Colosseum, and Willie Mays, who had delighted Bronx youngsters by turning up unannounced for stickball games, played before strangers from Sausalito and Menlo Park. A year later, Old Glory added two more stars when Hawaii and Alaska entered the union. No longer a continental nation of contiguous states, the United States had admitted to equal status the outposts of empire.

While the country's population increased 33 percent between 1940 and 1960, statistics for the Pacific states climbed an astonishing 110 percent. By 1960 half of the native citizens of the Far West were living in a different state from the one in which they were born. In the 1950's, one-fifth of the nation's population expansion was accounted for by the single state of California, which had become, as the British historian Arnold J. Toynbee said, the New World's New World, and in the 1960's Orange County, with the Anaheim of Disneyland and the California Angels, sustained a stupendous 102 percent growth to reach a 1,420,000 total. By 1963 California had moved past New York to be the number 1 state in population.

Other sections prospered too. Agreement to complete construction of the St. Lawrence seaway, which would make ocean ports of Chicago and Duluth, quickened expectations throughout the Midwest. After the army moved Wernher von Braun and his German rocket specialists to Huntsville, Alabama, that town of 30,000 in 1950 reached 115,000 in 1963. Huntsville tore down its Confederate monument and put up nineteen shopping centers. Space became the third-ranking industry in Florida, following tourism and citrus fruits. From 1950 to 1961 the personal income of Floridians rose a fantastic 187 percent, and in metropolitan Atlanta manufacturing employment in the 1950's increased 64 percent. French visitors, expecting to find "a Scarlett O'Hara land of cotton plantations" in the South, were surprised to see instead "oil, natural gas, helium, steel, magnesium, atomic energy and chemical plants." In the Houston–Beaumont–Port Arthur complex, there arose a huge petrochemical industry, and in the 1950's in Texas natural gas more than tripled in value to pass the half-billion-dollar mark. But despite all these regional gains, the performance of the Pacific coast remained the most impressive. The westering migrants, one eye on the main chance, the other on the high style of life in the sun country, pro-

News that statehood has been achieved is hawked before Iolani Palace, Honolulu. Statehood legislation for Hawaii was approved on August 21, 1959, eight months after Alaska became the forty-ninth state on January 3, 1959.

vided both a mobile work force for new industries and a seemingly insatiable demand for the products of those industries.

These multitudes with their augmented incomes made the cash registers chatter even more noisily because of the ready availability of credit. From 1946 to 1958 short-term consumer credit, particularly for buying Fords and Chevvies on the installment plan, rose from $8.4 billion to almost $45 billion. So easy did credit become that scores of pawnshops were driven out of business. In 1950 Diners' Club introduced the credit card; within fifteen years, it had more than a million card-carrying members, as did American Express.

Largely in response to consumer demand, capitalists risked billions of dollars in new investment. Even when government spending fell from $83 billion to $31 billion from 1945 to 1946, the economy did not collapse because corporation ventures and high consumption sustained it. Cured of the depression "psychosis" by the shock therapy of World War II, the private sector proved much more resilient than New Deal economists had anticipated. From 1946 to 1958, industrialists put an average of $10 billion a year into new plant and machinery, three times the pace set in the "golden twenties." The phenomenal rise in output per man-hour (35 to 40 percent a decade) was made possible by investment in mechanization and in the application of power. In the two decades after 1940, the generation of electric energy increased 340 percent.

Application of power did less to increase productivity than a dramatic new step in scientific management—automation. A term apparently first coined in 1946, "automation" originally signified the automatic handling of parts between successive stages of manufacturing but soon came to refer more particularly to the use of self-regulating electronic mechanisms to run complex operations, even immense strip mills in the steel industry. Automation made its greatest advance with the evolution of the computer, erected at Harvard and the University of Pennsylvania during World War II and first marketed in 1950, after the development in 1948 by Bell Telephone Laboratories of an indispensable component, the transistor. So great was the demand for computers that IBM, the industry's leader, could not turn them out fast enough. The twenty computers of 1954 had multiplied to more than 1,250 in 1957 and over 35,000 a decade later. When instructed, computers could remember, select, and give orders; they could write beatnik poetry, compose an avant-garde suite, and even devise original strategy at checkers to beat the human who had taught them the game. The computer, declared Dr. Herbert A. Simon of Carnegie Tech, represented "an advance in man's thinking processes as radical as the invention of writing." Computers were utilized to speed airline reservations, process bank check hieroglyphics, forecast election returns, advise sausage makers which meats to select in concocting salami, and figure out for Billy Graham the rate of "decisions for Christ" at his revival meetings. They were even able to increase inefficiency in college registration. Electronic data-processing machines, whose factory sales jumped from $25 million in 1953 to $1 billion in 1960, transformed the modern business office by performing the mundane but invaluable function of coping with the mountains of paper that were threatening to strangle the businessman like the snakes encoiled around Laocöon.

The word "automation" struck fear in the hearts of the American workingman. "The worker's greatest worry," explained a writer, "is that he will be cast upon the slag heap by a robot." The very point of automation was to eliminate labor. As *Business Week* stated flatly, "The art and science of going through as many stages of production as possible with as little human help as possible is called automation." From 1947 to 1961 employment in textiles, an industry especially susceptible to automation, declined 35 percent. Although automation offered openings to the college-trained, it took a heavy toll of unskilled laborers, farmhands, and inexperienced young manual workers who had dropped out of school; disproportionate numbers of these were black. One student of the subject claimed: "Automation is today the same kind of menace to the unskilled—that is, the poor—that the enclosure movement was to the British agricultural population centuries ago." However, employers countered that automation, while making some jobs obsolete, would create new opportunities, as indeed it did.

Much of this technological advance owed a debt to research and development, for it was the laboratories of companies like Bell Telephone and IBM that turned out many of the new products that sparked the postwar economy. Between 1953 and 1964, spending for "R & D" nearly quadrupled. Fast-spreading industries such as electronics and chemistry depended heavily on the university labs at Caltech and Stanford and along "Research Row" on the banks of the Charles in Cambridge, Massachusetts. Businessmen learned that graduate school training was a crucial source of economic growth and profit increments, and science departments in turn became enmeshed in corporation and government contracts. Some of them were for military purposes; in the late 1950's aircraft and guided missiles made the greatest use of R & D. A big chunk of investment went directly into laboratories like GE's in Schenectady and RCA's in Princeton, and only the very big firms could afford operations of these dimensions.

Most of the corporations of the postwar world bore familiar names like General Electric and United States Steel, but they had so expanded that they were different not in degree but in kind from their prewar counterparts. The giants of the 1950's, not yet the behemoths of the 1970's, did ten times the business of their predecessors in the 1920's and possessed resources vaster than the domains of many heads of state. General Motors, the world's biggest corporation, had a payroll of nearly 700,000 by the mid-1960's, and

American Telephone and Telegraph referred to its weekly board conclaves as "cabinet meetings." In 1957–1958, 574 corporations (out of a national total of 573,000) received over half of the net income of American industry. Corporations accounted too for the enlargement of the gaudy "growth industries" like chemicals and electronics.

In 1950 *Fortune* called chemicals "the premier industry of the United States," because none could match it "in dynamics, growth, earnings, and potential for the future." Since 1937, E. I. DuPont de Nemours & Co., the world leader, had doubled, Monsanto had quadrupled, Dow Chemical had expanded seven and a half times. Operated by chemists and engineers, these enterprises prospered by plowing back earnings into research, which yielded a never-ending array of new products for the consumer culture—Aerosol bombs, Dacron suits, synthetic tires, laundry detergents. In the five years after the war, DuPont tripled its nylon capacity and in 1950 began production of another synthetic fiber, Orlon, one of a series of discoveries that radically altered the textile business. The most spectacular gains came in plastics, a branch of the chemicals industry that by fashioning products such as Vinyl curtains, melamine dishes, and Teflon skillets grew a stunning 600 percent in a decade. Little wonder that when in the 1960's the secret of life was confided to Dustin Hoffman in *The Graduate,* the talisman was "plastics."

Chemicals also led all other manufacturing enterprises in direct foreign investment with 17 percent of the 1959 total. During the 1950's its overseas investment more than tripled, a slightly more rapid increase than that for American business generally. Especially remarkable was the penetration by the United States of the Canadian economy, accounting for one-third of the entire United States direct foreign investment, more than in all of Latin America. By 1957 Americans owned no less than one-half of its northern neighbor's manufacturing assets and mines and three-fourths of its oil and gas.

Nurtured by government contracts, the electronics industry came to maturity as a war baby and continued to thrive on war and rumors of war. In 1939, electronics, with total sales of less than $1 billion (mostly radios), ranked only forty-ninth in the country. By 1956, less than two decades later, it was America's number 5 industry, with $11.5 billion annual sales and a work force of 1.5 million, some ten times that of 1939. It had doubled since 1950 and was enlarging at a pace of more than $1 million a day. So avidly did electronics corporations recruit new talent that a single issue of *The New York Times* carried nearly six pages of want ads, forty-five full columns.

The favorite child of Mars, the electronics industry had flourished in World War II thanks to radar and after the war because of the demand for costly weapons systems. The $3 billion market in 1956 for military items (forty times the sales of 1947!) was twice as large as that for consumer goods like television sets and electronic kitchen ranges.

As the experience of the electronics industry indicated, if corporations played a stellar role in promoting economic growth, they had to share the limelight with government. Welfare benefits, minimum wage statutes, and farm subsidies built a base of purchasing power, and stock exchange regulation helped stabilize the securities markets. Manipulation of rediscount rates and reserve requirements regulated the money flow, and spending and taxing policies rechanneled it. Even enterprises that seemed to be "private" often rested on a government base. Some businesses got a head start in the postwar boom when the federal government disposed of its wartime holdings in shiny new plants — 50 percent of the country's machine tool facilities and aluminum capacity; 90 percent of aircraft construction, shipbuilding, and magnesium processing; and 97 percent of synthetic rubber production. Of spending for research and development at the end of the 1950's, Washington financed one-half. Consumer credit hinged on government bonds in the vaults of financial institutions, and the ex-GI's home in the suburbs depended on federal guarantees of mortgages. The government also intervened in more direct ways. In 1929 Washington's expenditures for goods and services totaled little more than 1 percent of the GNP; in 1953, they amounted to nearly 17 percent, marking the government as the nation's number 1 buyer. In 1956 alone the United States government spent more on highways than the entire worth of the economy of Norway. That year Congress took the first steps toward building a national, limited-access highway system to facilitate high-speed travel. Government had also become a major employer, with public jobs at all levels more than doubling between 1950 and 1970, when close to 13 million drew government paychecks. Uncle Sam's payroll underpinned the four most prosperous counties in the United States — Montgomery County in Maryland and Arlington and Fairfax counties in Virginia, all encapsulating bedroom communities of Washington, D.C., and Los Alamos County, which embraced New Mexico's atomic site.

High employment and the growth in productivity redounded to the benefit of large numbers of Americans. While the economy

Cars crowd the parking lot at the Crenshaw shopping center in Los Angeles. Widespread ownership of automobiles not only made it possible for industry to draw workers from a large area but was indispensable to the consumer culture.

was absorbing an increase in the civilian labor force from 54 million in 1945 to 78 million in 1970, real weekly earnings of factory employees rose 50 percent. Some workers had even attained the security of a guaranteed annual wage, a reform promoted by Walter Reuther, leader of the automobile union, and first instituted in 1955. Most industrial workers also enjoyed "fringe benefits" such as hospitalization insurance. In the 1950's the sums in private pension funds quadrupled; by 1959, they totaled $44 billion.

The distribution of income gave the American social structure the shape less of a pyramid than of a diamond, with a vastly expanded middle class. The proportion of families and unattached individuals with an annual income of $10,000 or more (in standard 1968 dollars) rose from 9 percent in 1947 to 33 percent in 1968, while that below $3000 fell from 34 percent in 1947 to 19 percent in 1968.

Nothing measured access to the middle class so well as the op-

Average Income of Families and Individuals

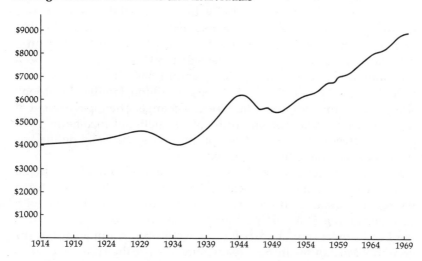

Source: From *Rich Man, Poor Man* by Herman P. Miller. Copyright © 1971 by Harper and Row Publishers, Inc. By permission of Thomas Y. Crowell.

portunity to win a college diploma. In 1870 the campus had been largely the preserve of the well-to-do: Less than 2 percent of young people in the eighteen to twenty-one age group attended any institution of higher learning. The ensuing seventy years saw important gains; yet as late as 1940 only 1.5 million Americans (15 percent of their age cluster) went beyond high school, which meant that the remaining 85 percent would have virtually no chance of becoming professionals and little more of rising in the corporation or government worlds. After World War II, the situation changed dramatically. By 1960, college enrollments had increased to 3.6 million, and in the ensuing decade campus populations exploded. From the mid-1950's to 1969, registration tripled; in just one year in the 1960's the growth was greater than the total attendance in all universities in Great Britain. By 1970 five times as many Americans were on college campuses as in 1940. They comprised 40 percent of their age group, 60 percent in California, which had more college students than did France, a nation with three times as many people. And for all the alarums about dropouts, three students out of four in 1970 were graduated from high school, while in 1929 three out of four did not get beyond the eighth grade.

These developments led some enthusiasts to conclude that the United States was moving rapidly toward a classless society as a consequence of the accelerating redistribution of income. In 1955 *Fortune* asserted, "Though not a head has been raised aloft on a pikestaff, nor a railway station seized, the United States has been for some time now in a revolution," and in *America in the Sixties* the periodical's editors claimed that only a million families "still look really poor." In truth, there had been a change. The top 5 percent of the population raked in one-third of the national income in 1929, only 15 percent in 1968, and the proportion statistically defined as impoverished markedly diminished.

However, extreme disparities in income distribution continued to characterize American society. The economist Paul Samuelson wrote, "If we made an income pyramid out of child's blocks, with each portraying $1,000 of income, the peak would be far higher than the Eiffel Tower, but almost all of us would be within a yard of the ground." Most of the income readjustment since the 1920's had taken place before 1945, and in the postwar years new riches were accumulated. A study by Robert J. Lampman found that the top 1.6 percent of the adult population in 1953 held 90 percent of corporate

Unemployment Among Nonwhite Men, 1955-1963

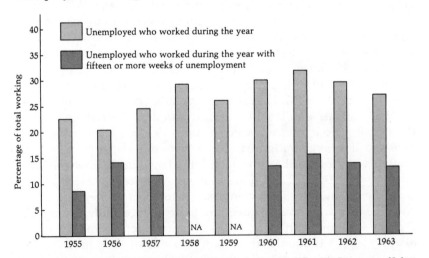

Source: Daniel Patrick Moynihan, *The Negro Family: The Case for National Action*, U.S. Department of Labor, Office of Policy Planning and Research, March 1965, p. 23.

Ben Shahn's 1948 painting *Miner's Wives* illustrates the hard times that were the lot of millions even in an affluent society. Like Jackson Pollock a beneficiary of New Deal art projects, the Russian-born Shahn was also an excellent photographer and a gifted muralist.

bonds and almost all state and local government bonds. By 1968, 153 Americans held nine-digit fortunes, including Dr. Edwin H. Land, the self-made chairman of Polaroid, and, despite steep estate taxes, one of the centimillionaires was a sixteen-year-old who had inherited a chunk of the Duke tobacco treasure. Nor did increases in income for the less well-to-do always guarantee a rise in class position. The sociologist Eli Chinoy learned that automobile workers had relinquished the "American Dream" of upward mobility and were settling instead for lateral mobility — a fancier car, a nicer house.

Moreover, millions still languished in want — Puerto Ricans in what Oscar Lewis called the "culture of poverty" in New York City, Mexican-Americans in the California lettuce fields, Indians wasting away on reservations with a death rate three times the national average, Negroes consigned to menial labor as busboys and janitors, whites in mountain hollows and lonely boarding houses. A report by the Survey Research Center in cooperation with the Federal Reserve Board concluded that in 1959 45 percent of spending units had less than $200 in liquid assets such as savings accounts. As late as the boom year of 1968, an estimated 25 million to 30 million Americans subsisted below the poverty line, three times the population of Belgium.

In the 1950's the Joint Economic Committee concluded that one-fourth of the poor were sixty-five years of age or older, a group particularly threatened by rising prices. The consumer price index (1957–1959 = 100) jumped from 62.7 in 1945 to 127.7 in 1969. Most of the increase in the 1945–1960 period came in two early spurts, during reconversion and at the outset of the Korean War, but prices continued to drift upward in the 1950's as well. Government spending, union demands (especially in service industries and municipal bureaucracies where wage boosts outran increased productivity), and monopolistic practices all drove prices up. When budget-minded administrations sought to preserve the dollar, they did so at the cost of heightened unemployment and retarded growth, and with mixed success in curbing price rises. Inflation cut cruelly into the pocketbooks of individuals who were not organized to win compensatory wage hikes and of people like pensioners who were on fixed incomes and who found it hard to absorb the spiraling costs of medical care.

Of those who lived below the "poverty line," one-fourth worked on farms at a time when many found agriculture unrewarding. From 1948 to 1956, the farmer's share of the national income fell from

The Purchasing Power of the Dollar, 1950-1965

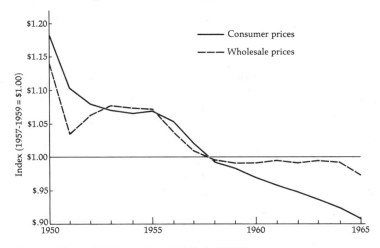

Source: U. S. Bureau of the Census, *Pocket Data Book, USA 1967.*

almost 9 percent to scarcely more than 4 percent, and as surpluses mounted, net farm income dropped from $3667 in 1946 to $2640 in 1960. Mechanization, a boon to wealthier growers, drove field hands off the land. Farm workers comprised over 40 percent of the male labor force in 1900, under 10 percent in 1960. Since tenant farmers, sharecroppers, and small growers lacked the capital to exploit technological changes or to cope with rising costs, many gave up the struggle. From 1940 to 1960, a time of prodigious population growth, the farm community declined by nine million, almost one-third. In 1935, 25 percent of the nation lived on farms; in 1969, only 5 percent did. The rich farm state of Iowa was scarred with crumbling villages that were once bustling trade centers: churches gone, the high school closed down, the bandstand in the square in ruin.

Yet these years, which carried such unhappy tidings to so many American farmers, brought piping times to others. By investing great amounts of capital to cultivate huge acreages, "corporation farmers" took advantage of a technological revolution. In 1945 for the first time the number of tractors exceeded the total of horses and mules. Mechanical pickers harvested cotton and corn, labor-saving machines spread chemical fertilizers, and airplanes dusted crops with new pesticides. As a result of such innovations, agricultural

Farm Production, 1947-1960

Source: The Life History of the United States, Volume 12, *The Great Age of Change* by William E. Leuchtenburg and the Editors of Time-Life Books. © 1964 Time Inc.

output per man-hour doubled in the fifteen years after the war. In happy contrast to their ordeal in the Depression, some farmers in the postwar years lived high on the hog. When Truman came to Dexter, Iowa, to speak at a plowing contest in the 1948 campaign, he found fifty private airplanes there. Soviet delegates watched popeyed while an Iowa farmer drove up to the Coon Rapids golf links, unloaded clubs from an electric cart, and teed off in a foursome.

Even the poverty-stricken had come a long way from the age of Social Darwinism. Old age benefit coverage was extended from 1.9 million persons in 1950 to 9.6 million in 1959, while average monthly benefits nearly tripled, though they were still far from generous. In the fifteen years following the end of World War II, welfare payments sextupled, and from 1960 to 1968 they increased another two and a half times. Over the two decades after 1940 the life expectancy of nonwhites rose ten years, the number of Negro college students and professionals more than doubled, and wage-earnings for blacks increased four and a half times. Of American families with pretax annual incomes of less than $4000 in 1959, 40 percent owned their homes. In 1964 in Harlan County, Kentucky, long regarded as a down-and-out mining district, 42 percent of the families had telephones, 59 percent owned automobiles, 67 percent TV sets, and 88 percent washing machines. In the consumer culture game, a minority of the players held the bulk of the vouchers, but most of the players had at least some vouchers to spend.

The Consumer Culture

The booming economy enabled millions of Americans to take part in the burgeoning consumer culture. With unprecedented amounts of disposable income, consumers devoted much of their time to institutions that catered to their needs and whims—shopping malls with hanging baskets of flowers and piped music, suburban department stores with civic auditoriums, supermarkets with row on row of brilliantly colored cartons. Shopping, while still often a chore, also became a kind of avocation. Husbands found release in "impulse buying," and the poet Randall Jarrell wrote of a housewife "Moving from Cheer to Joy, from Joy to All." After the advent of television in the late 1940's, millions each week turned their dials to a show that featured contestants who raced through the aisles of a supermarket competing to see who could accumulate the greatest value of goods in his shopping basket, and *Life* rejoiced at customers who wandered around a "$5 million grocery store, picking from the thousands of items on the high-piled shelves until their carts became cornucopias filled with an abundance that no other country in the world has ever known."

Foreign nations that in the 1920's had sent emissaries to Detroit to study the wizardry of America's industrial productivity now paid tribute to the magnetic consumer culture of a country "rich beyond the dreams of Marx." A Swiss department store chain, displaying a broad selection of products from the United States, admonished its customers, "Live like an American." At Uppsala in Sweden, a distinguished literary critic from Yale drew an audience of only thirty while in the next room three hundred were giving close attention to an address by his wife on the American kitchen. Yugoslavians gathered around TV sets to watch "Peyton Place," "Batman" became a big hit in Tokyo and Buenos Aires, and two avid admirers of "Bonanza" were Kenya's Tom Mboya and South Vietnam's Nguyen

Cao Ky. In Frankfurt, advertising men shamelessly borrowed a chestnut from Madison Avenue: "Ziehn wir's am Flaggenmast hoch und sehn wir wer grüsst" ("Run it up the flagpole and see if anyone salutes").

The consumer culture even made its mark on the cold war. In the competition for the allegiance of the Third World, the United States scored points when at the Jakarta trade fair in 1955 Indonesians showed more interest in an American toy train than in machine tools from Communist China. United States intelligence tried to weigh the significance of the fact that Ho Chi Minh had switched from Philip Morrises and Camels to Salems, and Soviet policy makers fretted over the popularity of rock music in Leningrad and Budapest. One of the Kremlin's first acts following Stalin's death was to re-open GUM, the State department store, and immediately after Nikita Khrushchev returned from his visit to the United States in 1959 the Russian government ordered a rapid acceleration of the out-

Land of plenty. To foreign observers, few aspects of American life were more striking than the well-stocked shelves of a supermarket. Stores like this one served as models for the burgeoning consumer societies abroad.

George Silk. LIFE Magazine. © 1951 Time Inc.

The consumer culture meets the cold war. On July 25, 1959, Vice-President Richard M. Nixon and Soviet Premier Nikita Khrushchev sip Pepsi-Cola before exchanging hot words at the model kitchen of the American National Exhibition in Moscow. In America the "kitchen debate" enhanced Nixon's reputation as a Cold Warrior, but the Russian people seemed more interested in the display of new household appliances from the homeland of capitalism.

put of television sets, refrigerators, and other consumer goods, "to match the best foreign samples."

The most noteworthy face-to-face encounter between cold war leaders in the 1950's took place neither on the battlefield nor at the negotiating table but in front of the kitchen of a model ranch house at the United States exhibition in Moscow in 1959. After sipping some Pepsi-Cola, Nikita Khrushchev and Richard Nixon engaged in a shouting match about washing machines and military machines. During the next six weeks nearly 3 million Russians looked in on the kitchen, where an automatic polisher popped out of an electronic console and dishwashers careened across the floor at the press of a housewife's thumb.

When the Paris editor of *U.S. News and World Report* came home to the United States in 1960 after twelve years abroad, he was astonished at the changes that had been wrought in his absence. He marveled at such manifestations of affluence and the consumer culture as small boats featuring electronic depth finders and automatic pilots, cocktails ready-mixed in plastic envelopes, and that ultimate evidence of a society with millions of its members far removed from subsistence concerns, striped toothpaste. He had been living in an advanced Western nation where only one family in ten had a bathtub with hot running water, and he was coming home to a country where, in some sections of California, at least one family in ten owned a swimming pool in the back yard.

The economy not only turned out an abundance of goods for the American consumer but gave him more leisure to enjoy them. As recently as the "prosperous" 1920's, the average industrial employee had been granted no paid holidays and had toiled fifty-two weeks a year without vacation. By 1970, the work week for production employees in manufacturing had been reduced to a little under forty hours. One study estimated that a typical employee enjoyed each year "1,500 more free, awake hours" than his counterpart in the mid-nineteenth century. Although in many countries of the world the Saturday workday was a regular feature, some American firms had begun to experiment with a four-day week. By 1963, paid holidays had risen to eight a year (double the 1946 figure), and many employees accrued paid sick leave too. In the 1960's almost all workers could count on an annual paid vacation (which most had not received in 1940), and the typical vacation ran at least two weeks, contrasted with one week on the eve of World War II. "Trade unions that once had a hard time getting clean toilets for their members are now plugging three-week package tours in Europe," noted Robert Bendiner. When steelworkers went out on strike in 1919, one of their "radical" demands was for one day's rest in seven. In 1963 the United Steel Workers secured a contract that provided for a "sabbatical" leave for the senior half of its members of thirteen weeks every five years.

Even the pace of work seemed more easygoing, as befit what the sociologist Pitirim Sorokin called a "late sensate society." The "coffee break," which before the war would have been frowned on as soldiering on the job, became a standard institution, and no office was complete without a water cooler, which served the purposes formerly met by the cracker barrel of the general store. At construction sites and in office buildings, caterers' trucks made their rounds each day with coffee and pastry. Many workers migrated to states like Florida and California because they offered a balmier climate for the pursuit of pleasure and amenities such as lighted tennis courts when the day's labors were over. By 1950, the country was already spending one-seventh of the gross national product (twice the expenditure for rent) on pleasure, and in 1971 Merrill Lynch, Pierce, Fenner and Smith estimated the value of the leisure market at better than $150 billion a year.

Yet these developments failed to persuade all writers that the change was as fundamental as it seemed. Some employees, including numbers of the steelworkers, took advantage of their "leisure time" to swell their incomes by "moonlighting" (working at a second job), and not a few would have been readily recognized by the go-getters of Sinclair Lewis' *Dodsworth*. In *Of Time, Work and Leisure,* Sebastian De Grazia derided the "myth" that the heavily committed modern man had more leisure than his grandfather, who worked much longer hours, and in *Couples,* John Updike wrote of "a climate still *furtively* hedonist." David Riesman, the *savant nonpareil* of the new society, cautioned: "But an attenuated puritanism survives in his exploitation of his leisure. He may say, when he takes a vacation or stretches a weekend, 'I owe it to myself' — but the self in question is viewed like a car or house whose upkeep must be carefully maintained for resale purposes."

As a consequence of higher income, longer vacations, and advances in commercial aviation, middle-class Americans traveled to places that had long seemed the destinations only of the well-heeled. In July 1955, *Newsweek* commented that "the Passport Office in New York's Rockefeller Center was as jammed as a department-store white sale," and one year later *Time* noted: "In Manhattan, liners packed to the last berth with tourists edged daily from their docks into the Hudson's high slack water." Families who had once counted it an adventure to take the San Francisco ferry thought nothing of crossing the Bosporus or riding the hydrofoil from Copenhagen to Malmö. The Piazza San Marco swarmed with camera-toting tourists from Fort Wayne and Passaic, and each August the Parisians abandoned their city to the peaceful invaders from the West. By the 1960's the beaches of San Juan and Montego Bay were so crowded in February by Americans who had come to consider a winter sojourn in the

Caribbean as much their right as the familiar summer jaunt that an increasing number of Yankees were planting themselves on the more remote shores of Acapulco and Ipanema.

The traveler, who in prewar days had been compelled to put up with fly-specked tourist "cabins," bedded down in luxurious motels boasting kidney-shaped swimming pools, saunas, chuck-wagon buffets, and the inevitable television set in every air-conditioned room. For a quarter the weary driver could stretch out on his double bed, with its decorator-coordinated spread, and be jiggled out of his tensions by a relaxing machine. In Vladimir Nabokov's *Lolita,* Humbert Humbert sang the praises of "the Functional Motel—clean, neat, safe nooks, ideal places for sleep, argument, reconciliation, insatiable illicit love," of "stone cottages under enormous Chateaubriandesque trees," and of the twin-bedded "cell of paradise, with yellow window shades pulled down to create a morning illusion of Venice and sunshine when actually it was Pennsylvania and rain." So attentive did the motels become to the spiritual needs of the wayfarers that Holiday Inns introduced a "chaplain on call" service and in Shreveport even a motel chapel and a meditation garden. Yet spirituality, too, paid homage to the opulence of the consumer culture. The ubiquitous Gideon Bible in the motel drawer appeared in hues such as bittersweet, beige, walnut, and olive, and when a Playboy Hotel requested 350 Bibles in the original black (to harmonize with the black and white motif that was a Hugh Hefner trademark), the Gideon functionaries had to scour a warehouse to find enough copies of the Good Book in the required color.

Air travel, once largely confined to the wealthy, became so commonplace in the postwar world that pilots, the glamorous fly-boys of the 1930's, were put down as "bus drivers." By 1956, airlines, which in prewar years had carried only 5 percent as much passenger traffic between cities as railroads, pulled even with their rivals. Two years later, a Boeing 707 introduced the country to the greater speed and comfort of jet aircraft. Both the prop planes and the jets, with their shapely stewardesses, piped music, in-flight movies, and stabs at gourmet dining, catered to a public that was being taught to expect luxury wherever it went. Braniff even painted its planes in gorgeous colors and clad its stewardesses in Pucci bloomers. One traveler, Jean Shepherd, recounted the experience of "floating gently on a sea of barely audible Muzak, the sweet Karo Syrup of Existence. . . . Muzak rises to a crescendo and we take off. Instantly we are high over this big chunk of land, and the world has become a blurred

Kodachrome slide. . . . Silently the red velour is rolled out and baby-blue and silver *houris* are plying me with stuff to eat—which if my mother knew I was eating she would really know I have gone to hell. By God, caviar and Moët *brut* and diced lamb's-liver pâté at 8:17 A.M., over Altoona."

The vast output of industry did not begin to satisfy the demands of the American consumer, and in the 1950's the United States moved past the United Kingdom as the world's leading importer. A country with the lion's share of the earth's goods and resources now acquired more from foreign lands than any other nation. Domestic sources no longer sufficed for the multitude of customers who coveted Simcas and Jaguars, preferred Heineken to Budweiser, furnished their homes in Danish modern, and counted on buying Carnaby Street fashions at J. C. Penney's.

The American household in the postwar years adopted a style of consumption that was more sophisticated, more worldly, more diversified, one appropriate to a nation that was not only affluent but imperial. A 1969 account observed: "Thirty years ago the average Midwesterner had never heard of pizza, sukiyaki, or South African lobster tails. He had never seen a foreign car, a Vietnamese, or a reproduction of Van Gogh's *Sunflowers.* It would have surprised him to see teak furniture in a neighbor's living room, let alone African tribal masks on the walls, or Thai silk at the windows. Now such former exotica are taken for granted."

The new style revealed itself most conspicuously at the dinner table, for in a decade wine purchases doubled, and millions of Americans learned to serve Chateauneuf du Pape (or more likely, Almadén's Cabernet Sauvignon) with the boeuf Bourguignonne and a chilled Pouilly-Fuissé with the frozen halibut. Before the war, the grocer's shelves offered little more in prepared foods than mundane items such as Heinz spaghetti and Del Monte spinach; after it, the frozen food locker of the supermarket was brimful of delicacies like frogs' legs and cannelloni. To meet the expectations of different ethnic groups, one new product was labeled both "Kreplach" and "Won Ton Soup." By 1971 "fancy food" was a billion-dollar industry, and *Gourmet* magazine's circulation had reached 550,000, more than twice what it had been four years before.

Although these changes affected most classes, differentiation in consumption styles (and, of course, in income distribution) remained critical. When the lower middle class protagonist from Newark, New Jersey, of Philip Roth's novella *Goodbye, Columbus* visited the up-

Growth in Production of Prepared Foods, 1947-1958

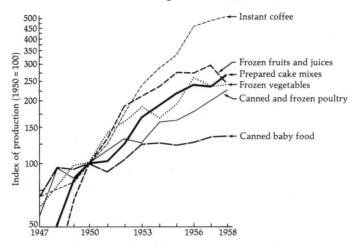

Source: Elmer Smith for Fortune Magazine, September 1959.

wardly mobile Patimkins in Briarpath Hills, he marveled at their refrigerator, which no longer held herring in cream sauce but "greengage plums, black plums, red plums, apricots, nectarines, peaches, long horns of grapes, black, yellow, red, and cherries, cherries flowing out of boxes and staining everything scarlet. And there were melons—cantaloupes and honeydews—and on the top shelf, half of a huge watermelon, a thin sheet of wax paper clinging to its bare red face like a wet lip. Oh Patimkin! Fruit grew in their refrigerator and sporting goods dropped from their trees!"

But not only the Patimkins moved into new homes. After enduring a critical housing shortage when they returned stateside in 1945, millions of GI's and their young families created a demand for shelter that both sparked the economy and sharply upgraded accommodations for millions of Americans. By 1950 over $18 billion was being invested in the construction of nonfarm, private residences. Life insurance companies erected large-scale urban projects like Stuyvesant Town and Peter Cooper Village in New York City, while national agencies such as the Federal Housing Administration and the Veterans Administration underwrote suburban developments. Washington also pumped money into public housing for lower-income groups, although much too parsimoniously and with urban renewal frequently carried on at the expense of the dislocated slum dweller. Nonetheless, during the 1950's, dwelling units were constructed at a record rate of better than a million a year, faster than the growth of new households. Of all the housing in America in 1960, one-fourth had been built during the 1950's, when for the first time in this century more Americans owned their homes (even if mortgaged) than lived in rented premises. While the well-to-do were adding amenities like air conditioning (in 1 percent of residences with electricity in 1953, in 13 percent by 1960, in 37 percent in 1968), the less prosperous were moving into dwellings with modern bathrooms; between 1940 and 1960, housing units lacking bathtub or shower fell from 39 percent to 12 percent. During these same years, the mechanization of the home advanced at a pace inconceivable in the 1920's when the process first began. Less than 1 percent of homes with wiring boasted a refrigerator in 1925; 98 percent had them in 1960; and in 1955 alone, sales of electric clothes dryers, first marketed in 1946, totaled 1.2 million, double the figure of only two years earlier.

To many American artists, the consumer culture permeated the urban landscape, and hence their conception of reality, much as trees and farmland had impressed themselves on the consciousness of Constable and Breughel. Willem de Kooning affixed a smile from a Camel ad on one of his many "women," Claes Oldenburg entitled a work *Hamburger with Pickle and Tomato Attached,* and in 1964 Andy Warhol created *Brillo.* Oldenburg even stocked a "store" with plaster replicas of familiar objects. But it was Warhol who made "pop art" the *dernier cri* with two paintings of repeated images that caught the nation's fancy—one of Campbell's soup cans, as though on a supermarket shelf; the other, as in a redundant film strip, of the love-object Marilyn Monroe.

Both critics and the public puzzled over the meaning of "pop art." Gallery-goers, unaccustomed to finding such works hanging in collections with Rembrandts and Giottos, wondered uneasily whether they were, in a phrase of the day, being "put on." Some critics saw "pop art" as a delightful way of poking fun at the severity and earnestness of abstract art. More prevalent was the view that "pop art" was a kind of social criticism, a parody of "the materialism, spiritual vacuity, and ludicrously sexualized environment of affluent America." Perhaps. Yet Warhol would soon be making ludicrously sexualized movies, and Oldenburg expressed an outspoken fondness for the objects of the consumer culture. "I am for Kool Art, 7-Up Art,

Pepsi Art, Sunkist Art," he said. "I am for the white art of refrigerators and their muscular openings and closings."

The affluent society made possible a spectacular "culture boom," which gratified uncritical admirers of the American way as much as it depressed the mordant mandarins who watched over the country's aesthetic well-being. The cold facts seemed to give the boosters all the better of it. Between 1952 and 1961, the sale of books more than doubled, to no small degree because of the "paperback revolution." The unbreakable, long-playing record, a postwar arrival, helped swell purchases of classical albums as well as of popular

4 Campbell Soup Cans, a 1962 still life by Andy Warhol, reveals how the consumer culture served the purposes of pop art. "Warhol's art uses the visual strength and vitality which are the time-tested skills of the world of advertising that cares more for the container than for the thing contained," a critic explained. "He selects examples from this commercial affluence which best evince our growing sameness."

Leo Castelli Gallery. Photograph by Rudolph Burckhardt.

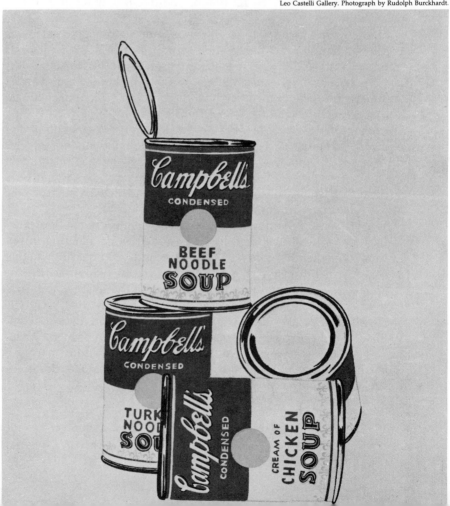

discs. Americans spent greater sums on tickets to classical concerts than to baseball games, and more on records and hi-fi equipment than on all spectator sports. Yehudi Menuhin performed in Naperville, Illinois; Byron Janis in Wartburg, Iowa; and Isaac Stern at Fort Hays, Kansas; while booming, oil-rich Houston boasted a symphony orchestra that Sir Thomas Beecham conducted. Art movie theaters, a rarity in 1945, had become fixtures by the 1960's, and Americans who had never seen a foreign language film before the war talked knowingly of Bergman and Fellini. Yet for all this, many major cities lacked even one adequate book store; television huckstered hours of dross each week; and the "middlebrows" sometimes hugged art so tightly that they squeezed it to death. The critic Dwight Macdonald, who warned that "a tepid ooze of Midcult is spreading everywhere," wrote: "There seems to be a Gresham's Law in cultural as well as monetary circulation: bad stuff drives out good, since it is more easily understood and enjoyed."

The pacesetters for much of the popular culture, America's teenagers, appropriated a huge segment of the country's productive machinery to turn out goods to conform to their tastes in consumption. In 1963 in the United States adolescents spent the staggering sum of $22 billion, twice the gross national product of Austria. They created a specialized market for a wide variety of goods from surfboards and transistor radios to *Glamour* and *Seventeen*, but especially for pop records. When Bill Haley and the Comets' "Rock Around the Clock" burst upon the country in *The Blackboard Jungle* in 1955, the national merchandising of rock culture began. By 1965, teenagers would be shelling out over $100,000,000 for forty-fives, and in 1968 people under twenty-five would spend $1.2 billion on records. In the 1960's rock would be intimately connected to the counter culture and social protest, but in the 1950's it was more tepid. For all his pelvic gyrations, Elvis Presley, a consumer culture hero with his gold lamé suits and pastel Cadillacs, neither smoked nor drank, respected his parents, and went to bed each night after saying his prayers. Dick Clark, the clean-cut emcee of the television show "American Bandstand," which 20 million watched each week to see singers lip-synch their songs and adolescents do the twist or the frug, explained, "What I'm trying to defend is my right and your right to go to a church of our choice, or buy the record of our choice."

Television exploded on the postwar world like a bomb with a delayed-action fuse. There were in 1946 fewer than 17,000 sets in use, and viewers were concentrated in a small number of cities where

Elvis the Pelvis. Born in Mississippi in 1935, Elvis Presley hit it big in 1955 with "Hound Dog" and "Blue Suede Shoes." The suggestive gyrations of his torso helped to associate rock and roll with sexual abandon and to rocket Presley to success in Hollywood films in which he sang tunes that were instantly forgettable.

they were offered a narrow choice of fare. In 1947, the fuse grew short, and in 1948, a Californian recalled: "Sometimes at night when a blind wasn't pulled all the way down we noticed mysterious blue light flickering in a living room across the street. Occasionally it was accompanied by sound of laughter or gun shots." In 1949, the bomb burst; as many as a quarter of a million sets a month were installed. A trade association ad in 1950 warned: "There are some things a son or daughter won't tell you. . . . Do you expect him to blurt out the truth—that he's really ashamed to be with the gang— because he doesn't see the same shows they see? . . . How can a little girl describe the bruise deep inside? . . . How can you deny television to your children any longer?" The following year, television went coast to coast, and 3 million at home and about as many in bars saw the Yankee-Dodger World Series in October.

By 1953 two-thirds of American families owned television; 7 million sets were manufactured in that year, compared to six thousand in 1946. Four years later, the country boasted 40 million sets and 467 TV stations. Antennas sprouted over slum tenements, and one writer reported in 1955, "In isolated rural Mississippi, we saw unpainted Erskine Caldwell shacks topped by aerials." During the mid-1960's, 94 percent of American households owned at least one TV set, and millions possessed more than one; in 1971, 90 million sets were in use. Color TV, a luxury in under 3 million homes in 1965, had been installed in 24 million (38.2 percent) by 1970.

The history of the quarter-century after World War II could readily be told in kinescopes of TV programs—the voices of gangsters at the Kefauver hearings ("I haven't got the lease idea"), Everett Dirksen's growl at the 1952 Republican convention ("Tom Dewey, we followed you before and you took us down the road to defeat"), Nixon's Checkers speech ("And you know the kids, like all kids, love the dog"), the army-McCarthy hearings ("Point of order, Mr. Chairman"), John Glenn on the launching pad at Cape Canaveral ("10-9-8-7 . . ."), and then, as though speeded up at much too intense a pace, the snarling police dogs in Birmingham, the motorcade in Dallas, the slumping body of Lee Oswald, the vociferous students on Telegraph Avenue, the howling delegates at the Cow Palace wearing "Stamp Out Huntley-Brinkley" buttons, the machine-gun fire from Vietnam, the clubs flailing at cameramen and reporters in Chicago, Nixon's inscrutable smile at the Great Wall.

The consumer culture even affected the political process. In 1952, the Eisenhower forces introduced a new wrinkle into campaigning

TV antennas frame the Statue of Liberty in New York harbor. Ownership of a television set became such a status symbol during the 1950's that it was said that some householders raised antennas to impress their neighbors before they could afford to acquire a TV. John Wayne later observed that "there sure has never been any form of entertainment so . . . available to the human race with so little effort since they invented marital sex."

by employing a Manhattan advertising firm to sell the general. Rosser Reeves, who saturated the channels with "spot" commercials for Ike, explained: "I think of a man who hesitates between two levers as if he were pausing between competing tubes of toothpaste in a drugstore. The brand that has made the highest penetration on his brain will win his choice." "Space merchants" like Reeves were inclined to exaggerate their influence, for determinants like income and ethnicity remained of critical importance in shaping electoral decisions and programmatic differences continued to be salient. But it is also true that candidates became increasingly concerned about their "image," a piece of Madison Avenue argot, and some of their audience appraised them as they assessed the rival claims of deodorants. The 1958 gubernatorial campaign in New York appeared to turn less on issues than on the degree of finesse with which the two candidates could devour blintzes and other ethnic delicacies. W. Averell Harriman, who had served with distinction as United States envoy in the leading chancelleries of Europe, lost to Nelson Rockefeller, who made a political asset out of the gusto with which he devoured bagels in the Bronx and spaghetti in the Italian sections of Buffalo and Syracuse.

"If we were to sum up the differences between elections past and present, it could be said that the United States had moved from the politics of the country store to the politics of the supermarket," wrote Karl Meyer. "In 1960," Meyer added, "our two living ex-Presidents, Herbert Hoover and Harry Truman, seemed like nostalgic remnants of the era of the country store," in contrast to the two young candidates "who stepped briskly into and out of the shopping centers. During the campaign, it often seemed as if the country were caught in a sales war between Safeway and the A & P." The highlight of the campaign in 1960 was a series of TV debates in which Nixon was said to have been put at a disadvantage because his pancake makeup failed to cover his "five o'clock shadow" and he looked like "a sinister chipmunk." In 1968 a more experienced Nixon staff would circulate passages from Marshall McLuhan warning that "politics and issues are useless for election purposes since they are too specialized and hot" for a "cool medium" like TV.

The Homogenized Society

In the 1950's critics launched a devastating attack on the consumer culture for fostering a docile, standardized nation. Wherever they looked—toward woman's place in the home or the antiseptic one-class suburb or the comatose campus—America seemed phlegmatic and routinized. One writer described the United States as " 'The Packaged Society,' for we are all items in a national supermarket—categorized, processed, labeled, priced, and readied for merchandising." In fact, the nation was livelier and more heterogeneous than these writers suggested. Nor were the 'fifties—the decade of Korea and McCarthyism, of the Montgomery bus boycott and Little Rock—an altogether tranquil time. Some of the outcry against affluence represented only another stage in the prolonged warfare of intellectuals against a prospering middle class. Yet America did pay a price for the consumer culture. It served to engender a preoccupation with private concerns and induce a complacency about public affairs that had unfortunate consequences.

Long characterized as a polyglot society, the United States increasingly became a homogeneous nation. In 1940, 26 percent of the population were first or second-generation Americans; by 1960 only 18 percent were and 95 percent were native-born. Institutions once essential for maintaining a sense of ethnic identity lost their vitality. In the 1940's, one-third of the foreign language press disappeared. To be sure, the 1950's saw a greater immigration than any decade since the 1920's, although it was only a modest 2.5 million. Puerto Ricans filled every seat on the night flights from the island until there were more of their number in New York City than in San Juan, and Mexicans crowded the *barrios* of the Southwest until Los Angeles had a larger Hispano population than Guadalajara. Still, the United States had moved a good distance from the world of Mulberry Bend and the East Side ghetto.

Commentators found the United States not only homogeneous but homogenized. The typical American, social analysts complained, had become both conformist and bland. Each morning Mr. Jones put on a standard uniform of button-down shirt, sincere tie, and charcoal-gray flannel suit, and adjusted his perpetual smile. At night he read to his children from the "Little Golden Book" of Tootle the Engine, a cautionary tale with the admonition: "Always stay on the track no matter what." One mother was informed about her son's failings: "He was doing fine in some respects but . . . his social adjustment was not as good as it might be. He would pick one or two friends to play with—and sometimes he was happy to remain by himself." Conformity watchers fretted too about the corporation wife who was told to hide any journal discussing intellectual questions when another wife paid a call, and they noticed "more and more men prowling about in sports cars in which the driver nestles well down in the prenatal position." As ardent a Yankeephile as the French Jesuit philosopher Jacques Maritain described a dentist's office with nurses who gave him the feeling that "dying in the midst of these happy smiles and the angel wings of these white, immaculate uniforms would be a pure pleasure, a moment of no consequence. . . . I left this dentist, in order to protect within my mind the Christian idea of death." (Yet, Maritain conceded, "Deep beneath the anonymous American smile there is a feeling that is evangelical in origin— compassion for man, a desire to make life tolerable.")

The evangelist Billy Graham. At scores of revival meetings at home and abroad, he converted thousands
to the Christian faith, and millions watched his TV program,
"Hour for Decision." The favorite clergyman of the consumer culture and of
Republican Presidents, the handsome Baptist minister accepted God's call
on a Florida golf course, won the Horatio Alger award, and enjoyed the privilege
of free lodging at motels throughout the world.

" 'Religion' like many other things is booming in America; it is
a blue chip," reported the shrewd British observer, Denis Brogan,
in 1957. Five days before he was inaugurated, President-elect Eisenhower stared out of the window of his New York hotel room for several minutes absorbed in thought, then wheeled around and said to
the evangelist Billy Graham, "America has to have a religious re-

vival." One writer has observed, "Perhaps no other policy directive issued by Mr. Eisenhower during the next eight years was executed so promptly or enjoyed such widespread support." Ike's first year in office saw Les Paul and Mary Ford's "Vaya con Dios" and Frankie Laine's "I Believe" among the top ten hits. In 1954 Congress voted to add the phrase "under God" to the pledge of allegiance and in the following year made "In God We Trust" mandatory on all United States currency. Religion was merchandised like other products of the consumer culture through the mass media (TV spot commercials announced, "The family that prays together stays together") and by testimonials from satisfied users. "I love God," announced the bosomy film actress Jane Russell. "And when you get to know Him, you find He's a Livin' Doll." Book stores sold *The Power of Prayer on Plants,* the Ideal Toy Company offered a doll that, when stroked, genuflected, and jukeboxes blared "Big Fellow in the Sky."

Although many churchmen were pleased to count a full house each week, some theologians brooded about the shallow piety purveyed by men like the Reverend Norman Vincent Peale in *The Power of Positive Thinking* and the unconsidered response he won. "By and large," wrote Will Herberg, "the religion which actually prevails among Americans today has lost much of its authentic Christian (or Jewish) content." Still, a contentless creed of good fellowship, good works, and Thursday night bingo had one advantage: It diminished the sectarian discord that had so often envenomed small-town life. The "religious revival" was yet another occurrence that served to nationalize and homogenize the American people, an eventuality having benefits as well as costs.

"The Silent Generation" in American colleges in the 1950's appeared to be even more conformist and prudent than its elders. *Fortune* first detected the cautiousness of the young when it reflected that the men of the class of '49 "seem to a stranger from another generation, somehow curiously old before their time. Above everything else, security has become their goal. . . . The class of '49 wants to work for somebody else — preferably somebody big." In 1950, President A. Whitney Griswold of Yale told the graduating class, "I observe that you share the prevailing mood of the hour, which in your case consists of bargains privately struck with fate — on fate's terms." After examining a series of interviews, Riesman concluded that the typical class of '55 senior sought a place on the corporate ladder, planned which branch of the military he would enter (guided missiles was one favorite), and knew what his wife would be like at forty-five ("the Grace Kelly, camel's hair-coat type" who would do volunteer hospital work and bring culture into the home). By 1957, *Time* was reporting, "No campus is without its atrocity story of intellectual deadness," and Leslie Fiedler complained, "The young, who should be fatuously but profitably attacking us, instead discreetly expand, analyze and dissect us. How dull they are!" As late as 1962 so perceptive an observer of the young as Kenneth Keniston could write, "I see little likelihood of American students ever playing a radical role, much less a revolutionary one, in our society."

With such near-unanimity in the contemporary testimony, the historian has little choice but to accept this characterization of "the careful young men" of the 1950's, and perhaps he should. But one wonders if they may not have been given a bad rap. Even at the time, the sociologist Reuel Denney found them "about the freest generation of students in U.S. colleges in the 20th century," liberated from the "moral inflation" of the cults of the 1920's and 1930's. If they lacked the fervor of the activists of the 1960's who would succeed them, they also were without their arrogance. If they were less civic minded, they understood the value of a life style that was personal and not politicized. There was something to be said, too, for their feeling "that they have to know a lot more in their minds before they can become effectual." Besides, however quiescent the campuses were, "Silent Generation" does not characterize adequately the brawling street gangs who provided the *dramatis personae* for Leonard Bernstein's *West Side Story*, the juvenile delinquents who sent statistics on crimes of violence soaring, or all those "rebels without a cause" who made of James Dean's death a morbid remembrance.

In 1954, *McCall's* first employed the word "togetherness." So precise a term did it seem for the spirit of the 1950's that many thought that the word, first used in the seventeenth century, had been invented by the magazine. *McCall's* boasted: "From a little cloud, like a woman's hand, it has risen to blanket the consciousness of an entire nation, popping up everywhere from Macy's to the halls of Congress." "Togetherness" was variously defined as "the beat and rhythm of our times," "the tie that binds American families to their mothers," and "the only real definitive American market." The Reverend Norman Vincent Peale explained "togetherness" as the "creative mechanism which fuses the man and the woman into a team."

Publicists and educators celebrated woman's role as homemaker and helpmate and heaped scorn on feminists. In *Modern Woman: The Lost Sex*, Ferdinand Lundberg and Marynia Farnham depicted feminism as a "deep illness" caused by penis-envy; "the shadow of the phallus lay darkly" over those masculinized females who proselytized it. To erase the influence of such neurotics, they proposed to subsidize childbearing, encourage country skills like putting up preserves, and give annual prizes to the best mothers. The president of Mills College advocated a "distinctly feminine curriculum" in which post-Kantian studies would yield to the creation of paella, and the president of Stephens College, who touted his programs in interior decorating, home economics, cosmetics, and grooming, declared that for women "the college years must be rehearsal periods for the major performance" of wedlock. Their political assignment, Adlai Stevenson told Smith graduates, was to "influence man and boy" in the "humble role of housewife." For their part, women published articles with titles like "Homemaking Is My Vocation" and underwent instruction in natural childbirth. The editors of *Mademoiselle*, after analyzing hundreds of questionnaires, concluded that young women wanted to be well-rounded rather than to excel, viewed the family as "the ultimate measure of success," and looked forward to relaxed, uneventful marriages "of thoroughly barbecued bliss."

In the midst of these placid waters, stronger currents had begun to move. To the undiscerning eye, it appeared that Rosie the Riveter could not wait to bid good riddance to the war plant and resume her familiar duties at the hearthside. Yet, in fact, little noticed at the time, women's position in the job market was fundamentally shifting. Between 1940 and 1960, the proportion of working wives doubled, and of all persons who entered the labor market in the decade after 1949, three-fifths were married women. By 1960, some 40 percent of American women were employed, fully or part-time; even more striking, about the same proportion of mothers of school-age children held jobs. When the women's liberation movement erupted in the 1960's, it was in large part because, as William H. Chafe has noted, women "had already experienced profound change in their lives."

However, in the 1950's many wives worked less in order to achieve self-fulfillment than to add to the family income. The less a husband earned, the more likely it was that a wife would be employed. In the suburbs a second paycheck made it possible to turn the basement into a rumpus room. *Mademoiselle's* survey suggested that

The sizeable percentage of female employees in this photograph of an office at the Internal Revenue Service demonstrates that while national attention was focused on women in the home in the Eisenhower era, large numbers were holding down jobs. The photograph also suggests the growth of the white collar sector and the rapidly increasing importance of government as an employer.

young women did not view employment as a way of altering their "place." As Russell Lynes summed up their attitude: "A job is a way of meeting 'interesting' people, of keeping amused, a continuation of one's education, a way to live in Europe a year or two, but it must not be all-absorbing."

Much of the lamentation about conformity centered on the quality of life in the suburbs, for in the period after World War II the United States experienced the most extensive internal migration in its history. Scott Donaldson has listed the main influences: "practically universal car ownership, the expanding highway system, the baby boom of the forties, and most important of all, the availability of cheap homes, and cheap financing after World War II." By 1950, there were 37 million suburbanites; two decades later, the number had nearly doubled, after bulldozers plowed up the apricot groves of the Santa Clara Valley and cleared the way for ranch houses to be plunked in Long Island potato fields. As many moved to the suburbs each year as had come to the United States in the peak year of transatlantic migration. Increasingly the suburb became not just a collection of bedrooms but the hub of activities that had long been the pride of the city. The "Dallas" Cowboys played in Irving, the Minnesota Twins performed not in the Twin Cities but in Bloomington, and when the Patriots removed to Foxboro they even dropped "Boston" from their name. With more people living in suburbs in the 1960's than in cities or villages or on farms, the suburbanite became the representative American.

This great exodus had an exceptional racial characteristic; it was turning the United States into a nation of black cities and white suburbs. Analysts frequently wrote of "the flight" to the suburbs, and the movement was in fact motivated not only by the attraction of azaleas and green lawns but also by an aversion to the changing character of the city. Some whites wanted simply to escape crowded schools and foul air, but others undoubtedly left in response to the rapid influx of Negroes into the central cities. From 1940 to 1960, the number of blacks living outside the South more than doubled, in large part because of the mechanization of the cotton fields, and by 1969 only 52 percent of American Negroes still lived in Dixie (contrasted to 77 percent as late as 1940). In both North and South, the displaced persons of modern technology migrated to the city. Washington, D.C., 72 percent white in 1940, had become a predominantly black metropolis by 1960; a decade later, it had been joined by Newark, Gary, and Atlanta, and seven other cities were more than 40 percent black. Although well over a million Negroes moved to the suburbs in the two decades after 1950, the suburban population in 1970 remained more than 95 percent white.

To critics of the suburb, its racial homogeneity represented only one of its deplorable aspects. Shoddy housing developments, "conceived in error, nurtured by greed, corroding everything they touch," wrote John Keats in *The Crack in the Picture Window*, had been "vomited up" by conscienceless speculators who defaced the countryside with rows of "identical boxes spreading like gangrene." These excrescences bred "swarms of neuter drones . . . [who] cannot be said to have lives of their own." Nathan Detroit, in Frank Loesser's *Guys and Dolls*, sneered at the "Scarsdale Galahad, the breakfast-eating, Brooks Brothers type," while feature writers decried the truncated existence of people who dwelt in communities with no institutions more permanent than the supermarket and the filling station. In these misshapen matriarchies, where children

Levittown, Pennsylvania, and its counterpart on Long Island typify the suburban development in postwar America. On the lower left of the photograph one can see that part of the tract has not yet been landscaped. The picture is by Margaret Bourke-White, who began her distinguished career in photojournalism in 1927, won fame for her sensitive portraits of sharecroppers in the Great Depression, and received the American Woman of Achievement Award in 1951.

rarely saw their commuter fathers, harried mothers, it was said, were endlessly delivering children, "obstetrically once and by car forever after," to synthetic "activities." When writers were not taking suburbanites to task for insulating their children from contact with other races and classes, they were scolding them for running away from the crises of the city. One church in Old Greenwich,

Connecticut, noted John Brooks, even felt compelled to hold a symposium entitled "overcoming guilt about having deserted the urban core." "The very word, 'suburbia,' " as Donaldson observed, came to have "unpleasant overtones, suggesting nothing so much as some kind of scruffy disease."

More careful studies of "suburbia" indicated that these indictments were overdrawn. The critics, it became clear, had spun broad generalizations from a single type of suburb—the new, artificially created, one-class cluster—though there were, in fact, many different kinds. Some suburbs, like Secaucus, New Jersey, and Cicero, Illinois, had few of the attributes associated with "suburban" whereas sections such as New York City's Forest Hills and Philadelphia's Chestnut Hill within the incorporated areas of central cities had many. Suburbs like Oak Park outside Chicago were over a century old. Furthermore, one sociologist found that even in the archetypal Levittown on Long Island, residents had, by ingenious rearranging, modified the standardized boxes to reflect their own tastes. In another study, *Class in Suburbia,* William Dobriner reported that although Levittown may have been "monotonously middle class" at the outset, it rapidly acquired a more heterogeneous social mix. If blacks were still largely confined to the central cities, other ethnic groups fanned out as did Philip Roth's Jews, who "had struggled and prospered, and moved further and further west, towards the edge of Newark, then out of it, and up the slope of the Orange Mountains, until they had reached the crest and started down the other side, pouring into Gentile territory as the Scotch-Irish had poured through the Cumberland Gap."

A number of commentators asserted that changes in the structure of the economy, especially the evolution of the consumer culture, were producing a new character type. The psychoanalyst Erich Fromm wrote of the individual with a "marketing orientation" who thought acceptability hinged on "how well a person sells himself on the market, how well he gets his personality across, how nice a 'package' he is." In *White Collar,* C. Wright Mills declared: "When white-collar people get jobs, they sell not only their time and energy but their personalities as well. They sell by the week or month their smiles and their kindly gestures, and they must practice the prompt repression of resentment and aggression." William H. Whyte, Jr., in his best-seller *The Organization Man,* claimed that group-oriented Americans gave allegiance no longer to the individualistic Protestant ethic but to "an organization ethic," marked by "a belief in 'belongingness' as the ultimate need of the individual."

The most elaborate exposition of this interpretation came from the pen of David Riesman, notably in his highly influential 1950 volume *The Lonely Crowd.* In a consumption society, Riesman pointed out, characteristics honed in a scarcity order such as frugality and self-denial were no longer appropriate. What was required was "an 'abundance psychology' capable of 'wasteful' luxury consumption of leisure and of the surplus product." A child adapted in this new milieu not by internalizing traditional values but by sensitizing himself to the expectations of others, particularly peer groups but also strangers in the mass media. "Parents make him feel guilty not so much about violation of inner standards as about failure to be popular or otherwise to manage his relations with these other children," Riesman wrote. Indeed, in these changed circumstances, "parents who try, in inner-directed fashion, to compel the internalization of disciplined pursuit of clear goals run the risk of having their children styled clear out of the personality market."

Americans continued to think of their country as a citadel of individual entrepreneurs, but many more worked for organizations— corporations, government agencies, universities—than made it on their own. The proportion of self-employed (36 percent of the labor force in 1900) fell from 26 percent in 1940 to 16 percent in 1960. By the end of the 1950's some 38 percent drew their pay from organizations with more than five hundred employees, in contrast to only 28 percent in 1940. From 1950 to 1960 the employment rolls of state and local government increased 52 percent; in 1960 they accounted for nearly one-eighth of the nonagricultural work force.

In the 1950's, too, the United States evolved the world's first "service economy." The government announced in 1956 that white collar workers outnumbered blue collar workers. Most employees were engaged not in turning out tangible goods like coal and steel but in professional capacities or in distributive or promotional occupations—sales clerks, office workers, advertising personnel—to provide services to the consumer. From 1947 to 1957 the number of factory operatives fell 4 percent, clerical ranks grew 23 percent, and the salaried middle class increased 61 percent. On the TV show "What's My Line?" the panel learned to frame a critical question, "Do you deal in services?"

To social critics like C. Wright Mills this "new middle class" of white collar workers seemed menacing. The modern office reminded Mills of Herman Melville's description of a factory: "At rows of blank-looking counters sat rows of blank-looking girls, with blank, white folders in their blank hands, all blankly folding blank paper."

Indifferent or hostile to the impoverished, hungering for higher social status, the white collar people were the fulcrum of a world in which "political expression is banalized, political theory is barren administrative detail, history is made behind men's backs. Such is the political situation in which the new middle classes enact their passive role."

The work of writers like Riesman, Mills, Whyte, and Fromm sent through intellectual circles reverberations that have not yet ended. "The upper-middle-educated American became a fascinated voyeur of his own victimization," Cushing Strout has observed. "The relish with which so many academics devoured these depressing images of American society reflects a blend of self-congratulatory relief for not having 'gone into trade' and self-accusing recognition of their own fate in the struggle for tenure and grants in the affluent 'multi-versities.'" Riesman was widely misunderstood to be saying that most Americans were "other-directed" and that the "other-directed" man was more conformist than the "inner-directed" man. In fact, some sociologists and historians doubted that conformity was a new phenomenon or peculiar to America and questioned whether it was so pervasive in the United States as the faultfinders suggested. Uniformity of views clearly did not characterize the scholarly community, for though writers like Mills were disenchanted, others were more favorably disposed.

Intellectuals who had once heaped derision on the United States now sang its praises. In 1950 Samuel Eliot Morison told the American Historical Association that he was pleased to discern "a decided change of attitude towards our past, a friendly almost affectionate attitude," which he contrasted with the earlier "cynical, almost hateful" judgment. The new mood resulted in part from the fact that the dour prophecies intellectuals had made had not been fulfilled. The historian Richard Hofstadter later commented: "We were surprised by the fact that instead of having a tremendous depression after the war, which those of us who were mature in the '30s thought surely was coming, we entered upon one of the great boom periods of history." As an unanticipated by-product of this prosperity, lavish foundation grants bankrolled a good many intellectuals. One critic remarked, "They are almost never unemployed; they are only between grants." When *Partisan Review,* once a gadfly of the establishment, sponsored a symposium of intellectuals, it bore the remarkable title, "Our Country and Our Culture," nomenclature that would have seemed odd in the 1920's and would again in the 1960's. "For the first time in the history of the modern intellectual," observed one of the contributors to that symposium, the literary critic Lionel Trilling, "America is not to be conceived of as *a priori* the vulgarest and stupidest nation of the world."

In the Eisenhower years, liberals lost their dread of the mammoth corporation. It was hard to summon up the kind of hatred reformers had once felt for the Jay Goulds and direct it toward the virtuous executives who sponsored projects like the Pepsi-Cola art contest. Moreover, those who sang paeans for a pluralist social order observed that corporation leaders, unlike the despots of old, were restrained by the "countervailing power" (John Kenneth Galbraith's phrase) of government and unions. Nor could one gainsay the accomplishment of corporations in swelling the gross national product. As a consequence of all these developments, David Lilienthal, who had entered public life as a Brandeisian foe of the power companies, wrote, "Big business represents a proud and fruitful achievement of the American people," and Adolf A. Berle, Jr., who had once anatomized the uncontrolled power of the new managerial class, praised tycoons for their sense of social concern.

No longer did corporations present the image of the heartless robber barons of the 1880's or the vicious union busters of the 1930's. "The big, coldly menacing grizzlies of 1939," wrote John Brooks, became "the superbig, smiling, approval-seeking pandas of 1964." The nineteenth century's "dark Satanic mill" gave way to the bright, if antiseptic, plant in the "industrial park." IBM maintained country clubs for its employees; Richfield Oil built model homes; and American Cyanamid hired psychiatrists to minister to the emotional needs of its workers. In fact, corporations came to be criticized not because they were malevolent but because they had become too benign and were imprisoning their employees in brotherhood and "belongingness." As one reviewer summed up this argument, "The capitalist robber baron has turned out to be a love-starved aunt cramming cake into eager little mouths." The diminished animus toward corporations inevitably shifted politics in a conservative direction, for leftwing movements in the past had battened on antipathy to monopolies.

Radicalism had no significant form of political expression in the 1950's. The Progressive Party petered out after its poor showing in 1948, and in 1952 Henry Wallace resigned from the party to signify his determination to stand by his country in the Korean War. He denounced the Soviet Union, came out for massive rearmament, and approved using the atomic bomb if military necessity required it. In that year the Socialist Party drew less than one-third as many votes as the Prohibitionists, and "for all intents and purposes," wrote Irving Howe and Lewis Coser in 1957, "the American Communist Party is dead."

Those who hoped for a more militant political movement in the 1950's looked expectantly at the ranks of organized labor. The goal of a labor party on a European scale had long been the Big Rock Candy Mountain of American social democrats, and in the 1940's they eyed wistfully the nationalization experiments of British Labour. For a time, Walter Reuther, who came out of a Socialist background, contemplated creating such a party. This would have been inconceivable at the start of the Roosevelt era, but by 1945 union membership, only 3 million in 1932, had risen to nearly 15 million. In 1955, when Reuther of the Congress of Industrial Organizations and George Meany of the American Federation of Labor concluded merger negotiations, the new AFL-CIO claimed over 16 million members, and there were another 1.7 million in independent unions like the railway brotherhoods. In the late 1950's two-thirds of the production force in manufacturing was unionized. Furthermore, labor organizations had expanded their domain from wages and hours to negotiations over such a range of questions, from rest periods to health insurance to pensions, that economists spoke of "welfare bargaining."

Yet well before the merger had been carried out, Reuther recognized that there was no prospect for a vigorous labor party. After the turbulence that in 1946 cost 115 million man-days, union aggressiveness had subsided to such a point that by 1963 less time was lost to strikes than to coffee breaks. The young, class-conscious workingmen who had fought the battles of River Rouge and Flint in the 1930's had become middle-aged, enbourgeoised members of the PTA. Often the union leaders were even more removed from their working-class origins. Refractory steelworkers grumbled about the "tuxedo unionism" of their president, David J. McDonald. Dave Beck of the Teamsters could afford a stud, trainers, and jockeys. In Washington, Meany, who once plied the trade of plumber, rode in a chauffeured limousine, and the Hod Carriers Union shared the ground floor of the swank Carlton Hotel with a covey of stockbrokers. Furthermore, labor's stake in the prosperity of the weapons industries reinforced the inclination of union leaders to subdue protests that might seem to jeopardize national unity. Increasingly, social reform had a lower priority than loyalty to the government's aims in the cold war.

In part because of deficient leadership, but more as a result of changes in the structure of the labor market, union efforts to attract new recruits faltered. Although membership rolls continued to expand in the 1950's, they failed to keep pace with additions to the working force. The percentage of the nonagricultural laboring population in unions fell from 33.2 in 1955 to 28.4 in 1968. Labor was hurt by the movement of industry to the South and to other regions hostile to unionism and by shifts in the economy that reduced the number of bituminous coal miners in the 1950's from 344,000 to 149,000 and the highly unionized railroad force from 1,700,000 in 1929 to 800,000 in 1960. It was hit even harder by the rapid growth of the white collar segment. Labor organizations made little headway in signing up clerical employees, who regarded union buttons as stigmata of lower social status. By the early 1960's, unions confronted a sorrowful situation: Snooty white collar workers were composing an ever larger portion of the labor force at the same time that technological displacement was shoving union members into the ranks of the unemployed.

Through much of the 1950's, the United States lived, as the social critic Paul Goodman wrote, "in a political limbo." Serious questions, such as whether to recognize Red China, were treated as though they were beyond the bounds of decent discourse, and criticism of Eisenhower was reproved as lèse majesté if not blasphemy. The President reflected the wishes of a society that wanted a respite from public affairs, but he in turn helped to reinforce these sentiments. If the country did not agitate more vigorously for attention to pressing needs, this was partly because Eisenhower, by his own example, served to mute concern and to tranquilize the nation.

The more disaffected American intellectuals viewed Eisenhower if not as the agent of quiescence and even torpor in a homogenized society then as its representative figure. A Nebraska professor, bemoaning the passivity of the university student, observed, "The vague but comforting symbol of Eisenhower has seeped into the vacuum of this generation's mind," and Robert Lowell concluded his poem "Inauguration Day: January, 1953" by writing:

> Ice, ice. Our wheels no longer move.
> Look, the fixed stars, all just alike
> as lack-land atoms, split apart,
> and the Republic summons Ike,
> the mausoleum in her heart.

Ike. The smile and the waving hand convey the amiable reassurance that won overwhelming victory for Dwight D. Eisenhower in 1952 and approval of 69 percent polled in 1955. "Everybody ought to be happy every day," the President said. "Play hard, have fun doing it, and despise wickedness."

The Politics of Tranquility

Rarely has a public figure so suited a nation's mood as did Dwight David Eisenhower. At a time when many had wearied of partisan strife, he was a man unsullied by political experience. In 1948, he had thrown cold water on an attempt to draft him for the presidency by observing, "The necessary and wise subordination of the military to civilian power will be best sustained when life-long professional soldiers abstain from seeking high political office." Never had a general seemed so singularly lacking in the qualities associated with a martinet. His genial manner and his ready grin moved multitudes to shout, "I like Ike." So did his humble comportment. At a whistle stop he would say, "It's all a bit overwhelming to me to see a great crowd like this. My memory goes back to a barren Kansas prairie and six little boys running around barefooted in the dust. I never get over my astonishment that you want to know what I think." Yet as the victorious commander of the Allied forces in the war against fascism, the general appeared ideally qualified to bring the Korean episode to a satisfactory termination.

Eisenhower had little difficulty in overcoming his opposition in the 1952 campaign. As the favorite of the internationalist, moderate eastern seaboard wing of his party, he won the Republican nomination by subduing Robert Taft, the idol of the more nationalist, conservative hinterland. (From 1936 until 1964, Corn Belt conservatives dominated the GOP bloc in Congress but failed to win the presidential designation.) The Democrats came up with a reluctant nominee of their own in Adlai Stevenson, Illinois governor and former New Deal functionary. Although Stevenson's wit and eloquence delighted readers of the *Atlantic Monthly*, he was no match for Ike. Stevenson's admirers had a moment of hope when it was revealed that Eisenhower's running mate, Senator Richard Nixon of California, had benefited from a "millionaires' fund." But Nixon turned this to his advantage with a "soap opera" performance on television in which he told about receiving an unsolicited gift, a black and white cocker spaniel which his six-year-old daughter Tricia named Checkers. Consumption styles also seemed relevant, for Nixon's reference to his wife's simple cloth coat was offered as a measure of his probity in contrast to the mink-coated spouses of Democratic officials. Apart from Eisenhower's personal popularity, the critical development of the campaign came on October 24 in Detroit when the general promised, "I shall go to Korea." Few any longer thought the Democrats could terminate the "police action." In balloting featured by a sharply increased turnout, Eisenhower rolled up 34 million votes (55.1 percent) to Stevenson's 27 million (44.4 percent).

The 1952 elections revealed affection for Ike rather than for his party. Despite his whopping plurality, the Republicans barely won control of Congress, the Senate only by the Vice-President's tie-breaking margin. Indeed in the 1950's the GOP not once got as much as 50 percent of the total national popular vote for the House; in 1958, when Vermont sent the first Democrat to Congress in 106 years and Missouri gave Senator Stuart Symington a lopsided 66 percent, the Republican share fell to the lowest level since 1936. In 1956, Eisenhower would defeat Stevenson a second time with the slogan "Everything's booming but the guns," but the Democrats would sweep both houses of Congress—the first time since Zachary Taylor's victory in 1848 that a presidential candidate had triumphed without his party's carrying at least one house. However, Eisenhower's appeal did contribute to the nationalization of American politics. The general captured four southern states in 1952. In 1956, he added Louisiana, which had been Democratic since 1880. Since 1944, the Democrats have not been able to count on their old standby, the "Solid South."

Some hoped that when Eisenhower entered the White House he would use his enormous popularity to lead the country toward a solution of pressing social problems, but the new President had quite a different expectation. He believed that his Democratic predecessors had impaired the dignity of the office in legislative brawls and that a President who assumed the role of chief legislator was transgressing the prerogatives of Congress. "I don't feel like I should nag them," he explained. At times he carried his conviction to the point of refusing even to comment on pending bills. The political scientist Louis W. Koenig has called this conception of the presidency "the greatest retreat in the national experience since the first battle of Bull Run." Eisenhower thought of his chairman-of-the-board stance as a neutral attitude, but it inevitably had programmatic consequences. As Earl Latham has noted, "The weak-President model of the Executive office is congenial to an economic philosophy in which the major decisions are to be left in private hands." When, after the death of John Foster Dulles in 1959 and the departure, in a cloud of obloquy, of the President's trusted aide Sherman Adams, Eisenhower did take a firm hold on the reins, it was in order to diminish government action—an attempt, as Richard Rovere said, to use "mastery in the service of drift."

Election of 1952

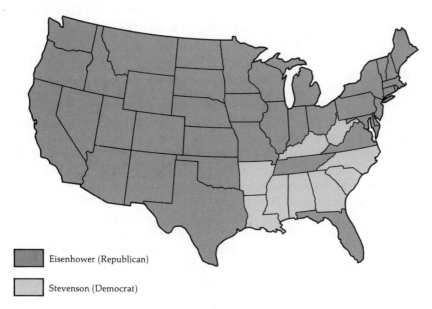

Eisenhower (Republican)

Stevenson (Democrat)

Election of 1956

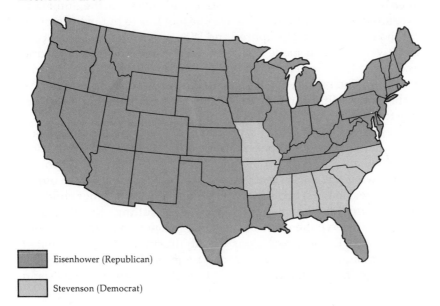

Eisenhower (Republican)

Stevenson (Democrat)

For those who had conceived of Eisenhower as leader of the GOP's liberal wing, his appointments came as a shock. To his Cabinet he named no fewer than three men with ties to General Motors — Charles E. Wilson, president of GM, as secretary of defense, and two auto distributors, Douglas McKay to the Interior Department and Arthur Summerfield as postmaster general. He filled other slots with conservatives such as George Humphrey of Mark Hanna's old company, who became secretary of the treasury. The one exception was the president of the plumbers union, Martin Durkin, chosen secretary of labor; within eight months he would give way to a businessman. "Eight millionaires and a plumber," *The New Republic* wrote, and Adlai Stevenson remarked that "the New Dealers have all left Washington to make way for the car dealers."

When Secretary Humphrey hung Andrew Mellon's portrait behind his desk, some feared that the nation was in the hands of 1920's reactionaries. Asked whether he had read Ernest Hemingway's *The Old Man and the Sea,* Humphrey responded, "Why would anybody be interested in some old man who was a failure and never amounted to anything anyway?" Humphrey's mother, it was learned, insisted on spelling Franklin Roosevelt's name with a small *r.* Secretary Wilson added to the uneasiness by saying that "what was good for our country was good for General Motors, and vice versa," and by likening the unemployed to "kennel-fed dogs." In Washington, the story circulated that the former GM executive had invented the automatic transmission so that he would have one foot free to put in his mouth. Yet though men like Humphrey and Wilson were undoubtedly conservative, most had made a separate peace with the New Deal and recognized that they could not undo developments such as industrial unionism. The President relied on these spokesmen for the "Practical Right"; of the fifty-three in the highest circle of the administration, only four were professional politicians.

Eisenhower advertised his program as "dynamic conservatism," which implied being "conservative when it comes to money and liberal when it comes to human beings." (Stevenson gibed: "I assume what it means is that you will strongly recommend the building of a great many schools to accommodate the needs of our children, but not provide the money.") By budget-cutting, the President hoped to preserve the value of the dollar through reducing inflationary pressure. Even in recessions the administration opposed deficit financing and large public works projects; Eisenhower warned against "going too far with trying to fool with our economy" and

setting up "huge federal bureaucracies of the PWA or the WPA type."
The President deliberately sought ways to reduce the role of the
federal government in the economy by increasing opportunities for
private corporations and turning national functions back to state
and local governments. After the conservative Senator Taft, his
former rival, explained the proposals for social legislation he was
sponsoring, Ike responded, "Why, Bob, with those views you're
twice as liberal as I am."

When the President attempted to apply these doctrines to natural
resources, he came to grief. He did win congressional support for
handing over to the adjacent states the oil-rich offshore "tidelands,"
which the Supreme Court had ruled belonged to the federal government. But the administration's efforts to hem in the Tennessee Valley
Authority (Eisenhower actually wanted to sell it) by negotiating an
arrangement with the Dixon-Yates utility syndicate embroiled it in
a costly fiasco. So objectionable were the circumstances of the deal
that the government wound up in the embarrassing position of suing
to cancel as "contrary to public policy" the contract it had negotiated.

Outside of natural resources, the Eisenhower administration made
limited attempts to turn back the clock. Although little of the New
Deal or Fair Deal was dismantled, the Reconstruction Finance
Corporation was liquidated, the Korean war economic controls
were abruptly ended, and Secretary of Agriculture Ezra Taft Benson
attempted to reduce farm subsidies. The new emphasis was apparent in the policies pursued by business-minded officials on
regulatory commissions and other government agencies, often with
deplorable results. When Secretary of Commerce Sinclair Weeks fired
the head of the Bureau of Standards for refusing to sanction the
marketing of a defective battery additive, he raised an outcry against
business influence on government, and when Secretary of Health,
Education and Welfare Oveta Culp Hobby opposed the free distribution to schoolchildren of the new vaccine for polio developed by
Dr. Jonas Salk, the resulting furor led to her resignation.

In Eisenhower's second term, as criticism of the lack of attention
to national needs mounted, the President stiffened. He vetoed two
public housing measures, two anti-recession public works bills,
an area redevelopment proposal, anti-pollution legislation (pollution was a "uniquely local blight"), and by the threat of the veto
deterred Democrats who wanted to push Fair Deal legislation. At
his behest, Congress changed a labor reform measure sponsored
by Senator John F. Kennedy, as a consequence of hearings that ex-

posed the "hoodlum empire" of Dave Beck and Jimmy Hoffa's Teamsters, into the Landrum-Griffin Act, a statute that settled some old scores with unions but left the Teamsters virtually unscathed. Intimidated by the President's insistence on budget-cutting, the Democratic leaders—Lyndon B. Johnson in the Senate and Sam Rayburn in the House—squandered the opportunities for advanced legislation provided by the big Democratic gains in the 1958 elections.

Yet Eisenhower's legislative agenda also found room for moderate reform measures, in part because the President accepted the need for a degree of government responsibility, in part because of the insistence of Democrats and pressure groups. In the Eisenhower years, Congress greatly expanded social security and unemployment compensation coverage, raised the minimum wage, authorized the construction of the St. Lawrence seaway in cooperation with Canada, and in 1953 established a Department of Health, Education and Welfare. (As secretary of the new department, Mrs. Hobby became the second woman, and first Republican of her sex, to hold a Cabinet post. The first female Cabinet member, Secretary of Labor Frances Perkins, had been appointed by Franklin D. Roosevelt in 1933.) Eisenhower did little substantial to develop federal programs in housing and education, but he did suggest that government initiative in these fields was appropriate. In sum, Eisenhower, although his actions generally ran in a contrary direction, helped encourage an important sector of "modern Republicans" to acknowledge that national responsibility for social welfare was something other than New Deal heresy.

In spite of Eisenhower's commitment to diminish the suzerainty of the federal government, Washington was playing at least as great a role at the end of Eisenhower's tenure as it had when he took office. When, on three occasions, the administration encountered recessions, it resorted, however queasily, to some of the devices associated with the New Dealers—government spending (albeit for highways that leveled the countryside), easier credit, tax cuts, depreciation allowances, and welfare payments. If Eisenhower was hardly the Keynesian some writers have described him as being, and if recovery resulted more from built-in stabilizers and inadvertent deficits than from the President's efforts, he did make clear that a Republican administration would pursue at least limited countercyclical policies in a slump. Moreover, not only did the President's attempt to decentralize authority fizzle but his campaign to slash federal spending ran into a series of obstacles—the voracious demands of military and foreign aid programs, the baleful effect on the economy of reductions in government outlays, and the unacceptable political and economic costs of denying benefits to groups such as farmers. Under Eisenhower, the federal administrative budget, which totaled $39.5 billion in 1950, a Truman year, reached $76.5 billion in 1960, and the national debt rose from $266 billion in 1953 to $286 billion in 1960. At the end of the 1959 fiscal year, Eisenhower's administration was running the highest deficit ever accumulated by an American government in peacetime.

History (or at least historians, who hold letters patent from the Muse) has judged Eisenhower more harshly than did his contemporaries. During his two terms in office, millions of Americans admired him as a man and for his emphasis on defusing the cold war while promoting the consumer culture. Although there were swelling numbers of Ikonoclasts at the end of his reign, few doubted that if Eisenhower had been a candidate in 1960 he would have won another resounding victory. However, two years later a poll of seventy-five historians placed him between Chester Arthur and Andrew Johnson. Eisenhower's achievements lay in his performance as a bringer of tranquility, a kind of peace abroad, a respite from strife at home. Yet calm bore a high price tag—the public sector shortchanged, the national estate deteriorating, the legal rights of Negroes disregarded, and an accumulation of unsolved social problems that would overwhelm his successors in the 1960's.

The Struggle for Civil Rights

The consumer culture made a profound impact on an upheaval from which it might have been thought quite remote, the campaign for Negro equality. Some of the most important battlefields of the civil rights movement would be motels, dime store eating places, and laundromats. Michael Walzer found that sit-in participants had materialistic as well as moral ends and were "willing to take risks in the name of both prosperity and virtue." At times cold war and consumer culture aspects were linked together by a single graphic incident. When the finance minister of Ghana ordered orange juice at a Howard Johnson's in Dover, Delaware, only to be told that Negroes could not drink or eat on the premises, Washington was embarrassed in its relations with the third world. The vivid display of the affluence of white society on television screens in black ghettos helped arouse anger at the maldistribution of wealth and a demand for a fairer share. To be sure, for most of the world's ghetto dwellers possession of a TV set would have seemed the ultimate luxury, but in a land of superabundance Negroes understandably felt a sense of relative deprivation. Moreover, the fact that many lived well above the subsistence level meant that increasing numbers were exposed to additional forms of discrimination when they sought to spend their cash. As a foreign observer noted, "Only people who are relatively well off in the first place worry about service and treatment at a lunch counter."

The campaign to give Negroes a central place in American society gained greatly increased momentum in the postwar era as the NAACP, the organization of aspiring middle-class Negroes, carried its brilliant strategy of ending racial discrimination through litigation to its culmination. For a generation a battery of lawyers, Negro and white, had been adroitly chipping away at the "separate but equal" doctrine in education, not by assaulting separateness but by insisting on absolute equality. The NAACP's attorneys won a series of victories in higher education, sorely trying the ingenuity of the segregationists. "You can't build a cyclotron for one student," conceded the president of the University of Oklahoma. In 1950 the court ruled that even if Texas built a separate law school for its lone Negro applicant it would not be providing equality.

With little left of the "separate but equal" doctrine on the campus, the NAACP leveled its guns directly at the principle of separateness, and not in the university but in the much more socially sensitive institution of the public school. It was conceded that in Topeka the separate black system that eight-year-old Linda Carol Brown attended was substantially equal to the white schools, but the NAACP's counsel, Thurgood Marshall, offered sociological evidence to demonstrate that segregation harmed children, both black and white, and argued that classification by race violated the Fourteenth Amendment.

On May 17, 1954, Eisenhower's new appointee, Chief Justice Earl Warren, spoke for a unanimous Supreme Court in *Brown* v. *Board of Education.* The Court, reversing *Plessy* v. *Ferguson,* stated that "in the field of public education the doctrine of 'separate but equal' has no place." To separate schoolchildren "solely because of their race," Warren averred, "generates a feeling of inferiority as to their status in the community that may affect their hearts and minds in a way unlikely ever to be undone." In one footnote, Warren cited several sociological works, adding: "And see generally Myrdal, *An American Dilemma.*" By a subsequent order the Court asked not for immediate total compliance but for action "with all deliberate speed." The border states, as well as idiosyncratic localities in Kansas and Arizona, responded readily, and large cities like Washington and Baltimore rapidly overhauled their entire school systems to end racial discrimination. The success in Washington owed much to President Eisenhower, who moved firmly in areas where federal authority was unquestionable — veterans' hospitals, navy yards in Norfolk and Charleston, as well as schools and other institutions in the District of Columbia.

But Eisenhower refused to perform the much more important task of persuading the South to abide by the Court's rulings. Skeptical of the value of coercion, fastidious about not overstepping his authority, the President would not even say that he supported the Court. "I am convinced that the Supreme Court decision *set back* progress in the South *at least fifteen years,*" he told an aide. "The fellow who tries to tell me you can do these things by *force* is just plain *nuts.*" He insisted: "No matter how much law we have, we have a job in education, in getting people to understand what are the issues here involved." Yet it was precisely the "job in education" that he would not carry out, and as Eisenhower faltered, moderates in the South who wanted to obey the law of the land were left leaderless, and racist opposition gained momentum.

Within a year, the federal courts faced a hostile phalanx in the southern press, almost all of Dixie's political leaders, and the newly formed White Citizens' Councils. In 1955 the Richmond *News Leader,* one of the country's most respected newspapers, trumpeted:

> In May of 1954, that inept fraternity of politicians and professors known as the United States Supreme Court chose to throw away the established law. These nine men repudiated the Constitution, spit upon the Tenth Amendment, and rewrote the fundamental law of this land to suit their own gauzy concepts of sociology. If it be said now that the South is flouting the law, let it be said to the high court, *You taught us how.*

In eight southern states in 1955 not one Negro pupil attended school with a white child. The following year a pugnacious Southern Manifesto was signed by 101 members of Congress, including the former Rhodes Scholar and university president J. William Fulbright and every Senator from the states of the Confederacy save Lyndon Johnson of Texas and Tennessee's Estes Kefauver and Albert Gore.

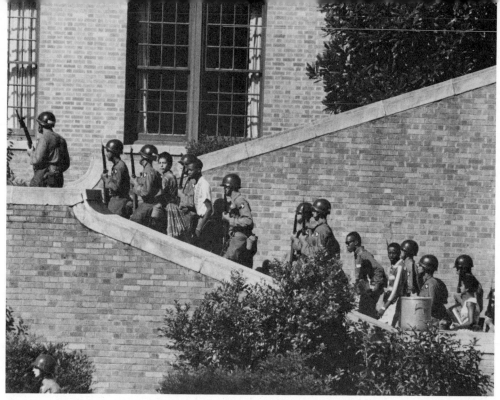

Bayonet-wielding paratroopers escort Negro students at Little Rock Central High School in September 1957, after the governor of Arkansas, Orval E. Faubus, had used National Guardsmen to bar their entry. Critics of the governor gibed: "Would you want Orval Faubus to marry your daughter?"

As Anthony Lewis wrote: "The true meaning of the Manifesto was to make defiance of the Supreme Court and the Constitution socially acceptable in the South—to give resistance to the law the approval of the Southern Establishment."

Encouraged by such sentiment, Governor Orval Faubus of Arkansas in 1957 raised the most serious challenge to federal authority since the Civil War. When Little Rock, a New South city under moderate leadership, acceded to a federal court order to admit nine Negroes to Central High School, Faubus sent in the Arkansas National Guard to bar their path. One child made an unforgettable impression. Fifteen-year-old Elizabeth Eckford, neatly dressed in a white short-sleeved blouse, a cotton skirt, bobby socks, and ballet slippers, got off a bus at the corner of 14th and Park Streets carrying her notebook. Head held high, she made her way through the hostile crowd to the line of soldiers, who raised their rifles. Turned away, she walked back through the gauntlet of guardsmen, followed by jeering students and

Coretta King and Martin Luther King sit in front of the courthouse at Montgomery, Alabama, where the young Baptist minister led a successful year-long boycott against segregated buses. A year before he took over the pastorate of the Dexter Avenue church in Montgomery, King married Coretta Scott, an Antioch graduate who was studying at the New England Conservatory of Music.

adults. For thirty-five minutes she stood at the bus stop harried by the threatening crowd, until a bus came by and took her home. As the crisis built, Eisenhower had offered no guidance and had even remarked on the southern concern about "mongrelization of the race." When he conferred with Faubus at his vacation headquarters in Newport, Rhode Island, he failed to bring the governor to heel. A second attempt to secure admission for the students was frustrated when a howling mob ringed the school and refused to heed a presidential order to disperse.

With the prestige of his office at stake, Eisenhower acted straightforwardly in defense of national supremacy. He placed the Arkansas National Guard under federal authority and sent in a thousand paratroopers. On the morning of September 18, an armed detachment led Elizabeth Eckford and the other eight young blacks into the school. For a while soldiers with bayonets escorted Negro students through the corridors of Central High School. Eisenhower, who had been unwilling to sanction any force, had ended up outraging the white South by becoming the first president since Reconstruction to dispatch federal troops in support of the rights of Negroes.

Even this did not end the turmoil. Faubus shut down Little Rock's high schools altogether in 1958 and 1959, and to open the schools required still another federal court edict. Virginia, too, sanctioned closing schools to forestall integration, but a series of federal and state court decrees terminated "massive resistance" in 1959, the year the walls of segregation were breached in Florida. Still, it was only token integration. A decade after the *Brown* decision, merely 1 percent of the Negro pupils in the South went to school with white children.

Congress did even less than the President to speed integration, but the little it did was hailed as epic-making. In 1957, for the first time since 1875, Congress enacted a civil rights statute. The law authorized federal suits in support of Negroes denied the right to vote and set up a Commission on Civil Rights. A second Civil Rights Act in 1960, which overcame a southern filibuster of 125 consecutive hours, further strengthened national authority over suffrage. For his role in securing passage of these modest measures, which sidestepped the issue of segregation, Lyndon Johnson was hailed as master legislator. In truth neither Congress nor the President gave much aid to the beleaguered judges or the harried black students, and as a consequence only slow headway was made in the Eisenhower years.

Yet the courageous Negro youngsters (and their white allies on bench and school board) did help win an increasing number of Americans of all races to the cause of civil rights. As Alexander M. Bickel of Yale Law School wrote of the school clashes: "Here were grown men and women furiously confronting their enemy: two, three, a half-dozen scrubbed, starched, scared and incredibly brave colored children. The moral bankruptcy, the shame of the thing, was evident." The movement to desegregate the schools also encouraged Negroes to move on other fronts to regain the rights they had enjoyed during Radical Reconstruction but had been deprived of thereafter.

One year after the Court handed down the *Brown* decision, an episode on a Montgomery, Alabama, bus turned the civil rights movement in a new direction. On December 1, 1955, Mrs. Rosa Parks, a Negro seamstress weary from a day's work, refused to give up her seat to a white man. She was arrested and ordered to stand trial. Leaders of the Negro community met the next night in the Dexter Avenue Baptist Church; there to take up his first pastorate had recently come a young Atlantan trained in theology at Boston University, Reverend Martin Luther King, Jr. Under King's leadership, Montgomery's Negroes organized a massive boycott; for months, buses rolled nearly empty through the streets of the Cradle of the Confederacy. At first, King's Montgomery Improvement Association was willing to settle for maintaining the custom of Negroes sitting in the back of the bus so long as seats were on a first-come first-served basis, but as the months went by the whole Jim Crow system came under attack. The long boycott ended in victory when on November 13, 1956, the Supreme Court unanimously affirmed a lower court ruling invalidating Alabama's segregation statutes. In the end, Jim Crow met death through traditional methods—litigation in federal courts by an elite of NAACP attorneys—but the protest also marked the beginning of a new style of mass action led by young, indigenous black southerners.

King, who would eventually become a Nobel Peace Laureate, attracted national attention by his skillful direction of the boycott and his eloquent espousal of the doctrine of nonviolent resistance. On the night after he was indicted in Montgomery for violating Alabama's anti-boycott law, he said: "If we are arrested every day, if we are exploited every day, if we are trampled over every day, don't ever let anyone pull you so low as to hate them. We must use the weapon of love. We must have compassion and understanding for those who hate us."

King's preaching combined the rhetoric of evangelical Christianity with the lessons of Gandhi's Satyagraha campaign against the British *raj* in India, and when in 1957 the young minister founded the Southern Christian Leadership Conference (SCLC), Negro churches played old movies of the Mahatma. King sensed not only that nonviolence was an appropriate technique for a caste-ridden minority but that it could make a unique contribution to reuniting "the broken community." He assured his followers: "If you will protest courageously, and yet with dignity and Christian love, when the history books are written in future generations, the historians will have to pause and say, 'There lived a great people—a black people—who injected new meaning and dignity into the veins of civilization.'"

The passive resistance movement took on added dimensions when on February 1, 1960, four Negro freshmen from North Carolina Agricultural and Technical College—Ezell Blair, Jr., Franklin McCain, Joseph McNeill, and David Richmond—sat down at a Woolworth's lunch counter in Greensboro, North Carolina, and, having been refused service, remained in their seats. They were soon joined by other students, white and black, some fifty thousand in all, who organized similar "sit-ins" in restaurants, theaters, and laundromats, as well as "kneel-ins" in churches and "wade-ins" in pools. Although the Congress of Racial Equality (CORE) had organized a sit-in in Chicago as early as 1942, it had not succeeded in eliciting such a broad-gauged, largely spontaneous response. Well-mannered, well-groomed, the students shunned violence even when provoked by tormentors who burned them with lighted cigarettes, and their comportment impressed segregationists as well as partisans. The editor of the Richmond *News Leader* wrote:

Here were the colored students, in coats, white shirts, ties, and one of them was reading Goethe and one was taking notes from a biology text. And here, on the sidewalk outside, was a gang of white boys come to heckle, a ragtail rabble, slack-jawed, black-jacketed, grinning fit to kill, and some of them, God save the mark, were waving the proud and honored flag of the Southern States in the last war fought by gentlemen. *Eheu!* it gives one pause.

The sit-ins fundamentally transformed both the mores of public accommodation in the upper South and the structure of the civil rights movement. Before 1960 had run its course, lunch counters in 126 cities had been desegregated, and the total would reach 200 in the next year. The demonstrations had an even more consequential long-range impact by shifting the focus of activity from the court-room to the streets and from the prestigious NAACP to SNCC, the Student Nonviolent Coordinating Committee, organized in April 1960 at a conference called by Martin Luther King, although the NAACP Legal Defense Fund would continue to prove indispensable to the students. At its birth "Snick" embraced King's philosophy of peaceful, interracial protest, but it would soon be marching to a different drum.

The Warren Court

With the President exerting little leadership and Congress stalemated, the main engine of social action in the Eisenhower era, and even later, turned out to be the least likely of the three branches, the Supreme Court, under Chief Justice Earl Warren. Reformers had long viewed this "undemocratic" institution, with its robed dignitaries insulated from popular control, as a bulwark for reaction, and the "Constitutional Revolution of 1937" had marked a triumph for liberalism precisely because it had circumscribed the powers of the High Bench. New Dealers rejoiced, and conservatives moaned, when the Court accepted the doctrine of "judicial self-restraint." But after Eisenhower in 1953 named California's three-time governor to the chief justiceship, the "Warren Court" (which embraced seventeen justices during Warren's sixteen-year tenure) astonished the nation by intervening in areas traditionally thought to be beyond its scope. The appointment of Warren ("biggest damfool mistake I ever made," Eisenhower later said) brought to the High Court a "Swedish Jim Farley," gregarious and politically astute, who had an instinct for governing. However, because he had opposed reapportionment, ardently advocated the internment of Japanese-Americans during World War II, and flayed the Truman administration for "coddling" Reds, few in 1953 anticipated that under Warren's leadership the Court would revamp the apportionment system and protect the liberties of minorities and radicals. The Court's wide-ranging decisions resulted in a historic flip-flop, with conservatives denouncing the judiciary for meddling and liberals hailing it as the instrument of democratic change.

The Warren Court, which first kicked up a storm with the decisions putting it in the business of desegregating schools and other social institutions, stirred another tempest over its rulings on sub-

Noel Clark from Black Star

Above the bespectacled Chief Justice of the United States, Earl Warren, stands Associate Justice William J. Brennan, Jr. Eisenhower appointed Warren, the popular California governor, in 1953 and named Brennan, a New Jersey judge, to the "Catholic seat" on the Supreme Court in 1956, but both quickly adopted positions well beyond those held by the President.

version. To be sure, the Supreme Court has customarily defended civil liberties from encroachment by the national government in wartime and in other periods of stress only after the main peril has passed, and the Warren Court proved no exception. Not until 1957, the year Joe McCarthy died, did it act forthrightly. On "Red Monday," June 17, Justice William J. Brennan, Jr., another Eisenhower appointee, spoke for the court in the *Jencks* opinion, which held that the accused had the right to inspect the government's files. In dissent, Justice Tom Clark protested that the decision afforded the accused "a Roman holiday for rummaging through confidential information as well as vital national secrets." Two weeks later, the Justices, on what C. Herman Pritchett called "one of the most memorable decision days in the history of the United States Supreme Court," handed down rulings in the *Yates, Watkins,* and *Sweezy* cases, modifying the *Dennis* holding and curbing legislative investigatory powers; several Communists were freed. Under a barrage of criticism, some of it fomented by the Eisenhower administration, the Court retreated in the 1958–1959 term, but as Walter F. Murphy has observed, it was "a tactical withdrawal, not a rout." By 1964 the Warren Court would be taking a bolder line when it wiped out a section of the Subversive Activities Control Act of 1950 forbidding passports to Communists as an unconstitutional denial of the right to travel.

If the Court sometimes behaved circumspectly on national security questions, it moved daringly on other civil liberties matters, often by embracing ideas earlier advanced for the Court's minority by Hugo Black and William O. Douglas. The Court greatly expanded First Amendment protection, notably in cases like *New York Times Company* v. *Sullivan,* making it all but impossible for a public figure to win a libel action. In the 1964 *Times* opinion, Justice Brennan remarked on the "profound national commitment to the principle that debate on public issues should be uninhibited, robust, and wide-open." *The New York Times* would provide the occasion for another important ruling in 1971, when the Court held that the federal government could not enjoin that newspaper or *The Washington Post* from publishing material from a classified study of Vietnam policy.

The Warren Court also gave new meaning to Fourteenth Amendment guarantees. In 1966 the High Bench enjoined the Georgia legislature from excluding Julian Bond, a properly elected black member who had angered lawmakers by voicing "sympathy and support for the men in this country who are unwilling to respond to a military draft." Two years later in *Katzenbach* v. *Morgan* the Court sanctioned federal legislation outlawing New York state's requirement that a prospective voter demonstrate literacy in English. The Court invaded a still more delicate area when it ruled on sexual and marital relations. It struck down a Connecticut statute banning the sale of contraceptives, a Virginia act outlawing racial intermarriage, and a Florida law penalizing sexual relations between whites and blacks.

Through another series of decisions, the Warren Court drastically reshaped the code of criminal justice. In 1957 it unanimously upset the conviction of a Negro in the District of Columbia for the brutal rape of a white woman because his confession had been secured only after extended grilling and he had not been promptly arraigned. Seven years later Justice Arthur Goldberg spoke for a divided Court in voiding the murder confession of Danny Escobedo, who had been denied permission to see his lawyer, a year after the Court, in *Gideon* v. *Wainwright,* ruled that a pauper must be provided with an attorney at public expense. In 1966 the Court brought this line of reasoning to a climax in the bitterly controverted *Miranda* opinion, which required police to advise a suspect of his right to remain silent and to have counsel present during interrogation.

Considerations of judicial restraint had inhibited previous courts from examining "political questions" of the sort involved in the malapportionment of legislatures, but the Warren Court was not deterred. In the 1962 case of *Baker* v. *Carr*, it insisted that Tennessee, which had not reapportioned its legislative seats since 1900, act to reflect changes in the population, especially the movement from the country to city and suburb. *Wesberry* v. *Sanders* in 1964 established the principle of "one man, one vote," and in that same year *Reynolds* v. *Sims* held that in apportioning legislative seats no allowance could be made for geographical diversity within the state. "Legislators represent people, not acres or trees," Warren stated. In a companion ruling, the Court stipulated that these guidelines be followed even when the people of the state had approved a different system in a referendum, a decision that the Court's critics viewed as a new high in arrogance.

Each departure from precedent added more recruits to the forces opposed to the Warren Court. For some, it was the cold war decisions that stuck in the craw. Congressman Rivers called the Justices "a greater threat to this Union than the entire confines of Soviet Russia." Others were so provoked by the desegregation opinions

that they plastered huge "Impeach Earl Warren" posters on billboards along southern and western highways. Rulings on pornography offended people fretful about public morals, and they
were likely to be the most distressed, too, by the Court's interdiction
of Bible-reading and prayer in the schools, decisions that, to some,
appeared to align the Supreme Court with all the godless elements
subverting the American way of life. "They've put the Negroes in
the schools," cried an Alabama Congressman, "and now they've
driven God out."

Even some of the Court's defenders conceded that the Judges were
often cavalier in drafting opinions and that they seemed concerned
less with the legal merits of a case than with seeing that the better
cause won. Anthony Lewis, Supreme Court correspondent of *The
New York Times,* wrote, "A Warren opinion, characteristically, is a
morn made new—a bland, square presentation of the particular
problem in that case almost as if it were unencumbered by prece-
dents or conflicting theories, as it inevitably must be. Often the
framework of the argument seems ethical rather than legal." Its
methods, friendly critics feared, needlessly antagonized the bar,
"jeopardized acceptance of its commands," and impaired "the
credibility of the judicial process." "Earl Warren," Lewis concluded,
"was the closest thing the United States has had to a Platonic
Guardian, dispensing law from a throne without any sensed limits
of power except what was seen as the good of society." Yet he added:
"Fortunately, he was a decent, humane, honorable, democratic
Guardian."

The Quest for National Purpose

For all its political achievements and for all the indications that the
United States was a confident, prosperous nation, many observers
detected signs of an underlying anxiety. Both the cold war and the
consumer culture contributed to the feeling of unease. The Soviet
Union's rapid recovery from the devastation of World War II shook
America's conviction of superiority, for the 1950's were punctuated
by Russia's explosion of a hydrogen bomb early in the decade and
its seizure of the lead in the "space race" in the latter half. Those
fearful that America might fall to the number 2 spot among the
world's powers sharply questioned the desirability of consumer
sovereignty, which, it was said, sacrificed national needs to private

indulgences. Others viewed with disfavor the value system of the consumer culture. Creative writers spoke out against what one literary critic called "the sentimental, supermarket humanism and homogenized morality of modern America." Before Eisenhower left office, public figures would be sending out search parties to rediscover the lost sense of national purpose.

Commentators found hard evidence for an "age of anxiety" in the burgeoning of psychoanalysis, the manifestations of mental illness, and the bull market in tranquilizers, often some form of meprobamate like "Miltown." In upper middle class circles in the 1950's it seemed as though almost everyone was saying, "I've got to hurry or I'll be late for my hour," and that prototypical literary character Holden Caulfield tells his story from the perspective of a period of psychiatric treatment. Admissions to mental hospitals nearly doubled between 1940 and 1956, and by the latter year mental patients occupied more hospital beds than all other patients combined. That same year Americans consumed over a billion tranquilizer pills, and during the last part of the decade one out of every three prescriptions included a tranquilizer.

The anxiety resulted in no small degree from the gains America had achieved. A people who could roam freely from place to place found it hard to establish the community stability of a more fettered society. "Opportunities for mobility and morbidity go together," wrote *Time*. And the relative emancipation from the boundaries of class and status took its toll in depriving people of a sense of certainty about what was expected of them. "Nobody truly occupies a station in life any more," observed the central figure of Saul Bellow's *Henderson the Rain King*. "There are displaced persons everywhere."

In an individualistic society, men and women often experienced a sense of isolation not only from their world but from themselves. Psychoanalysts reported an increase in a new kind of neurosis characterized by doubts that life has meaning and by an atrophying of the capacity to feel, a desperate awareness of entrapment in an empty cosmos that the theologian Paul Tillich called the fear of "nonbeing." James Jones in *From Here to Eternity* ruminated about "the song of the Great Loneliness, that creeps in like the desert wind and dehydrates the soul"; Paddy Chayefsky's *Marty*, a TV drama later made into a movie, evoked the lonesome wanting of unglamorous ordinary people; and the poet Richard Wilbur wrote, "We are this man unspeakably alone." In *The Catcher in the Rye* by J. D. Salinger,

George Tooker's *The Subway* (1950) portrays the dreadful alienation and fragmentation that many experienced in urban America. Tooker's work hangs in the permanent collections of the Museum of Modern Art, the Whitney Museum of American Art, and Dartmouth College.

who better than any other author of his time understood that dolorous rite of passage, American adolescence, Holden Caulfield revealed that he was "lonesome as hell. No kidding"; and the poet Robert Bly delineated "the loneliness hiding in grass and weeds / That lies near a man over thirty, and suddenly enters." From such an angle of vision, America would inevitably seem, as John Updike observed in his novel *The Centaur*, "a paralyzed patch of thankless alien land." "I dunno what to think of things now, Cora," confessed Rubin Flood in William Inge's drama *The Dark at the Top of the Stairs*. "I'm a stranger in the very land I was born in."

Through much of the literature of the period ran the themes of disillusion, desolation, and even disgust. The era opened in 1945 with Tennessee Williams' affecting "memory play," *The Glass Menagerie*, which included the stage direction: "The apartment faces an alley, and is entered by a fire-escape, a structure whose name is a touch of accidental poetry, for all of these huge buildings are always burning with the slow and implacable fires of human desperation." The following year came the poet Robert Lowell's *Lord Weary's Castle*, an exploration of a ruined world. In Edward Albee's drama *The Death of Bessie Smith* (1959), Nurse cried: "I am sick of everything in this stupid, fly-ridden *world*. . . . I am sick of

going to bed and I am sick of waking up. . . . I am tired of my skin.
. . . I WANT OUT!" That same year, William Burroughs' *Naked Lunch*
reached a nadir in the imagery of decay: "Smell of chili houses and
dank overcoats and atrophied testicles. . . . A heaving sea of air
hammers in the purple brown dusk tainted with rotten metal smell
of sewer gas." In 1963, a year when everything began to come apart,
the poet Louis Simpson, in *At the End of the Open Road*, stood on a
Pacific beach musing on the "same old city-planner, death." And
in that year, too, the brilliant young expatriate poet Sylvia Plath,
who, haunted by the horror of the Nazi extermination chambers,
had written of the moon "of complete despair, I live here," took her
life.

The playwrights of the theater of the absurd and the novelists of
black comedy depicted a world of pointlessness, in which there was
no order to history, no pattern to life, no relationship between intention and outcome. In plays like Edward Albee's *The Sand Box* and in
novels such as John Barth's *The Sot-Weed Factor*, life was devoid of
any meaning save what might be gained from the perception that
people are helpless players in a cosmic farce. Yet if the subject of
these works is Everyman, and if they have a strong kinship to those
of European writers like Samuel Beckett, it is often the world of the
American consumer culture they are ridiculing. *Catch-22,* Joseph
Heller explained, "is about the contemporary, regimented business
society," and Lenny Bruce's savage "sick humor" found targets in
the Lone Ranger and the Avon Lady.

In 1957, with the publication of Jack Kerouac's *On the Road*, there
burst on the bourgeois world of Eisenhower's America that disturbing phenomenon to which Kerouac gave the designation "beat."
It was a term with varied resonances. "Beat" suggested the quest for
beatitude, a life style of inner grace often pursued through the cult
of Zen Buddhism. It appeared to refer as well to the special state of
blessedness attained by those who were down and out, especially
the drifters. And it reverberated too with a musical connotation, not
only in the obvious synonym but in the affinity of the beat movement for the "cool jazz" of Lester Young, Stan Getz, and Gerry Mul-
ligan, whose rhythms seemed "disengaged." In each sense of the
word, the beats rejected the canons of respectability—organized religion, striving for material success, homage to the state. Lawrence
Ferlinghetti, who owned the beats' hangout, the City Lights book
store in San Francisco, entitled one of his poems "Tentative Description of a Dinner to Promote the Impeachment of President

Eisenhower." The "beatniks," as the squares preferred to call them, shocked the bourgeoisie in other ways, too. The "Dharma bums" helped popularize marijuana among the young and made no secret of their promiscuity. Sometimes the male camaraderie of the boys on the road found homosexual expression, as in Allen Ginsberg's *Howl and Other Poems*, which celebrated sex with "saintly motor-cyclists."

In some respects, especially in their concern for self and their disengagement, the beats shared the values of the square world of the 1950's. "We're no action group, man," one explained. ". . . I stay cool, far out, alone. When I flip it's over something *I* feel, only me." The beats' oceanic compassion seemed to discourage political protest by embracing their adversaries. "We love everything—Bill Graham, the Big Ten, Rock and Roll, Zen, apple pie, Eisenhower—we dig it all," Kerouac explained. The beats even made a minor contribution to the California economy. With their beards and sandals, they became tourist bait in San Francisco, and it was possible to acquire "Beatnik kits." But however much the beats mirrored conventional society, their real significance lay in the fact that they had fired the first gun of the rebellion of the "counter culture" that would shake the 1960's.

Despite the preoccupations of writers and artists, not every commentator agreed that the postwar period was an especially anxious time. The increase in patients, it was pointed out, was less a sign of a rise in illness than of the diminished stigma attached to mental ailments and of the fact that when many more could afford professional care, fewer were willing to tolerate fear and depression. Nor was this the first era that had known stress. In the 1830's, a doctor remarked that "the population of the United States is beyond that of other countries an anxious one," and Tocqueville observed "that strange melancholy which often haunts the inhabitants of democratic countries in the midst of their abundance, and that strange disgust at life which sometimes seizes upon them in the midst of calm and easy circumstances." Yet much in the modern age was unsettling. If in Tocqueville's time the United States was a country of limitless prospects, in the 1950's Americans were coming to question the results of a century and a half of progress and to doubt that the world would continue to step to the tune of "Yankee Doodle Dandy."

On October 4, 1957, Radio Moscow reported an event that struck a savage blow at American pride. The U.S.S.R. announced that it had thrust a man-made satellite, *Sputnik I,* into orbit around the earth. A month later, *Sputnik II* circled the globe carrying a live dog of the Laika breed. Within less than two years, the Russians would plant the emblem of the hammer and sickle on the surface of the moon. The United States, the premier nation in industrial skill, the country that had unlocked the secret of the atom, had been beaten in the one area where it was certain it was supreme — technology. In truth, the United States was not so far behind as it seemed, but for many months Americans had to endure the ignominy of watching foreign observers gather at Florida's Cape Canaveral only to see United States rockets climb a foot into the air and topple over. Dismaying as this was to the nation's self-esteem, even more disturbing was the thought that Soviet armaments might soon be pointing down from the sky at Kansas rooftops. When the physicist Edward Teller was asked what American spacemen would find if they ever got to the moon, he answered, "Russians."

The *Sputnik* furor had its greatest immediate impact on the American school. The same month that Laika soared into space, Washington released a 200-page study, *Education in the U.S.S.R.,* which highlighted the disciplined training Soviet pupils received in science, mathematics, and languages. Little wonder, it was reasoned, their spacemen were ahead of ours. Critics had been telling the American public that this kind of intellectual rigor was missing from their schools, and writers like Arthur Bestor (*Educational Wastelands*) and Mortimer Smith (*The Diminished Mind: A Study of Planned Mediocrity in Our Public Schools*) now found an attentive audience for their assaults on the shortcomings of progressive education. None was more attentive than the United States Congress, which in September 1958 approved the National Defense Education Act (NDEA) to authorize government financing of programs in science, mathematics, and foreign languages. What a generation of liberals clamoring for federal aid to education had failed to achieve, the cold war accomplished almost overnight. Thanks to NDEA funds, schools acquired expensive hardware such as language laboratories, a response in part to the emphasis of the Harvard psychologist B. F. Skinner on programmed instruction. ("Any teacher who can be replaced by a machine should be," Skinner said.) The *Sputnik* crisis also led to a drastic reworking of the curriculum, with the introduction of the "new physics" of atomic structure, the "new biology" of DNA, and the "new math" of set theory, a unique contribution to the generation gap.

The United States reacted to the *Sputnik* challenge too with a massive effort to overtake the Russians in the "space race." In October 1958, the National Aeronautics and Space Administration (NASA) began its operations with funds that would climb rapidly from some $340 million in 1959 to more than $5 billion in 1965. By 1959 the country had already made the acquaintance of NASA's team of astronauts—handsome, crew-cut young fathers reared in Protestant families in small towns, with Anglo-Saxon craftsmen's names like Carpenter and Cooper and reassuring old-fashioned virtues of pluck, stamina, and technological prowess. Soon the nation would also be introduced to a new glossary—retro-rockets, A-OK, lift-off, Mission Control, T minus 2 and holding, we return you to Roger Mudd. Only a generation earlier, men had relegated stories of space travel to the comic book fantasies of a Flash Gordon or the suppertime radio of Buck Rogers, but on February 20, 1962, Lieutenant Colonel John Herschel Glenn, Jr., would orbit the globe in a five-hour voyage in which he would see three sunsets and experience nightfall over the Indian Ocean like a brilliant desert night "when there's no moon and the stars just seem to jump out at you." Glenn's message, "Cape is go and I am go," would spell success for three and a half years of exertion, but in the Eisenhower years, as failure was compounded by failure, the outlook appeared bleak.

Much of the censure for the miscarriage of the space enterprise fell on the President, who was charged with neglecting the national interest, for America's lag in the space race seemed as dangerous as it was humiliating. The U.S.S.R. was mistakenly believed to be far ahead of the United States in missiles, and, in announcing one of their space successes, the Russians crowed, "The present generation will witness how the freed and conscious labor of the people of the new socialist society turns even the most daring of man's dreams into a reality." The administration was upbraided for the low priority it had given to missile development as well as for its hostility to intellectuals and its contempt for basic research. After the success of the Soviet scientists, Postmaster General Summerfield's boast of "progress in rooting out eggheads" and Secretary of Defense Wilson's insistence that basic research is "when you don't know what you are doing" appeared especially ill advised.

Even that marvel of the country's industrial genius, the American economy, came under fire. Although the increment in the gross national product had been sizable, critics deemed the rate of growth unsatisfactory. Partly as a consequence of Eisenhower's policies, the growth rate fell from 4.3 percent in the 1947–1952 period to 2.5 percent in 1953–1960. Three "Eisenhower recessions" impeded the development of sustained advance, with a resultant loss of billions of dollars of productivity in idle machines and a rise in unemployment that neared 8 percent in Eisenhower's last year in office. By early 1961 the economy, wrote Walter Heller, was "in the position of the .300 hitter who started the season batting a weak .250, then slumped to .230."

The "sluggish" economy also had international implications. At a time when the country was already embarrassed by *Sputnik*, it was discomforting to be reminded that the Soviet rate of growth for 1950–1958 was 7.1 percent (in large part, to be sure, because Russia had started at a much lower level). Nor was worry limited to competition from cold war rivals. The European Common Market, once a ward of Uncle Sam, was jeopardizing America's world trade position, and the drain of gold to Europe led some economists to predict that in the foreseeable future the United States would have to devalue the dollar.

Dissidents objected not only that the administration's policies yielded a smaller GNP but that they reflected a distorted scale of values. Eisenhower's aversion to government spending begot, said Adlai Stevenson, "private opulence and public squalor." Crucial decisions on how to allocate resources were delegated to the shopper or to the advertiser who manipulated him. While the consumer was euchred into diverting the nation's metal resources to add tailfin excrescences on automobiles, school boards lacked the funds to erect critically needed new buildings. By Eisenhower's second term, social critics were deploring the very economy of abundance that was the President's pride. The historian Eric Goldman, with an ascetic intensity that rivaled Saint Simeon Stylites, complained, "We meander along in a stupor of fat." In *A Surfeit of Honey*, Russell Lynes grumbled, "Prosperity produces not only plenty but curiously empty values. . . . Cars get gaudier; hi-fi sets get hi-er; beer-can openers become mink-bearing."

Poets and novelists, too, raised their voices against the consumer society. Robert Lowell, in "For the Union Dead," wrote:

> . . . Everywhere,
> giant finned cars nose forward like fish;
> a savage servility
> slides by on grease.

In Thomas Pynchon's novel *V.*, Benny Profane felt bereft "in the aisles of a bright, gigantic supermarket, his only function to want," and Allen Ginsberg, in "A Supermarket in California," suffered a headache when he entered a store until he found Walt Whitman "poking among the meats in the refrigerator and eyeing the grocery boys." Rabbit, John Updike's protagonist in *Rabbit, Run,* mused ruefully on a world with no consciousness of tragedy as he watched his wife on her hospital bed absorbed by "Queen for a Day" on a rented TV set. In this "air-conditioned nightmare" (Henry Miller's term), one had to commit one's self to a deliberate act of rejection of the consumer culture. The projective poet Charles Olson, in "The Songs of Maximus," urged:

> In the midst of plenty, walk
> as close to
> bare
>
> .   .   .
>
> In the land of plenty, have
> nothing to do with it.

By the end of the decade, publicists were charging that the United States, in the catch phrase of the day, had lost its sense of national purpose. Eisenhower responded to this reproof forthrightly: He appointed a commission to ascertain what the country's aims were. In the commission's reports and in popular journals there ensued a "debate" about national purpose that resulted in more high-minded thinking than Americans had witnessed in many a year. Like Puritan divines scourging a colony of sinners, the tribunes of purpose flailed away at a people who put private pleasure ahead of national goals. Some of the scolding centered less on the quality of life in the United States than on the country's role as a world power, for critics alleged that the United States had given the consumer culture higher priority than the cold war. The failure of the Russians to match the American outpouring of consumer goods, once a source of rejoicing in the United States, was taken as evidence of Soviet dedication and the explanation for Uncle Sam's debility. Adlai Stevenson asked, "With the supermarket as our temple and the singing commercial as our litany, are we likely to fire the world with an irresistible vision of America's exalted purposes and inspiring way of life?"

A good deal of the concern about the quality of American life focused on the city, for the transition of the United States from a rural to an urban society continued at a rapid pace. Even though almost all the largest cities were losing population to the suburbs (Boston had fewer people in 1960 than in 1920), the total metropolitan agglomerations grew relentlessly. Of the population gains in the 1950's, they accounted for no less than 97 percent. In 1940, 48 percent of the nation lived in metropolitan areas; by 1969, 64.5 percent did. Flying at night, pilots who used to be able to pick out each cluster of lights that separated city from countryside found the urban areas indistinguishable; from Newport News north to New York was a single ribbon of light. It was estimated that by the year 2000, 85 percent of the country's 300 million people would live in urban centers, and many of them would be clustered in four huge concentrations whose parameters were already evident in the postwar years—"Boswash," from Boston to Washington; "Chipitts," from the Windy City to the Golden Triangle; "San San," running south from San Francisco all the way to San Diego near the Mexican border; and "JaMi," a megalopolis stretching the length of Florida's east coast, from Jacksonville to Miami.

The cities had long been the nation's nerve centers. Like powerful magnets attracting iron filings, they drew black tenant farmers to Gary's steel mills, Chicanos out of the sugar beet fields to the metropolises of California and Texas, Navaho and Zuñi to the streets of Gallup, girls from Columbus (as in Leonard Bernstein's *Wonderful Town*) to Greenwich Village, because for all they offered at least the illusion of a new beginning. Painters who once found their subject matter in the countryside—the Hudson River School, "Motif No. 1" on the New England shore—set up their easels along urban thoroughfares. Franz Kline and Frank Stella painted New York bridges; Larry Rivers designed the cover for Frank O'Hara's lengthy poem *Second Avenue*. As the artist John Ferren explained, "It is not accident that contemporary painting used lots of black and white. It didn't come from the sunlit fields—it came from white lofts in dirty buildings on dirty streets and from the inner resources of the mind. Its beginning was urban, of the city."

Yet many also viewed the city as the country's number 1 problem, indeed the very embodiment of the nation's ills. There were the festering sores of racial antagonism, the warrens of crime, the breeding places of a hundred social maladies. The fragmented life of the city, critics wrote, resulted in what the French sociologist Emile Durkheim termed *anomie*, the vacuum characterized by the absence of an accepted value system. Los Angeles was taken to be the leading instance of a distended town lacking authentic community—"six suburbs in search of a city," one observer called it. The metropolis, which existed only because of the achievements of technology, seemed to have reached the point where it was throttling the very mechanisms it needed to keep going. Passengers whisked across the country at over 700 miles per hour were moved at a snail's pace from the airport to their downtown destinations. And when in 1965 power failures plunged New York into darkness and trapped hundreds in unlighted subway tunnels, some even came to doubt whether Gotham would survive. To the gloomiest Cassandras, the American city, like Nineveh and Tyre, seemed doomed to perish as had the centers of other civilizations that had lost their sense of national purpose.

Although many of the national purpose diatribes hit home, they also included a fair amount of malarkey. It was not clear to all that a nation ought to have a "purpose." As Britain's Prime Minister Harold Macmillan observed, "If people want a sense of purpose, they should get it from their archbishops." The concentration on vulgar consumption distracted attention from the millions with low incomes, and, as Stephan Thernstrom has noted, it was particularly ungracious often to have "the loudest complaints against tailfins . . . voiced by people whose own Spartan mode of transportation was a Porsche." Nor were the critics altogether fair in their assessment of the nature of American society in the 1950's, although they helped establish a mode of interpretation of those times that may never be seriously altered.

Bland, vapid, self-satisfied, banal—all true of Eisenhower's America, yet not the whole truth. The political life of the decade was undernourished, but Adlai Stevenson made important contributions to the advances of the 1960's, and both the Supreme Court and the civil rights movement broke new ground on race. As a result of the efforts of mayors like New Haven's Richard Lee, Ford Foundation executives such as Paul Ylvisaker, and political scientists like Robert Wood, the country was beginning to accept the need for national action on behalf of the cities. Those who concentrated their attention on the shortage of classrooms gave too little notice to the impressive gains in education. And although many of the by-products of economic growth were deplorable, the soaring GNP lifted millions out of poverty.

A culture allegedly hostile to creativity, it nonetheless found room for the inventive sculpture of David Smith, the architectural genius of Minoru Yamasaki and Eero Saarinen, and brilliant paintings like Joseph Albers' *Homage to the Square*. During this "arid" period Ralph Ellison published *Invisible Man*, and Tennessee Williams' *A Streetcar Named Desire* had its premiere. The barbs at mass culture were often well directed, and in retrospect this has come to seem a period of little save paint-by-the-number kits, Liberace's smirk, Lassie, and the Nelson family. But the popular culture of the time also had its special pleasures—Edward R. Murrow's "See It Now," Gian Carlo Menotti's *Amahl and the Night Visitors*, Phil Silvers breaking them up as Sergeant Bilko, Rodgers and Hammerstein's *The King and I* and Loewe and Lerner's *My Fair Lady*, Bill Russell sweeping the boards, and Paul Hornung bursting off tackle on a Green Bay power sweep.

Even the value system of the 1950's had its virtues. If children raised by parents with one eye on Dr. Spock's manual were overindulged, they were also spared the mindless tyranny of some earlier kinds of upbringing. Critics were depressed by the hero of Sloan Wilson's *Man in the Gray Flannel Suit*, who rejected an offer to become a top executive so that he might spend more time with his family, but such a decision may have indicated less an attenuation of character than a sensible turning away from the go-getter striving of primitive capitalism. Yet despite all the buncombe the national purpose debate brought forth, it did serve to raise questions about the shortcomings of the consumer culture and to point the country toward different emphases in the 1960's.

The participants in the debate on national purpose looked toward the 1960 presidential campaign for new directions. Without exception, they emphasized the importance of government leadership. "It is time," said the political scientist Hans Morgenthau, "for the President to reassert his historical role as . . . the initiator of policy." But the two young candidates (the Democrat, Senator John F. Kennedy, was forty-three; the Republican, Vice-President Richard M. Nixon, forty-six) had both been identified with the unadventurous politics of the 1950's.

In 1956 alarm over Eisenhower's health after the President suffered a heart attack and ileitis had led the Republicans to unveil a "new Nixon." The Vice-President was revealed to be a man of such modest demeanor that none could confuse him with the unshaven mudslinger Herblock had made the butt of his cartoons. In his "high level" campaign that year, Nixon shunned all controversy; "I lean to the Dodgers, but my wife is a Yankee fan," he confided.

His critics were unimpressed. Nixon, said Adlai Stevenson, had "put away his switchblade and now assumes the aspect of an Eagle Scout." However, observed Stevenson, "This is a man of many masks. Who can say they have seen his real face?" In 1960, too, many who opposed the Vice-President did so less because they disagreed with his views, or even because they recalled resentfully his role in the McCarthy era, than because they thought he typified the hollow man of a synthetic society. Often Nixon appeared to be manipulating himself in order to gain a temporary advantage; in one address, he soberly explained how much preparation had to go into a spontaneous talk and stressed the importance of "seeming sincere." The question, noted one editor, was not whether the real Nixon was the old Nixon or the new Nixon but "whether there is anything that might be called the 'real' Nixon, new or old."

Kennedy, many of these same critics claimed, was a "Democratic Nixon," a man wanting in strong convictions. In view of the fact that he had not stood up to Joe McCarthy, the Massachusetts Senator opened himself to ridicule by publishing *Profiles in Courage*, a study of the valor of resolute legislators. During the McCarthy era, Kennedy, it was said, should have shown less profile and more courage. He won the 1960 nomination by defeating Minnesota's Senator Hubert Humphrey, who in a decade when moderation was the national style had boldly taken forthright positions. Kennedy's victory over him in the primaries was interpreted as further evidence that the nation would not countenance an outspoken candidate in 1960.

"The 'managerial revolution' has come to politics," wrote the television commentator Eric Sevareid, "and Nixon and Kennedy are its first completely packaged products. The Processed Politician has finally arrived." Recalling his experience in the 1930's when he had been deeply aroused by the Republic Steel massacre and the fate of the Spanish Loyalists, Sevareid added:

I can't find in the record that Kennedy or Nixon ever did, thought or felt these things. They must have been across the campus on Fraternity Row, with the law and business school boys, wearing the proper clothes, thinking the proper thoughts, cultivating the proper people. I always sensed that they would end up running the big companies in town but I'm damned if I ever thought one of them would end up running the country.

Much about the 1960 campaign served to confirm these misgivings. The public response to the four television confrontations between

Paul Schutzer. LIFE Magazine. © 1960 Time Inc.

John F. Kennedy debates Richard M. Nixon in the camera's eye. The four confrontations
in the 1960 presidential campaign, which helped determine the outcome of the election,
marked the culmination of the impact of the new medium of television on American politics.

the two candidates centered less on their ideas than on which
man was the more "telegenic." So little choice did some detect that
the veteran political writer Gerald Johnson saw the contest as "Burroughs Against IBM."

Yet during the campaign Kennedy did take up the themes of national purpose, especially by emphasizing that the cold war should

Election of 1960

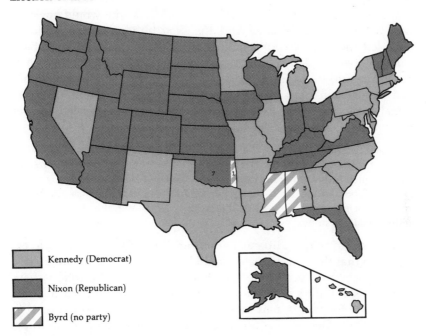

Kennedy (Democrat)

Nixon (Republican)

Byrd (no party)

have higher priority than the consumer culture. In asserting the need to "get America moving again," he insisted that America must make a choice "between the public interest and private comfort." "I run for the Presidency because I do not want it said that in the years when our generation held political power . . . America began to slip," Kennedy declared. "I don't want historians writing in 1970 to say that the balance of power in the Nineteen Fifties and the Nineteen Sixties began to turn against the United States and against the cause of freedom."

The country gave little indication that it was in a heroic mood or that it was ready to give either candidate a decisive mandate. So evenly did the electorate distribute its ballots on election day that after a long night of television-viewing the nation was still not certain of the outcome. Kennedy's victory margin in the popular vote (two-tenths of 1 percent) was the smallest since 1880, although his edge in the Electoral College was more emphatic, 303 to 219. The first triumph of a Roman Catholic nominee was taken as proof of the country's freedom from bigotry, despite the fact that Kennedy may have lost over 4 million votes of Democrats who would not support a Catholic candidate. And the distribution of congressional seats left the pivotal conservative coalition essentially undisturbed.

Eisenhower ended his eight years in office with a symbolic act. He left behind for his successor an official paper that attempted what had never been tried so self-consciously before—to define the national goals. But in the same year that Kennedy was elected, Daniel Bell wrote in *The End of Ideology:*

Thus one finds, at the end of the fifties, a disconcerting caesura. In the West, among the intellectuals, the old passions are spent. The new generation, with no meaningful memory of these old debates, and no secure tradition to build upon, finds itself seeking new purposes within a framework of political society that has rejected, intellectually speaking, the old apocalyptic and chiliastic visions.

For many American liberals, however, Kennedy's election offered the hope that the United States could leave behind the torpid Eisenhower years and face up to the challenge of critical public issues. Kennedy's admirers pointed out that when Martin Luther King had been jailed for taking part in a sit-in at the Magnolia Room restaurant of Rich's Department Store in Atlanta, Nixon had done nothing but Kennedy had intervened to secure his release. They noted too that Kennedy had campaigned on a platform calling for elimination of racial discrimination, federal aid to education, medical care for the aged and government action to foster economic growth. With a program embodying so much of the Fair Deal agenda, with a vigorous chief executive committed to the doctrine of a strong presidency and eager to regain a sense of national purpose, liberals looked forward with confidence to what awaited them in the 1960's.

SUGGESTED READINGS

Few historians so far have attempted to assess the quarter-century after 1945. The most judicious brief account is Carl N. Degler, *Affluence and Anxiety* (1968). Eric F. Goldman, *The Crucial Decade And After—America, 1945–1960* (1961), is a lively narrative of the Truman-Eisenhower era. A somewhat longer period is covered by John Brooks, *The Great Leap* (1966), an effervescent social history. More political in focus is Walter Johnson, *1600 Pennsylvania Avenue* (1960), which begins in 1929 and terminates in 1959. Herbert Agar, *The Price of Power* (1957), is a volume in The Chicago

History of American Civilization, edited by Daniel Boorstin. Chester E. Eisinger, ed., *The 1940's: Profile of a Nation in Crisis* (1969), compiles original sources for that decade; and Joseph Satin, ed., *The 1950's: America's "Placid" Decade* (1960), performs the same task for the succeeding ten years.

There are extended essays on each of the postwar elections through the 1968 contest in volume 4 of Arthur M. Schlesinger, Jr., and Fred L. Israel, eds., *History of American Presidential Elections* (4 vols., 1971). In the first of these essays, Richard Kirkendall analyzes the 1948 election. For the minor parties in that contest, see Karl M. Schmidt, *Henry Wallace: Quixotic Crusader* (1960), a rather uncritical view of the Progressive candidate, and V. O. Key, Jr., *Southern Politics in State and Nation* (1949), a major work which includes material on the Dixiecrats. Key also wrote *The Responsible Electorate* (1966) in support of his contention that voters are more rational than many political scientists concede. Paul David et al., *Presidential Nominating Politics in 1952* (1954), is an exhaustive five-volume study. The succeeding presidential election is dealt with in Charles A. H. Thomson and Frances M. Shattuck, *The 1956 Presidential Campaign* (1960), a Brookings monograph. Heinz Eulau, *Class and Party in the Eisenhower Years* (1962), examines the data on politics and social structure for the 1952 and 1956 elections. The Democratic candidate in both years, Adlai Stevenson, is the subject of Kenneth S. Davis's *A Prophet in His Own Country* (1957). The 1960 election is described in Theodore H. White, *The Making of the President* (1961), and in Paul T. David et al., *The Presidential Election and Transition, 1960–1961* (1961). Richard M. Dalfiume, ed., *American Politics Since 1945* (1969), is one of a number of skillfully edited collections of articles that first appeared in *The New York Times*. Angus Campbell et al., *The American Voter* (1960), a summary of the work of the Survey Research Center of the University of Michigan, has had a pervasive influence. Samuel Lubell's *The Future of American Politics* (rev. ed., 1956) and his *Revolt of the Moderates* (1956) are contributions of a hardworking journalist. For the legislation of the period, *Congressional Quarterly's* bulky *Congress and Nation* (1965) is a mine of information. Donald R. Matthews, *U.S. Senators and Their World* (1960), dissects the upper house, while Richard Bolling, *House Out of Order* (1965), offers the perspective of an able liberal Congressman from Kansas City on the House of Representatives.

Literary developments in the beginning of this period are surveyed in John W. Aldridge, *After the Lost Generation* (1951), which deals with the war writers, and Chester E. Eisinger, *Fiction of the Forties* (1963). Howard M. Harper, Jr., *Desperate Faith* (1967), analyzes brilliantly the novels of Bellow, Salinger, Mailer, Baldwin, and Updike. Malcolm Cowley, *The Literary Situation* (1954), offers the judgments of a veteran critic. For the beats, see Lawrence Lipton, *The Holy Barbarians* (1959), and Jane Kramer, *Allen Ginsberg in America* (1969). Sidney Finkelstein, in *Existentialism and Alienation in American Literature* (1965), approaches his subject in a single-mindedly Marxist manner. Stephen Stepanchev, *American Poetry Since 1945* (1965), and M. L. Rosenthal, *The New Poets* (1967), which covers British as well as American writing since World War II, are excellent. Alvin B. Kernan, ed., *The Modern American Theater* (1967), pulls together essays on drama. Exceptionally wide-ranging is Richard Kostelanetz, ed., *The New American Arts* (1965). Barbara

Rose, *American Arts Since 1900* (1967), has a substantial section on postwar developments, which is also the subject of an anthology, Gregory Battcock, ed., *The New Art* (1966). There are important documents too in Barbara Rose, *Readings in American Art Since 1900* (1968). For architecture, see John Burchard and Albert Bush-Brown, *The Architecture of America* (1966).

Richard S. Kirkendall, ed., *The Truman Period as a Research Field* (1967), a collection of essays, is the best introduction to the Truman era. Barton J. Bernstein and Allen J. Matusow, eds., *The Truman Administration: A Documentary History* (1966), is a painstaking anthology. Another useful collection is Louis W. Koenig, ed., *The Truman Administration* (1956). The Washington correspondent Cabell Phillips has written *The Truman Presidency* (1966). For the politics of the veterans issue, see Davis R. B. Ross, *Preparing for Ulysses* (1969). Stephen K. Bailey, *Congress Makes a Law* (1950), details the legislative history of the Employment Act of 1946. Another landmark of political science is David B. Truman, *The Congressional Party* (1959), on the Eighty-first Congress. Questions of labor policy in the postwar era are aired in R. Alton Lee, *Truman and Taft-Hartley* (1966), and H. A. Millis and E. C. Brown, *From the Wagner Act to Taft-Hartley* (1950). The Fair Deal has already spawned several monographs including Allen J. Matusow, *Farm Policies and Politics in the Truman Years* (1967), and Richard O. Davies, *Housing Reform During the Truman Administration* (1966). Alonzo L. Hamby will soon publish an ambitious study of American liberalism in the Truman period. Some of his preliminary findings appeared in "The Vital Center, the Fair Deal, and the Quest for a Liberal Political Economy," *American Historical Review* (1972). For the most formidable opponent of the Fair Deal, see James T. Patterson, *Mr. Republican* (1972), the first scholarly biography of Robert Taft.

Earl Latham, *The Communist Controversy in Washington: From the New Deal to McCarthy* (1966), provides a good historical background and takes a tough-minded view of the subversion question. Latham has also edited an anthology of essential essays, *The Meaning of McCarthyism* (1965). Three important monographs on the loyalty issue in the Truman era are Alan D. Harper, *The Politics of Loyalty* (1969); Robert K. Carr, *The House Un-American Activities Committee, 1945–1950* (1952); and C. Herman Pritchett, *Civil Liberties and the Vinson Court* (1954). Richard M. Freeland adds an international dimension in *The Truman Doctrine and the Origins of McCarthyism* (1972). David A. Shannon's *The Decline of American Communism* (1959) does justice to that subject. Alistair Cooke, *A Generation on Trial* (1950), contributes a British perspective to the Hiss case. The participants in that confrontation have each written their own accounts, Whittaker Chambers' disturbing *Witness* (1952) and Alger Hiss' much thinner *In the Court of Public Opinion* (1957). Truman's firing of MacArthur is covered by Richard Rovere and Arthur M. Schlesinger, Jr., *The General and the President* (1951); J. W. Spanier, *The Truman-MacArthur Controversy and the Korean War* (1959); and Trumbull Higgins, *Korea and the Fall of MacArthur* (1960). Richard Rovere, *Senator Joe McCarthy* (1959), is superb, but Jack Anderson and R. W. May, *McCarthy: The Man, the Senator, the "Ism"* (1952), is also of value. Robert Griffith, *The Politics of Fear* (1970), is a substantial analysis of McCarthyism and the Senate. Richard Fried's forthcoming study illuminates the Democratic Party's response to McCarthyism, while Ronald J. Caridi,

The Korean War and American Politics (1968), examines the impact on the Republicans of limited war. Daniel Bell, ed., *The New American Right* (1955), later revised as *The Radical Right* (1964), is a seminal but much controverted work by prominent intellectuals in the 1950's. Richard Hofstadter, who contributed an essay to that volume, returned to the subject in *The Paranoid Style in American Politics and Other Essays* (1965). Michael Paul Rogin, *The Intellectuals and McCarthy* (1967), raises doubts about the hypotheses in the Bell volume.

The impact of the cold war on American society requires more careful attention than it has so far received, but Edward Bernard Glick, *Soldiers, Scholars, and Society* (1971), sheds light on the influence of the military. Samuel P. Huntington is the author of both *The Soldier and the State* (1957) and *The Common Defense* (1961). Two other worthwhile books are Demetrios Caraley's exploration of *The Politics of Military Unification* (1966) and Edward A. Kolodziej, *The Uncommon Defense and Congress, 1945–1963* (1966). Lawrence Wittner, *Rebels Against War* (1969), dissects the peace movement. Seymour Melman, *Pentagon Capitalism* (1970), is one of a number of books that deplore the influence of the military-industrial complex.

The most comprehensive book on the economy in this period is Harold G. Vatter, *The U.S. Economy in the 1950's* (1963). Other important studies are John Kendrick, *Productivity Trends in the United States* (1961); Walter Adams and Horace M. Gray, *Monopoly in America* (1955); Walter Adams, ed., *The Structure of American Industry* (3d ed., 1961); and A. E. Holmans, *United States Fiscal Policy, 1945–1959* (1961). John Kenneth Galbraith's most influential books are *American Capitalism* (1952), which developed the notion of "countervailing power," and *The Affluent Society* (1952; rev. ed., 1969). Many of the best analyses of the economy appear not in books but in articles, notably those published in *Fortune,* such as William B. Harris' 1957 essays on electronics and computers. Harry M. Trebing, ed., *The Corporation in the American Economy* (1970), collects articles that originated with *The New York Times.* The role of the Council of Economic Advisers is the subject of Edward S. Flash, Jr., *Economic Advice and Presidential Leadership* (1965). E. L. Dale, *Conservatives in Power* (1960), looks at Eisenhower's economic policies. Norman Macrae, *The Neurotic Trillionaire* (1970), is an incisive commentary by the deputy editor of *The Economist.* Historians have given little attention to the consumer culture, but David M. Potter, *People of Plenty* (1954), and Daniel J. Boorstin, "Welcome to the Consumption Community," *Fortune* (1967), are suggestive. The best book on the difficult question of income distribution is Herman P. Miller, *Rich Man, Poor Man* (1971). The persistence of maldistribution is emphasized by Gabriel Kolko, *Wealth and Power in America* (1962); Michael Harrington, *The Other America* (1962); Letitia Upton and Nancy Lyons, *Basic Facts: Distribution of Personal Income and Wealth in the United States* (1972), a Cambridge Institute study; and Stephan Thernstrom, "The Myth of American Affluence," *Commentary* (1969). On urban developments, see Blake McKelvey, *The Emergence of Metropolitan America, 1915–1966* (1968), and Nathan Glazer, ed., *Cities in Trouble* (1970). Jane Jacobs, *The Death and Life of Great American Cities* (1961), is stimulating even to those who do not share the author's viewpoint. A forthcoming study by Mark Gelfand presents rich detail on the relationship of the federal government to the cities. Robert C. Wood, *Suburbia: Its*

People and Their Politics (1959), is the standard work on that subject, but see too Scott Donaldson, *The Suburban Myth* (1969), and Herbert J. Gans, *The Levittowners* (1967).

Bernard Rosenberg and D. M. White, eds., *Mass Culture* (1957), is an ambitious anthology. David Manning White, ed., *Pop Culture in America* (1970), is another useful collection, as is Eric Larrabee and Rolf Meyersohn, eds., *Mass Leisure* (1958). Erik Barnouw, *The Image Empire* (1970), the third volume of his History of Broadcasting in the United States, gives a provocative, if jaundiced, view of television. David Quentin Voigt, *American Baseball, Volume II: From the Commissioners to Continental Expansion* (1970), explores baseball's coming of age. In the superabundant literature on rock, see Jerry Hopkins, *The Rock Story* (1970), Carl Belz, *The Story of Rock* (1969), and Jonathan Eisen, ed., *The Age of Rock 2* (1970).

David Riesman et al., *The Lonely Crowd* (1950), deeply affected the interpretation of national character. Riesman was a prolific writer; among his many contributions, see *Faces in the Crowd* (1952), written in collaboration with Nathan Glazer, and "The Found Generation," in *Abundance for What?* (1964). C. Wright Mills, *White Collar* (1951) and *The Power Elite* (1956), and William H. Whyte, *The Organization Man* (1956), also had a huge influence. Thomas L. Hartshorne, *The Distorted Image: Changing Conceptions of American Character Since Turner* (1968), examines the impact of Riesman and others. Clyde Kluckhohn, "The Evolution of Contemporary American Values," *Daedalus* (1958), is an important survey. Eric Larrabee, *The Self-Conscious Society* (1960), is insightful, as is D. W. Brogan, "Unnoticed Changes in America," *Harper's* (1957). Karl E. Meyer, *The New America* (1961), offers a melancholy estimate. Seymour Martin Lipset takes a longer look in "A Changing American Character," in Lipset and Leo Lowenthal, eds., *Culture and Social Character* (1961).

Among the studies of Eisenhower, Marquis Childs, *Eisenhower: Captive Hero* (1958), and Emmet John Hughes, *The Ordeal of Power* (1963), are highly critical, while Merlo J. Pusey, *Eisenhower, The President* (1956), and Arthur Larson, *Eisenhower: The President Nobody Knew* (1968), are approving. R. J. Donovan, *Eisenhower: The Inside Story* (1956), and Richard Rovere, *Affairs of State: The Eisenhower Years* (1956), are the best sources for Ike's first term. Dean Albertson, ed., *Eisenhower as President* (1963), puts together some of the important essays. Richard M. Nixon, *Six Crises* (1962), gives the viewpoint of Eisenhower's Vice-President. For the legislation of this period, James L. Sundquist, *Politics and Policy: The Eisenhower, Kennedy, and Johnson Years* (1968), is indispensable. Eisenhower's attitudes toward natural resources may be approached through E. R. Bartley, *The Tidelands Oil Controversy* (1953), and Aaron Wildavsky, *Dixon-Yates* (1962). For farm and labor policies, consult Lauren Soth, *Farm Trouble in an Age of Plenty* (1957), and Alan K. McAdams, *Power and Politics in Labor Legislation* (1964).

Most of the literature on the civil rights revolution concentrates on the period beginning with the *Brown* decision in 1954. Important studies of developments in the postwar era prior to 1954 are Clement E. Vose, *Caucasians Only* (1967), and Richard M. Dalfiume, *Desegregation of the U.S. Armed Forces* (1969). Harvard Sitkoff examines the political contours in "Harry Truman and the Election of 1948: The Coming of Age of Civil Rights in American Politics," *Journal of Southern History* (1971). Albert P. Blaustein and Clarence Clyde Ferguson, Jr., *Desegregation and the Law* (rev. ed., 1962), discusses the *Brown* decision. Benjamin Muse, *Ten Years of Prelude* (1964), and Anthony Lewis and *The New York Times, Portrait of a Decade: The Second American Revolution* (1964), are the best sources for the reverberations of the Court's decision. See, too, Robert Harris, *The Quest for Equality* (1960). *Race Relations in the USA, 1954–68* (1970), is one of the many useful Keesing's Research Reports. The leader of the Montgomery bus boycott, the Reverend Martin Luther King, Jr., states his views in *Stride Toward Freedom* (1958). C. Eric Lincoln, ed., *Martin Luther King, Jr.* (1970), is a useful anthology. J. W. Anderson, *Eisenhower, Brownell, and the Congress* (1964), presents a legislative history of the 1957 civil rights statute. Richard H. Sayler et al., eds., *The Warren Court* (1968), is an excellent anthology on the tribunal that delivered the *Brown* decision. C. Herman Pritchett, *Congress versus the Supreme Court, 1957–1960* (1961), and Walter F. Murphy, *Congress and the Court* (1962), analyze the attempt to shackle the Court. Among the many first-rate appraisals by constitutional lawyers, see Archibald Cox, *The Warren Court: Constitutional Decision As An Instrument of Reform* (1968); Herbert Wechsler, *Principles, Politics and Fundamental Law* (1961); Alexander M. Bickel, *The Supreme Court and the Idea of Progress* (1970); and Philip B. Kurland, *Politics, the Constitution, and the Warren Court* (1970).

Significant Statistics

	1900	1920	1932	1945	1960
Population	76,094,000	106,466,000	124,949,000	139,928,000	180,684,000
Percentage urban	39.7	51.2	NA	58.6	69.9
Percentage rural	60.3	48.8	NA	41.4	30.1
Percentage non-white	12.0	10.0	10.0	10.0	11.0
Life expectancy					
White	47.6	54.9	63.2	66.8	70.6
Nonwhite	33.0	45.3	53.7	57.7	63.6
Gross national product (current dollars)					
Total (billions of dollars)	17.3	88.9	58.5	213.6	503.7
Per capita (dollars)	231	835	468	1,526	2,788
Defense spending (millions of dollars)[a]	332	4,329	1,688	84,311	51,334
As percentage of GNP	1.9	5.0	3.0	40.0	10.0
Military personnel on active duty	125,923	343,302	244,902	12,123,455	2,476,435
Labor union membership	791,000	5,034,000	3,226,000	14,796,000	18,117,000
Birth rate (per 1,000 live births)	32.3	27.7	19.5	20.4	23.7
Advertising expenditures (millions of dollars)	542	2,935	1,627	2,874	11,932
Motor vehicle registrations	8,000	239,161	24,391,000	31,035,420	73,869,000
Persons lynched					
White	9	8	2	0	0
Nonwhite	106	53	6	1	0
High school graduates (as percentage of all persons over 16 years old)	6.4	16.8	NA	NA	65.1

Sources: *Historical Statistics of the United States, Colonial Times to 1957; Statistical Abstract of the United States,* 1970; and *Digest of Educational Statistics,* 1970.

[a] Includes veterans spending; excludes interest.

The Travail of Liberalism

At 12:51 P.M. on January 20, 1961, Chief Justice Earl Warren administered the oath of office to the thirty-fifth President of the United States, John Fitzgerald Kennedy, at a ceremony appropriate to Liberalism Ascendant. In the brilliant sunshine on snow-swept Capitol Hill, each of the elements of the New Deal tradition (notably its hospitality to diverse faiths and to intellectuals) found acknowledgment. Richard Cardinal Cushing intoned the invocation to take cognizance of the accession of the first Roman Catholic chief executive, and the benediction was read by the president of the Hebrew Union College of Cincinnati, Rabbi Nelson Glueck. Out of gratitude for the invitation to men of letters, Robert Frost wrote a verse tribute to the new administration for

> Summoning artists to participate
> In the august occasions of the state.

Kennedy's inaugural address, much admired despite its affecta-
tions, made clear that the cold war, too, was near high noon and that
the tribunes of national purpose had won a convert. In his acceptance
speech at Los Angeles in 1960, Kennedy had indicated a resolve
to move the country away from the values of the consumer culture
and toward a commitment to engagement. The "New Frontier," he
explained, "sums up, not what I intend to offer the American people,
but what I intend to ask of them. It appeals to their pride, not their
pocketbook." During one of his TV debates he had scolded Nixon
for telling Khrushchev, "You may be ahead of us in rocket thrust,
but we're ahead of you in color television," for rocket thrust was
more important. In his inaugural oration, the new President admonished, "Ask not what your country can do for you. Ask what you can
do for your country."

The youngest man ever elected to the presidency, Kennedy
emphasized that "the torch has been passed to a new generation of
Americans—born in this century, tempered by war, disciplined by
a hard and bitter peace, proud of our ancient heritage." In 1917, the
year of his birth, his predecessor Dwight Eisenhower (at seventy the
oldest man ever to occupy the White House) was already a captain
in the United States army, Konrad Adenauer was chosen lord mayor
of Cologne, and Nikita Khrushchev was soldiering for the czar.
Kennedy appointed young men to the highest posts in the government, notably the attorney-generalship, to which he named his
thirty-five-year-old brother Robert. When critics deplored the
appointee's apparent lack of qualifications, the President, in a
characteristic jest, said, "I don't see what's wrong with giving
Bobby a little experience before he goes into law practice." President
Kennedy found young people responsive to such new departures as
the Peace Corps, and he helped turn their energies toward public
affairs and activities like the civil rights movement.

The young judged attractive not only the "vigor" of the new administration but also its vivacious style and the welcome extended
to intellectuals and to novel ideas. Of the two hundred most important posts in the government, three times as many went to men from
the university world under Kennedy as under Eisenhower. If neither
the President nor the First Lady were the intellectuals they were
sometimes imagined to be, they did read widely, patronize the arts,
and exhibit solicitude about the quality of American life. Richard
Rovere observed, "Kennedy's concern with motels was not only
with whether Negroes should get into them but with the *idea* of

President-elect John F. Kennedy and his wife Jacqueline look radiant as they walk through
snowclad Washington on the way to Kennedy's inauguration. The
society of the New Frontier seemed to some like the *Camelot* of the musical by Alan Jay
Lerner and Frederic Loewe based on T. H. White's *The Once and Future King*.

motels—with their function, with the way they looked, with the strange names they bore, and with what they revealed about us." In a single short speech at the University of Wisconsin in 1959, Kennedy had quoted Goethe, Emerson, Swift, Faulkner, Tennyson, Woodrow Wilson, Lord Asquith, Artemus Ward, Finley Peter Dunne, and Queen Victoria, and when Jacqueline Kennedy accompanied the President to Paris, she visited the Jeu de Paume with Malraux and talked blithely of the Duc d'Angoulême with De Gaulle. Kennedy's summons to national service reminded some of Henry V's salutation to his forces before Agincourt in Shakespeare's drama, and some even fancied they saw in the White House circle the Arthurian idyll of Camelot.

Yet Kennedy's fondness for a dashing style also led him to admire the Green Berets, his penchant for vigorous action would result in his approving the ill-fated Cuban invasion, and Jackie's *haute couture* and *haute cuisine*, her much-copied coiffeur, and her conspicuously consuming jet set would bring to the White House the consumer culture writ large. Indeed, the sensibility of the Kennedy years frequently blended the value systems of the consumption society and the cold war, notably after the Berlin crisis fostered a craze for fallout shelters. *The New York Times* ran a two-page ad from Hammacher Schlemmer for "Shelters for Living" (one room would cost around $14,000), and in Dallas, the Lone Star Steel Company marketed a shelter with a window painted on the wall showing an outdoor scene; it even came equipped with a shade that could be pulled down at night. Before Kennedy's administration was cut short, some sixteen thousand young men would be demonstrating in Vietnam what they could do for their country.

The cold war figured too in Kennedy's economic policy. Increased military and space expenditures exercised a leavening influence on the economy, and appeal to the national interest served to exalt the administration's anti-inflation campaign. When steel magnates hiked prices, the President thundered: "In this serious hour in our nation's history, when we are confronted with grave crises in Berlin and Southeast Asia . . . , the American public will find it hard, as I do, to accept a situation in which a tiny handful of steel executives whose pursuit of private power and profit exceeds their sense of public responsibility can show such utter contempt of the interests of 185 million Americans." Browbeaten by Kennedy, the steel companies backed down, and the administration won that particular battle to maintain the price level. But business never forgave him for this dressing down or for his private utterance: "My father always told me that all businessmen were sons of bitches, but I never believed it till now."

To "get America moving again," Kennedy gave much of his attention to the sluggish economy. In part out of worry over the balance-of-payments exigency, he acted with such restraint at the outset that the Kennedy government was contemned as "the third Eisenhower administration." However, Kennedy's policies—a moderate climb in federal spending, a trade expansion act, stable interest rates—helped account for a $100 billion increment in the gross national product without an appreciable price rise. Furthermore, Kennedy became, asserted the economist Seymour Harris, "the most literate of all Presidents in his understanding of modern economics and revealed great courage in his willingness to risk political losses in putting his economics to the test of the market place." He sought to educate the country in the heresies of the New Economics and asked Congress for a multi-billion-dollar slash in taxes with the aim of deliberately augmenting a federal deficit in the expectation that this would stimulate growth. Congress bottled up the tax cut request, and the President was disappointed to find that despite the soaring GNP unemployment remained a melancholy 5.5 percent. Yet Kennedy could take satisfaction in knowing that he had brought the country out of the Eisenhower recession and started the longest sustained recovery in the nation's history.

Kennedy had less success in achieving a new frontier in social welfare. He did put through unemployment compensation, area redevelopment, public works, and manpower training legislation, as well as water pollution control and seashore acquisition programs. A raise in the minimum wage was extended to such consumer culture occupations as hotel and restaurant work. But Congress frustrated him repeatedly in his attempts to win approval for Fair Deal measures like federal aid to education and for new legislation such as his mass transit proposal. By 1963 the stalemate that had begun in 1938 was a quarter-century old, and Kennedy's biographer, James MacGregor Burns, was writing of *The Deadlock of Democracy*. Some blamed the conditions of stasis on the President. They pointed out that he enjoyed top-heavy majorities in both houses of Congress and charged that, in the columnist James Reston's words, "he didn't really know the deck on Capitol Hill." "In his relations with Congress," John Roche has contended, "Kennedy suffered from what Sören Kierkegaard once called the 'paralysis of knowledge.' He was temperamentally incapable of leading lost causes, or causes which seemed lost in a rational appraisal of the odds." Most commentators, however, conceded that he faced formidable impediments in the powerful bipartisan conservative coalition and the obdurate committee structure in Congress. Above all, he lacked a constituency for social change. As the economist George Stigler observed, "The trouble is that hardly anybody in America goes to bed angry at night." But some did go to bed hungry, and three days before his death Kennedy instructed Walter Heller, his principal economic aide, to draft battle plans for a war on poverty.

Lee Harvey Oswald's bullets left the question of Kennedy's place in history in the land of What Might Have Been. His admirers pointed out that in every area — civil rights, economic policy, foreign affairs — the young President was moving more confidently in his third year in office, and they anticipated that he would chalk up impressive achievements in his fourth year and in his second term. They remarked, too, on what he had already accomplished — his championing of civil rights and the New Economics, the defusing of the cold war, the renewed dedication to public service. But skeptics doubted that he had done much that was fundamental about the festering cities or the arms race and noted that most of his key proposals were stymied. Four days before his death, the *Congressional Quarterly* calculated that he had gained acceptance for less than one-third of his legislative program. The New Frontier, concluded the British critic Henry Fairlie, was no more than "a limited exercise in civilizing the status quo" and Kennedy "a Man of Only One Season." Still, there could be no doubt that Kennedy had, at least in some degree, gotten the country moving again and that he had made possible many of the successes, as well as some of the failures, of the Johnson administration.

The young felt a special sense of deprivation at Kennedy's death. The slain President had broken through the middle-aged complacency of the 1950's to give a feeling of hopefulness about American society and a free field to the idealism of young people. They had admired, too, the President's gallantry and the impression he conveyed of being a valorous adventurer who was, William Carleton wrote, in the romantic tradition of Achilles, Roland, Bayard, Raleigh, and Henry of Navarre. By any rational calculation, it was not the young of the 1960's but Kennedy's contemporaries, the Depression generation pushing fifty, who had grounds for grievance at being denied a leader. But as Richard Neustadt commented less

President Lyndon B. Johnson on his horse Lady M rounds up a Hereford yearling at the LBJ
ranch in Texas. Johnson put the LBJ brand on all he was associated with, including his daughters—Lynda Bird Johnson and Lucy Baines Johnson. His wife, Lady Bird,
had acquired her nickname as a child, and marriage made the LBJ symmetry complete.

than a year after the President's murder, "He left a broken promise,
that 'the torch has been passed to a new generation,' and the youngsters who identified with him felt cheated as the promise, like the
glamor, disappeared. What do their feelings matter? We shall have to
wait and see."

The assassination of John F. Kennedy brought to the White House
a man of unbounded ambition and prodigious skills in the craft
of politics. At fifty-five, only nine years older than his predecessor,
Lyndon Baines Johnson seemed to come from a different generation

as well as from a dissimilar social stratum. He had been raised not in the mansion of a multimillionaire financier but on a farm in the arid mesquite country of southwest Texas. "When I was young," Johnson once told reporters, "poverty was so common that we didn't know it had a name." A state director of the National Youth Administration who was first elected to Congress in 1937 as an FDR loyalist, he had trimmed sail in the 1950's but in 1963 was determined to outdo Roosevelt as liberal lawgiver, in fact to leave an indelible brand on the whole history of the presidency. Three flags unfurled at his Texas ranch — Old Glory, the ensign of the blue bonnet state, and his personal flag with LBJ lettered in white on a blue field. Toward the government he took a proprietary interest. When on one occasion an air force officer told him he was headed for the wrong helicopter at Andrews Field, Johnson replied, "Son, all of them are mine."

Johnson's dexterity as legislative tactician enabled him to exploit to the fullest the grief and remorse following the assassination. The new President put to good use what the columnists Rowland Evans, Jr., and Robert D. Novak dubbed the Johnson Treatment: "He moved in close, his face a scant millimeter from his target, his eyes widening and narrowing, his eyebrows rising and falling. From his pockets poured clippings, memos, statistics. Mimicry, humor, and the genius of analogy made the Treatment an almost hypnotic experience and rendered the target stunned and helpless." As chief executive, he followed the course of legislation in the most minute detail. "Not a sparrow falls," said one adulatory aide, "that he doesn't know about." In less than a year, Congress enacted a quantity of bills that had been stranded in the Kennedy era — a Higher Education Facilities Act, which authorized federal assistance for the construction of campus buildings and provided federal aid to graduate centers, appropriations for mass transit, the tax cut, an anti-poverty program, and, as a memorial to Kennedy, civil rights legislation.

In February 1964, Congress defied economic orthodoxy by approving a tax cut of more than $10 billion. Johnson succeeded in part because his emphasis on consensus and budgetary prudence had mollified business leaders, although they accepted the Keynesian rationale with some trepidation. The tax cut turned out to be a brilliant success. In the next six quarters consumer spending increased an unprecedented $45 billion, the gross national product soared, and the government took in more money under the new tax schedule than it had before. During the 1960's the total of goods and services increased some 60 percent. Fears of automation diminished as the economy developed 10 million new jobs, a rate of a million a year. From 1961 to 1968, over 14 million Americans moved above the "poverty line," as the proportion of the impoverished in the nation was halved from 22 percent to 11 percent. Median annual family income, under $4000 in 1958 when Galbraith's *The Affluent Society* was published, approached $8000 when a revised edition appeared a decade later, a gain of 85 percent after allowance is made for price rises. The figures for families earning $7000 a year, measured in 1966 dollars, rose from 22 percent in 1950 to roughly 55 percent in 1966, and by 1970, 30 percent of the families in the United States took in over $13,000 annually.

Liberal economists had exhilarating proof that they could put their theories into practice with gratifying results. Daniel P. Moynihan called the tax cut outcome "perhaps the most impressive demonstration that has yet occurred . . . of the capacity of organized intelligence to forecast and direct events." This feat of social engineering, said Secretary of Labor W. Willard Wirtz, marked "the ultimate triumph of the spirit of John Maynard Keynes over the stubborn shade of Adam Smith," and the country's leading conservative economist, Milton Friedman, conceded, "We are all Keynesians now."

On January 8, 1964, in his first State of the Union message, Johnson declared "unconditional war on poverty," another program that carried on initiatives first explored by his predecessor. Kennedy had been shocked by what he had seen in West Virginia during the 1960 primary campaign. "Imagine," he said one night, "just imagine kids who never drink milk." Kennedy and his advisers had also been influenced by Michael Harrington's *The Other America,* a small book that had a big impact. "The millions who are poor in the United States tend to become increasingly invisible," Harrington wrote. It required "an effort of the intellect and will even to see them." Accounts like Harrington's, and more scholarly assessments by Robert Lampman and Leon Keyserling, indicated that in an age of affluence, one-fifth of the nation existed, as Johnson said, "on the outskirts of hope" in "inherited, gateless poverty." Blacks made up a disproportionate number of the poor, but 70 percent were whites, many of them trapped in cul-de-sacs of distress such as Appalachia.

Johnson took Kennedy's slowly emerging plan, revamped it, and drove it through Congress with a blare of trumpets and a roll of drums. Reporters for London's *Sunday Times* commented that it "was not the most daring, but it was perhaps the most bellicose program of social reform in history. It was to be a *war* on poverty. Federal funds were to be 'fired in' to pockets of poverty in what was known in Washington as 'the rifle-shot approach.' . . . He actually spoke of 'throttling want.' " The Economic Opportunity Act of 1964 (a title that suggests the endurance of nineteenth-century ideas) appropriated nearly a billion dollars for projects such as Head Start to help preschoolers, the Job Corps for dropouts, a work-study program to assist college students, a domestic peace corps—Volunteers in Service to America (VISTA)—a Neighborhood Youth Corps, basic education and work experience activities to help adults, and, what would prove to be the most controversial departure, a Community Action Program stipulating "maximum feasible participation" by the impoverished. The Public Works and Economic Development Act in 1965 would add over $3 billion more and an Appalachian Regional Development Act another $1 billion to rehabilitate that section. "We are not helpless before the iron laws of economics," the President said. Although the war on poverty was inadequately funded, it was a hopeful beginning, and the Negro novelist Ralph Ellison would call Johnson "the greatest American President for the poor and for the Negroes."

In 1964 Johnson announced a conception of his own—the "Great Society." At Ann Arbor in May, he explained that the Great Society was "a place where men are more concerned with the quality of their goals than the quantity of their goods," thus challenging the ethos of the consumer culture while the tax cut was aggrandizing it. But Johnson's prospectus went beyond the preoccupations of "qualitative liberalism." The President stated, "The Great Society rests on abundance and liberty for all. It demands an end to poverty and racial injustice, to which we are totally committed in our time."

Johnson's Great Society confronted a challenge that fall from a die-hard reactionary, Senator Barry Goldwater of Arizona. A millionaire Phoenix department store owner, Goldwater thrived on the consumer culture, but his ideas were more appropriate to the entrepreneurial individualism of frontier America. In *The Conscience of a Conservative*, published four years earlier, he had called for the abolition of the graduated income tax and the sale of TVA, and he recommended that the national government abandon most of its functions at the rate of 10 percent a year. A spokesman for the new rich of Scottsdale, the retired officer corps of San Diego, and small-town Americans in retreat, Goldwater distrusted the cosmopolitan

East, with its solicitude for society's outcasts and its fussiness about nuclear war. He expected to win the presidency by putting together a regional combination of the South and West and, by offering the nation "a choice not an echo," to bring to the polls millions of dormant conservative, nationalist voters with the appeal, "In Your Heart, You Know He's Right."

Goldwater's campaign gave Lyndon Johnson the enormous advantage of running as a social reform candidate and still seeming the less "radical" of the two. By picking Senator Hubert Humphrey of Minnesota as his running mate, Johnson quieted lingering doubts about his commitment to liberalism, and by saying, "We are not about to send American boys nine or ten thousand miles from home to do what Asian boys ought to be doing for themselves," he emerged as the peace nominee. Moderate Republicans were disturbed by Goldwater's statement at the rowdy San Francisco convention that "extremism in the defense of liberty is no vice," a declaration that appeared to give benediction to the far-right John Birch Society, which even viewed Eisenhower as a Communist agent. Goldwater's missile-rattling created unease about whether he should have his finger on the nuclear button; as the Democrats put it, "In Your Heart, You Know He Might." Blacks were antagonized by Goldwater's covert countenancing of "white backlash," and old people were troubled by his hostility to social security. On election day, Johnson sent Goldwater down to a crushing defeat by gaining a record 61.1 percent of the popular returns and every electoral vote save those of Goldwater's Arizona and five Deep South states. In Congress the Democrats swelled their margin to 155 in the House and attained a 68 to 32 edge in the Senate, enough to nullify the conservative coalition and enhance prospects for a legislative performance that would rival the New Deal.

In rolling up the most impressive record of any Congress in three decades, the "fabulous Eighty-ninth" wiped clean the legislative slate of the Fair Deal. When Congress approved a Medicare program of health insurance for the aged under Social Security, Johnson flew to Independence so that Harry Truman could witness the signing. (Congress also provided Medicaid for the indigent.) Truman saw the effectuation of another of his goals with the enactment, also in 1965, of the Elementary and Secondary Education Act, which provided more than a billion dollars in grants for low-income pupils and authorized, for the first time, assistance to children in Catholic parochial and other private schools. This departure resulted from

Election of 1964

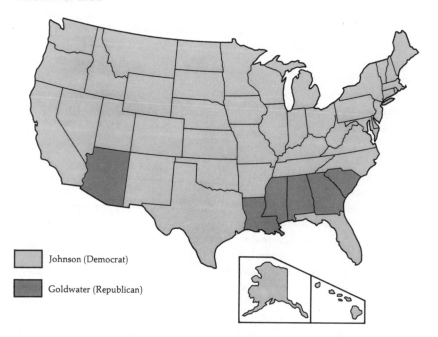

Johnson (Democrat)

Goldwater (Republican)

Kennedy's easing of fears about Catholics and the ecumenical spirit fostered by Pope John XXIII as well as from Johnson's acumen as chief legislator. Regarded by many of the literati as anti-intellectual, Johnson prided himself on being the Education President. That same year he shepherded through Congress the Higher Education Act for assistance to college students. In one year, the President claimed, Congress had done "more for the wonderful cause of education in America than all the previous 176 regular sessions of Congress did, put together."

The Eighty-ninth Congress, at Johnson's behest, also instituted reforms that went beyond the New Deal and Fair Deal. It established two new Cabinet-level departments, for Transportation and for Housing and Urban Affairs, in recognition of the railroad crisis occasioned by the ubiquitous automobile and of the fact that the United States had become a nation of cities. To carry out the Great Society's emphasis on the quality of life, legislation made provision for the beautification of highways, an abiding interest of the President's wife, Lady Bird Johnson, and, under the sponsorship of Senator Edmund Muskie of Maine, for the cleansing of air and rivers. Influenced by Ralph Nader's *Unsafe at Any Speed,* Congress adopted the Highway Safety Act and the Traffic Safety Act. The lawmakers agreed to the first important change in immigration policy since the 1920's when they ended the national origins system of quotas, which favored Northwestern Europe, while imposing a quota on nations in the Western Hemisphere for the first time. In response to recent episodes such as Eisenhower's illness, a resolution subsequently ratified as the Twenty-fifth Amendment outlined procedures in case of presidential disability. The Housing Act of 1965 enabled Washington to supplement the rent of poor tenants and in 1966 Congress set up a Demonstration Cities program, although neither was supported with adequate appropriations. This was the Congress, too, that made

The Fair Deal becomes the Great Society. On July 30, 1965, at the Truman Library in Independence, Missouri, former President Harry Truman, an early advocate of national health insurance, flourishes the signing pens after President Johnson puts his signature on the Medicare bill. Looking on are Lady Bird Johnson, Bess Truman, and Vice-President Hubert Humphrey, who bridged the two liberal eras.

Y. R. Okamoto

advances in civil rights and furnished additional rounds of ammunition for the war on poverty.

"The Congress of Fulfillment" completed almost the entire agenda of twentieth-century progressivism. Under Kennedy and more markedly under Johnson, the quarter-century deadlock had been broken. The Eighty-ninth Congress, wrote one Washington reporter, "brought to a harvest a generation's backlog of ideas and social legislation." Arthur Krock observed that it had "moved the country nearer to state collectivism at the federal level than in any previous period." For those who since the Great Depression had waited in vain for another era like that of the New Deal, the first half of the 1960's was a time for rejoicing, and the Eighty-ninth Congress recalled the halcyon days of 1935. "It is the Congress of accomplished hopes," declared Speaker John W. McCormack. "It is the Congress of realized dreams."

Black and White Together

The same sanguine ebullience animated the civil rights movement, which in those years reached the apogee of its power in an ambience of brotherhood, goodwill, optimism, and euphoria. Negroes took to the streets in hundreds of cities, south and north, and frequently whites joined them:

> Black and white together
> We'll walk hand in hand.

Often they enjoyed instant success. The Justice Department toted up three hundred cities in which lunch counters were desegregated in 1963 alone. Blacks pursued equality with an unshakable determination, and sizable numbers of whites became their allies. The National Opinion Research Center at the University of Chicago reported that the proportion of whites in the North who accepted integration of neighborhoods rose from 42 percent in 1942 to 72 percent in 1963 and that those favoring school integration increased from 40 to 75 percent. Both Kennedy and Johnson committed themselves by words and deeds to the civil rights revolution, and the Supreme Court, its patience gone, announced, "The time for mere 'deliberate speed' has run out." Even in the Deep South the times they were a-changin'; more than six hundred community leaders in McComb, Mississippi, called for compliance to civil rights legislation. With so many hopeful indicators, many could sing with conviction:

> Oh, deep in my heart I do believe
> We shall overcome some day.

And "some day" would be now.

In the early 1960's, racial prejudice, as Benjamin Muse has observed, "entered the catalog of unquestioned evils — like water pollution or reckless driving." To be sure, whites were often patronizing and even expected gratitude from Negroes for helping them win rights they should have been able to take for granted. Some of the change, too, was mere tokenism. The black comedian Godfrey Cambridge announced facetiously that he had organized a "Rent a Negro" organization so that every firm could have one temporarily on display in the reception foyer. Yet even the most awkward, self-serving gestures indicated a shift in what was regarded as socially desirable.

The cold war and the consumer culture continued to be instrumental in advancing racial equality. The needs of cold war (and limited war) in the 1960's served to justify national civil rights legislation. In his civil rights message to Congress in June 1963, President Kennedy would point out that "when Americans are sent to Viet-Nam or West Berlin, we do not ask for whites only." The consumer culture proved an even more significant base than it had in the 1950's. Negroes in Birmingham and other cities made effective use of the boycott to demonstrate the importance to white merchants of black consumer buying power, estimated as equivalent in the United States to that of all the people of Canada. In San Francisco militants seeking to increase Negro employment in supermarkets created disorder by piling their shopping carts high with groceries and abandoning them at check-out counters. An important measure of advance in the 1960's was to be the increasing numbers of blacks appearing in television commercials to sing the praises of detergents. Black nationalists touted the distinctive virtues of soul food, but the political future of the black mayor of Cleveland was jeopardized by a quarrel with militants over franchises for McDonald's hamburger drive-ins.

The motel provided the locale for stirring episodes in the civil rights movement. In Florida black and white activists dove into motel swimming pools to break the taboo on integrated bathing. Attorney General Robert F. Kennedy, guidebook in hand, would point out to a congressional committee that a black tourist could not find a room in Danville, Virginia, though a dog accompanied by a white man would be taken in by at least four hostelries. When Congress responded by legislating the Civil Rights Act of 1964, it was sustained in the *Heart of Atlanta Motel* case (as well as by the Court's ruling on Ollie's Barbecue in Birmingham). The Reverend Martin Luther King, Jr., won a sympathetic response from whites by telling what it was like "when you take a cross-country drive and find it necessary to sleep night after night in the uncomfortable corners of your automobile because no motel will accept you." By the late 1960's, King would no longer face this hardship, but in the spring of 1968 in Memphis he would meet death on a motel balcony.

John Kennedy has been hailed as the first President to make the cause of racial integration his own, but he came to his final position slowly and under duress. Of his antipathy to discrimination and his support of the *Brown* decision there was no doubt. But he hesitated to advocate civil rights legislation, for he feared it would fail and would pull the rest of his program down with it. (In fact, when in 1963 he did take a strong stand in the Alabama desegregation crisis, his comfortable margin for an area development measure melted away. When thirty-nine Congressmen switched abruptly, the bill lost by five votes.) Kennedy reasoned that he would have to rely on executive action and concentrate his attention on the federal establishment.

The President used his authority as chief executive to make the national government a staging area for the civil rights movement. He put together a committee headed by Vice-President Johnson to ferret out evidence of discrimination in federal employment and in industries with government contracts. Under his brother Robert the Department of Justice enlisted a remarkable crew of dedicated men— Byron R. White (raised to the Supreme Court in 1962), Nicholas de B. Katzenbach, Burke Marshall, Ramsey Clark, and John Doar, who on one occasion in Jackson, Mississippi, would create a legend by nervily walking into a mob like Gary Cooper gunless on the streets of Dodge City. They were a tough breed. When Ed Guthman, besieged at the University of Mississippi in 1962, reported on the phone to the attorney general, "It's sorta like the Alamo," Bob Kennedy retorted, "Well, you know what happened to those fellows." The President filled high government offices with distinguished blacks—Carl Rowan as ambassador to Finland, Robert Weaver to head the Housing and Home Finance Agency, Thurgood Marshall as United States Circuit Court Justice, and the first Negro district judges ever to serve in the continental United States. In the year ending June 1963, the appointment of Negroes to top-level federal posts increased 39 percent.

However, even in the orbit of executive authority, Kennedy encountered criticism from civil rights activists. He had said during the 1960 campaign that discrimination in federally financed housing could be ended by a stroke of the pen. But not until November 21, 1962, after numerous pens were mailed to him, did he issue an order, so circumscribed and so unenthusiastically administered that it had small effect. His excellent selections for judicial posts in the North were offset when he placed segregationists on the federal bench in the South. Even the Department of Justice was accused of preferring racial peace to the enforcement of rights and of failing to live up to its pledge to protect registration workers. In Mississippi, Allen J. Matusow has noted, "SNCC's only contact with federal authority consisted of the FBI agents who stood by taking notes while local policemen beat up SNCC members." Although some of the objections failed to take into account either political constraints or the limits imposed on federal action by state sovereignty, it is clear that the national government required the prod of the civil rights movement to push it to reaching the full extent of its powers.

The new Department of Justice team got its baptism of fire when it was called to the defense of the "freedom riders" four months after Kennedy took office. That spring the Supreme Court, in *Boynton* v. *Commonwealth of Virginia,* ruled that restaurants in bus stations could not discriminate against interstate travelers. On May 14, 1961, an interracial group from the Congress of Racial Equality set out for the Deep South to test the effectiveness of the decision. In Anniston, Alabama, a mob incinerated a Greyhound bus carrying one delegation (which barely escaped), and in Birmingham the rest of the party was savagely mauled as it left a Trailways bus. When a mob seized the Montgomery bus terminal, the attorney general dispatched hundreds of federal marshals under "Whizzer" White's command. Before order was restored, the mob beat the President's personal representative, John Seigenthaler, into semi-consciousness when he tried to protect a rider. Federal authority prevented a repetition of such episodes, but it could do nothing to help the riders when Mississippi shrewdly eschewed violence and resorted instead to mass arrests.

Nevertheless, the freedom rides did spur the Justice Department to move on two different fronts. The attorney general persuaded the Interstate Commerce Commission to issue an order banning segregation in carriers and terminals, and by government edict signs stating "Waiting room for colored" came tumbling down. The Justice Department also got thirteen of the country's fifteen segregated airports to desegregate voluntarily and filed suit against the other two.

Black and white volunteers challenge Jim Crow in the cradle of the Confederacy, Montgomery, Alabama, in May 1961. After the Greyhound bus pulled into the Montgomery station, a mob of a thousand clubbed and beat the freedom riders. The Kennedy administration dispatched hundreds of marshals, but order was not restored until the governor of Alabama belatedly called out the national guard.

To channel the energy of civil rights workers in less explosive, and it was thought more constructive, directions, the attorney general encouraged a drive to register black voters in the South. By the spring of 1963, Claude Sitton was writing:

There are harbingers of a new day: voting applicants standing patiently at the courthouse door in Greenwood for hour on endless hour, a Justice Department attorney shaking hands with a Negro while a white woman shivers with rage, the songs of freedom rolling out of the little Negro churches into the blackness of the Delta night.

The Department of Justice brought more than five times as many voting rights suits in its first two years as Eisenhower had in three years. The previous administration had left Mississippi alone; the Kennedys filed nineteen suits, even in Sunflower County, home of James Eastland, the mighty segregationist chairman of the Senate Judiciary Committee.

Mississippi provided the battlefield, too, for a confrontation with federal authority even more critical than the one at Little Rock. In 1962 James H. Meredith, the grandson of a slave and a cold war veteran with eight years in the air force, attempted to enroll at the University of Mississippi. To his aid came the able state secretary of the NAACP, Medgar Evers. But in defiance of a United States Circuit Court order, sustained by the Supreme Court, Governor Ross Barnett turned Meredith away and announced a doctrine of interposition reminiscent of John C. Calhoun. President Kennedy responded by sending to the campus of Ole Miss hundreds of federal marshals and, when they proved necessary, almost thirty thousand troops, including the federalized national guard. They were met by a mob who treated the forces of the United States as though they were enemy invaders. The rioters were led by a former major general, Edwin Walker, who, ironically, had commanded the troops at Little Rock five years earlier. In a night of terror, two were killed and 375 injured, including 166 federal marshals (twenty-nine with gunshot wounds) and thirteen members of the steadfast Mississippi National Guard, among them William Faulkner's nephew. Only at such a cost was it possible for one black man to go to the university of his native state.

In 1963 the alliance of the civil rights movement and the federal government overcame the final bastion of white supremacy, Alabama. On Good Friday, April 12, Martin Luther King led a massive demonstration in Birmingham, "the Johannesburg of America." The police commissioner, Eugene "Bull" Connor, shocked the nation, and indeed the world, by employing high-pressure water hoses, ferocious police dogs, and electric cattle prods against the marchers. Despite the intervention of the Justice Department, King won only limited concessions, and when his brother's home and the movement's headquarters motel were bombed, angry blacks rioted, an omen of things to come. However, newspaper photographs and televised accounts of Birmingham motivated still more Americans to align themselves with King.

In June the civil rights forces encountered a less volatile but more dangerous enemy than Connor, the governor of Alabama, George C. Wallace. Although he was slicker than Joe McCarthy, he conveyed the same image of a punisher. Golden Gloves bantamweight champion in 1936 and 1937, he had flown in B-29 bombing missions over Japan in World War II, then entered the Alabama political ring. After being defeated by a little-known racist in his bid for the governorship in 1958, Wallace said, "John Patterson out-nigguhed me. And boys, I'm not going to be out-nigguhed again." He pledged to the people of his state that he would stand in the doorway to prevent Negroes from entering the University of Alabama. But when the President federalized the national guard, Wallace, after putting up a farcical show of resistance, gave way. No longer did any state in the union have an exclusively white school system.

Two hours after Wallace capitulated, Kennedy spoke to the nation

Bull Connor's America. In April 1963 Martin Luther King led a direct-action campaign against segregation and discrimination in Birmingham, Alabama. Eugene Theophilus Connor, Birmingham's commissioner of public safety, horrified the world by using police dogs against Negro demonstrators.

Charles Moore from Black Star

in a televised address, much of it extemporaneous, which conveyed an intensity of emotional commitment that had not been manifest before. The President stated:

If an American, because his skin is dark, cannot eat lunch in a restaurant open to the public; if he cannot send his children to the best public school available; if he cannot vote for the public officials who represent him; if, in short, he cannot enjoy the full and free life which all of us want, then who among us would be content to have the color of his skin changed and stand in his place?

Who among us would then be content with the counsels of patience and delay? One hundred years of delay have passed since President Lincoln freed the slaves, yet their heirs, their grandsons, are not fully free. They are not yet freed from the bonds of injustice; they are not yet freed from social and economic oppression. And this nation, for all its hopes and all its boasts, will not be fully free until all its citizens are free.

He warned that "the fires of frustration and discord are burning in every city," leading to actions that "threaten violence — and threaten lives." The President's words gained added meaning, tragically, when that very night Medgar Evers was murdered by a cowardly assassin in the driveway of his home. A week later, Kennedy, who had said that "the time has come for this nation to fulfill its promise," asked Congress to enact the most comprehensive civil rights law in history.

To demonstrate their enthusiasm for the proposed legislation, which Congress showed no haste to pass, more than two hundred thousand gathered in the nation's capital on August 28, 1963, for an impressive March on Washington. Mobilizer of the march was Bayard Rustin, a veteran of the civil rights movement who had organized the original Aldermaston Ban-the-Bomb protest in England and had been in the front ranks of the marchers in the Sahara to halt a French nuclear test. Highlight of the occasion was a passionate speech by Martin Luther King. "Even though we face the difficulties of today and tomorrow, I still have a dream," he said. "It is a dream chiefly rooted in the American dream." He anticipated that "one day on the red hills of Georgia, the sons of former slaves and the sons of former slave-owners will be able to sit together at the table of brotherhood." Many in Washington had feared that violence would erupt. But London's *Daily Express* was able to headline its account, "The Gentle Flood," and Russell Baker commented, "The sweetness and patience of the crowd may have set some sort of national highwater mark in mass decency." There was reason enough to fear violence, but not there. In September a chill of horror went through the nation when in Birmingham a bomb took the lives of four Negro children at Sunday school, and two months later the President, too, would be gone, his civil rights legislation not yet enacted, King's dream far short of fulfillment.

In his initial address to Congress on November 27, 1963, Lyndon Johnson, the first President from a southern state since Reconstruction, stated emphatically: "We have talked long enough in this country about equal rights. We have talked for one hundred years or more. It is time now to write the next chapter, and to write it in the books of law." By July 1964, the President, with expert assistance from Hubert Humphrey, a long-time fighter for civil rights, and Everett Dirksen, a recent convert, had guided a more ambitious version of Kennedy's bill through both houses, after breaking a southern filibuster. Dirksen, known for his grandiloquent manner of speaking as "the Wizard of Ooze," proclaimed, after Victor Hugo, "Stronger than all the armies is an idea whose time has come."

The Civil Rights Act of 1964 outlawed racial discrimination in public accommodations like restaurants, motels, soda fountains, and filling stations, required equal access to public facilities such as stadiums and swimming pools, and authorized withholding federal subsidies from recipients like schools and hospitals that continued to evince prejudice. It prohibited discrimination in voter registration and established a sixth-grade education as presumptive of literacy. For the first time in some Deep South communities, Negroes sat in "white only" sections of movies and spent the night in hotels from which they had always been excluded. "The thing that the Act reaches," said Burke Marshall, "is the official caste system in this country."

Although the voting rights section of the 1964 act was an improvement, it still left hundreds of thousands of southern Negroes without a ballot. The total of Negroes registered in Alabama had risen from 6,000 in 1947 to 110,000 in 1964, but not one was registered in counties like Lowndes and Wilcox where whites were outnumbered 4 to 1. To dramatize the plight of the disfranchised blacks, King went to Selma, Alabama. Six days after being honored in Oslo as the youngest American ever to receive the Nobel Prize, he was in a Selma jail. The imprisonment of King served only to rally Alabama's Negroes, who sang:

> Police cars are the Berlin Wall,
> Berlin Wall, Berlin Wall,

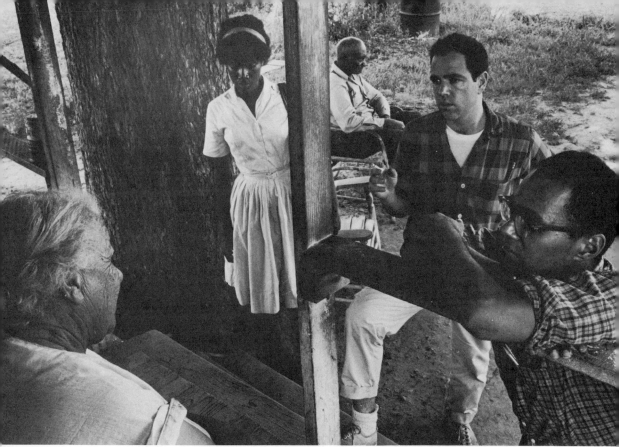

Danny Lyon, Magnum

Young civil rights workers of both races urge the older generation to register to vote. These efforts, reinforcing national legislation, proved so successful that Negro registration in Mississippi rose from 22,000 in 1960 to 285,000 in 1970.

Police cars are the Berlin Wall,
   In Selma, Alabama.
We're going to stand here till it falls,
   till it falls, till it falls,
We're going to stand here till it falls,
   In Selma, Alabama.
Love is the thing that'll make it fall,
   make it fall, make it fall,
Love is the thing that'll make it fall,
   In Selma, Alabama.

In the spirit of militant love, King organized yet another interracial demonstration, this time a march from Selma to the Alabama capital, Montgomery.

When local authorities harassed the marchers and Governor Wallace refused to safeguard them, President Johnson came to their aid in the kind of tandem between King and the chief executive that had proved so effective before. He federalized the Alabama National Guard, and on March 15, 1965, went before Congress to deliver one of the greatest addresses ever made by a President. He compared the struggle at Selma to that at Lexington, stated that equal rights was an issue that "lay bare the secret heart of America," told the legislators that "the real hero of this struggle is the American Negro," and promised to use the full power of his office to wipe out the prejudice he had once seen scar the children he had taught in a small Mexican-American school. Because local officials had calculatedly denied suffrage to Negroes, he was submitting a bill to "establish a simple, uniform standard which cannot be used, however ingenious the effort, to flout the Constitution." "And," the President said emphatically, "we *shall* overcome." That August, Johnson put his signature on the Voting Rights Act, which authorized federal examiners to register qualified voters and suspended devices like literacy tests.

The Voting Rights Act and related measures proved spectacularly successful in expanding Negro suffrage in the South and in encouraging black officeholding. The 1965 act marked the culmination of a series of such reforms — the 1957 law, the 1960 statute, the Twenty-fourth Amendment, ratified in 1964, which outlawed the poll tax in federal elections. (In 1966, the Supreme Court invalidated the poll tax altogether.) Two months after a federal examiner arrived in Dallas County (Selma), the percentage of voting-age Negroes registered rose from under 10 to 60. By spring, Alabama had added 166,000 Negro registrants, and black registration in Mississippi had increased fourfold. At the end of the decade, the country had fifty Negro mayors, heading municipal governments in cities such as Cleveland, Newark, Gary, and Wichita. In 1966, a year when pundits were accentuating the power of "white backlash" in the North, the Democratic state of Massachusetts, with a population less than 3 percent black, gave a Republican, Edward W. Brooke, III, an overwhelming 61 percent of its ballots. In defeating the patrician former governor Endicott Peabody, Brooke became the first Negro elected to the United States Senate since 1881. Black representatives sat in the state capitol in George Wallace's Montgomery, as well as in Atlanta and Columbia; blacks controlled Greene County, Alabama; and, to the consternation of white supremacists, the mayor of Fayette, Mississippi, was Medgar Evers' brother, Charles.

When on August 6, 1965, President Johnson signed the Voting

Rights Act, liberals of both races felt gratification, and whites took pride in the fact that virtually every piece of national legislation Negroes had requested had been adopted. A period of tranquility loomed, for, as *Time* observed, "there was a growing sentiment that perhaps it was time for the revolution to move off the streets." To be sure, there had been rumblings — rising disaffection among SNCC workers in the South, massive boycotts to terminate de facto school segregation in the North, even moderate-scale riots in Harlem and Rochester in 1964. James Baldwin had warned that "if we do not dare everything, the fulfillment of that prophecy, recreated from the Bible in song by a slave, is upon us: 'God gave Noah the rainbow sign, no more water, the fire next time.'" But that had been in 1963, and since then the movement had achieved much. As the civil rights lawmakers gathered about the President for the bill-signing ceremony at the White House on August 6, there was an air of liberalism triumphant. Five days later the Watts area of Los Angeles burst into flame; up in smoke with it went many of the assumptions and the expectations of the civil rights movement and of American liberalism.

The Fire Next Time

The Watts explosion detonated the first of four successive "long hot summers." Before the burning and looting in Los Angeles ended, thirty-four were dead, nearly four thousand arrested, and property damage had reached at least $35 million. The uprising stunned the evangels of the Great Society because Watts, for all its deprivation, was so much better off than other Negro districts that the anti-poverty program had been aiming at raising the level of black slum dwellers elsewhere to that of Watts. With tidy bungalows along palm-lined streets and nine public swimming pools, the black section of Los Angeles bore little physical resemblance to the typical grimy tenement ghetto. The National Urban League rated Los Angeles first among sixty-eight cities for Negroes, and delegates from Africa and Asia visited the city to study its success in race relations. White reformers, who had been stressing the importance of access to the democratic process, were puzzled that such a holocaust could occur in a place where Negroes boasted a Congressman, two assembly-men, and three city councillors, and held one-quarter of the jobs in the county government. Morever, the riots revealed a depth of anti-white bitterness that in the era of brotherhood anthems few

Burn, baby, burn! When the Watts district of Los Angeles exploded in August, 1965, arson and looting devastated many of the edifices of the consumer culture. The firemen who sought to save these blazing buildings arrived too late because they were delayed by bands of rock-throwing blacks, and the fire burned out of control.

liberals recognized existed. A governor's commission headed by John McCone concluded, "The existing breach, if allowed to persist, could in time split our society irretrievably. So serious and so explosive is the situation that, unless it is checked, the August riots may seem by comparison to be only a curtain-raiser for what could blow up one day in the future."

Following a series of outbreaks in 1966, notably in Chicago, where young blacks stoned white motorists and sniped at police, the summer of 1967 saw the most intense racial violence of modern times. During five days in July, twenty-six died and some twelve hundred were wounded in Newark, New Jersey. A week later, Detroit erupted in the worst upheaval in half a century; forty-three were killed, two thousand injured, and more than four thousand fires burned out a large part of the country's fifth largest city. After flying in a helicopter over the smoking ruins, Governor George Romney said that Detroit looked like "a city that has been bombed." As in a major war, too, tanks rolled through the streets, and machine guns raked snipers' nests.

The riots raised fundamental doubts about the liberals' policy strategy. Washington had spent more per capita on anti-poverty efforts in Newark than in any other northern metropolis. But Newark had long been a dead-end town. It was the Detroit disaster that was the shocker. The Motor City had a farsighted mayor, supported by Negro voters and responsive to ghetto problems, black officeholders, expensive anti-poverty and urban renewal programs, a high-wage industry, an anti-discriminatory union in Reuther's United Automobile Workers, and the stability indicated by the fact that 45 percent of the Negro families owned their homes. As Benjamin Muse observed, "There was probably more widespread affluence among Negroes in Detroit than in any other American city."

Civil rights activists, committed to the principle of "black and white together," found one emphasis of the 1967 riots especially

The Negro Revolt, 1965-1967

Source: Reprinted by permission of The Macmillan Company, New York, and Weidenfeld and Nicolson Limited, London, from *American History Atlas* by Martin Gilbert. Cartography by Peter Kingland. Copyright © 1969 by Martin Gilbert. Reprinted by permission of A D Peters and Company, Ltd.

perturbing, the cry of "Black Power!" The slogan first captured national attention as the unanticipated consequence of the determination of James Meredith to walk from Memphis to Jackson to inspirit Mississippi Negroes by his example. He got only ten miles across the border of his native state when, on June 6, 1966, he was shot from ambush (but not seriously wounded). On the very next day Martin Luther King and other civil rights leaders arrived in Mississippi to carry on Meredith's pilgrimage. Although Dr. King continued to stress racial integration and nonviolence, even when the marchers were stoned by white mobs and assaulted by the highway police, the young SNCC leader, Stokely Carmichael, sounded a different note when he said, "The only way we gonna stop them from whuppin' us is to take over. We been saying freedom for six years, and we ain't got nothin'. What we gonna start saying now is black power." When fifteen thousand marchers reached Jackson on June 26, many of them were shouting the new slogan, "Black Power!"

Not all who took up the chant agreed about what it meant. "At its inception in June 1966," Allen J. Matusow has noted, "black power was not a systematic doctrine but a cry of rage." By late August 1966 CORE's Floyd McKissick was explaining that "black power" implied self-determination based on six ingredients: "(1) political power; (2) economic power; (3) an improved self-image of the black man himself; (4) the development of young militant leadership; (5) the enforcement of federal laws, the abolition of police brutality; (6) the development of the black consumer bloc." In practice, black power exponents might aim at community control of the school system in northern ghettos or the election of Negro officials in the southern Black Belt. The phrase could convey little more than a plea for capital for aspiring black shopkeepers or the kind of precinct activity that the New York Irish had traditionally pursued through Tammany Hall. But increasingly "black power" acquired two features that were anathema to the civil rights activists—rejection of integration (coupled with hostility to whites) and a willingness to employ violence. Developments in the third world persuaded black nationalists in the United States that they were not a hopelessly outnumbered minority that had to accommodate to whites because they composed only 11 percent of the population. Instead, they concluded that they could afford to take a more militant stance as members of a potentially powerful community that made up two-thirds of the peoples of the earth.

Black leaders in the United States found inspiration in the successful nationhood movements in Africa. In 1960, the "African Year" when sixteen nations won their independence, Muslim luminaries welcomed the black American pilgrim Elijah Muhammad to Mecca. American black nationalists drew sustenance from Frantz Fanon's *Wretched of the Earth*, demanded instruction in Swahili in the public schools, and identified their own struggle with a worldwide process of decolonization. "At the rate things are going here," complained James Baldwin, "all of Africa will be free before we can get a lousy cup of coffee." However much they admired Africans like Nkrumah and Lumumba, most blacks recognized that they were indigenous Americans, and few save those fleeing prosecution expatriated themselves. LeRoi Jones, a black poet and playwright who would later change his name to Imamu Amiri Baraka, wrote about Africa as a "foreign place." He described the problems facing contemporary black Americans as directly related to black people's current situation in the United States rather than to the situation in their distant homeland.

Black nationalism, which had achieved a considerable following under Marcus Garvey in the 1920's, had recently gained new converts through the Black Muslims. Founded in 1930 by a mysterious Detroit peddler, W. Fard Muhammad, believed by his disciples to be the incarnation of Allah, The Lost-Found Nation of Islam in the Wilderness of North America flourished under his Messenger, Elijah Poole, who took the name of Elijah Muhammad. The Black Muslims preached that whites were agents of the devil, rejected Christianity as the creed of the slaveholder, denounced both the word "Negro" and Christian surnames as slavemaster's terms, and demanded territory from the United States in compensation for past wrongs in order to create a separate black nation. The order offered Negroes heightened self-esteem as well as the vision of a future society in which they would be ascendant and a hereafter when they would be resurrected first. It made greatest headway among the young black unemployed and the social outcasts of the northern ghettos, but it numbered among its adherents two prominent athletes, Jim Brown and Cassius Clay (Muhammad Ali).

Although in the early 1960's the Black Muslims probably did not have the allegiance of more than fifteen thousand fully involved members (but with several times that number of believers and sympathizers), they exerted a powerful impact on Negro thought despite, or perhaps because of, the fact that many of their doctrines mirrored those of their enemies. Like the Klansmen, they celebrated female chastity and racial immaculacy. "No nation that loves the purity of that nation desires any mixture of blood with any un-alike people," said Elijah Muhammad, adding, "We must use force, if necessary, to stop our people from destroying our race through intermarriages and intermixing." Advocates of a radical restructuring of society, they preached nevertheless a message of self-help, hard work, and sobriety that recalled the teachings of Booker T. Washington and Benjamin Franklin, and they established consumer culture ventures such as department stores, restaurants, and groceries. Outraged by racial discrimination against blacks, they fostered anti-Semitism by denouncing Jews as exploiters and the NAACP as the instrumentality of Zionists, and they preached hatred of whites. "How can Martin Luther, being the minister he claims of God, teach his people to love their enemy, when God Himself said he had set a day to deal with his enemies?" asked Elijah Muhammad. Yet the actions of the Black Muslims rarely matched their fiery rhetoric, and even opponents admired their success with the down-and-out whom the older civil rights organizations had not reached.

None of the Black Muslim leaders excited such adulation among young blacks (and apprehension among whites) as the son of an Omaha Garveyite, Malcolm Little, who, casting off his "slavemaster" final name, became better known as Malcolm X. At a time when other Negro leaders were preaching nonviolence, Malcolm asserted that a Mau Mau was required. He jeered at King's strategy. "You need somebody who is going to fight," he insisted. "You don't need any kneeling in or crawling in." In response to the March on Washington, he asked:

Who ever heard of angry revolutionists all harmonizing "We Shall Overcome . . . Suum Day . . ." while tripping and swaying along arm-in-arm with the very people they were supposed to be angrily revolting against? Who ever heard of angry revolutionists swinging their bare feet together with their oppressors in lily-pad park pools, with gospels and guitars and "I Have a Dream" speeches?

Whites were incensed by his tirades and took special offense at his chortling over President Kennedy's murder, and he came into even sharper conflict with blacks, including Elijah Muhammad, who broke with him in late 1963. On February 21, 1965, at a meeting of his new group, the Organization for Afro-American Unity, at the Audubon Ballroom in New York, three black men armed with a shotgun

"The shining black prince," Malcolm X, addresses a meeting of Black Muslims. In 1952 he enlisted under Elijah Muhammad, leader of the Nation of Islam, and became, as Louis Lomax observed, the "St. Paul" of the Black Muslim movement. In 1964 he founded a new organization, and on February 21, 1965, at a meeting in Harlem, he was murdered.

and revolvers gunned him down. Conflicting evidence suggests that Malcolm may have been moving toward a more integrationist stance in his final days, but it is as the shining prince of black nationalism that he left his mark, notably in his posthumously published, and widely read, autobiography.

During Malcolm's lifetime, most Negroes, as devout Christians, rejected his teaching, and the civil rights movement followed Dr.

King's star, but increasing numbers of embittered blacks were finding such ideas congenial because they had lost faith in white intentions. In James Baldwin's *Another Country* (1962), one character sneered that "white people go around jerking themselves off with all that jazz about the land of the free and the home of the brave." Baldwin, far from urging the integration of Negroes into white America, judged white civilization unfit to survive. As early as July 1963, Negroes in Cambridge, Maryland, fired shotguns at whites, and that summer too *Dissent* published a symptomatic essay, "The Black Man's Burden: The White Liberal." By the fall of 1963, an element in SNCC was muttering about expelling white volunteers from the organization.

While much of the country marveled at the rapid rate of change in the South, the young civil rights workers experienced deep frustration. Albany, Georgia, and Jackson, Mississippi, both showed that a city with enough jail space could foil peaceful efforts at desegregation. Token compliance proved even more troublesome; in 1967, four hundred thousand more Negro pupils attended all-black schools in the South than in 1954 when the *Brown* decision was handed down. The gains that were made came at a fearful cost — churches and homes bombed, civil rights workers brutally beaten and even murdered. Sometimes local authorities approved or covertly collaborated, as in the sickening slayings of James Chaney, Andrew Goodman, and Michael Schwerner in Mississippi in 1964.

Despite the sacrifices of whites like Goodman and Schwerner, radicalized blacks took a growingly cynical attitude toward white liberals. Whereas most white civil rights enthusiasts viewed the March on Washington as an epiphany, SNCC militants thought of it as an occasion that the Kennedy administration had turned to its political advantage by co-opting the leadership. Blacks in SNCC remembered bitterly that the speech of their leader John Lewis had been censored and that Negroes had been insulted by a humiliating edict closing down liquor stores and bars for the day. At the Democratic national convention in 1964, the SNCC-sponsored Mississippi Freedom Democratic Party scored an important victory over racism, but since the outcome was a compromise, the MFDP claimed that white liberals had sold them out. That summer proved to be the last in which white and black volunteers in the South were able to work together.

A faction of SNCC had been skeptical of the Mississippi Summer Project of 1964 from the outset on the grounds that blacks should carry out the job of registering blacks, and their doubts were reinforced by the coverage the national press gave the project. Julius Lester, a SNCC field secretary who would later publish *Look Out Whitey! Black Power's Gon' Get Your Mama!*, recalled:

The feature stories it wrote usually went something like, "Blop-blop is a blue-eyed blonde from Diamond Junction-on-the-Hudson, New York. She is a twenty-year-old junior at Radcliffe majoring in Oriental metaphysics and its relationship to the quantum theory, when the sun is in Saggitarius [*sic*]. This summer she's living with a Negro family in Fatback, Mississippi who has never heard of the quantum theory, etc., etc., etc." All summer the articles came about white boys and white girls living with poor Negroes in Mississippi. It didn't escape the attention of Negroes that seemingly no one cared about the Negro civil rights workers who have been living and working in Mississippi for the previous three years. Didn't anyone care about Willie Peacock, born and raised on a Mississippi plantation, who couldn't get back to his town because he was an organizer for SNCC and the white people would kill him if he went to see his mother? Apparently not.

Many of the whites in the summer project sympathized with these sentiments, but that failed to heal the breach. Michael Schwerner's young wife said that if the Negro Chaney had been the only one killed there would not have been the national expressions of outrage, and after attending a memorial service for Chaney in Mississippi a Connecticut girl wrote her family:

How the Negro people are able to accept all the abuses of the whites — all the insults and injustices which make me ashamed to be white — and then turn around and say they want to love us, is beyond me. . . . As a white northerner I can get involved whenever I feel like it and run home whenever I get bored or frustrated or scared. I hate the attitude and position of the Northern whites and despise myself when I think that way. Lately I've been feeling homesick and longing for pleasant old Westport and sailing and swimming and my friends. . . . And what is making it worse is that all those damn northerners are thinking of me as a brave hero.

To blacks like Lester and Carmichael such expressions of empathy had become depreciated currency because in the North as well as in the South white America was responding too slowly.

Although the North presented many fewer legal obstacles to the struggle for equality, it also revealed the limitations of familiar approaches. When Martin Luther King attempted to desegregate housing in Chicago by employing the techniques that had been successful in southern towns, he was rebuffed by angry mobs. More than brotherhood marches, or even new statutes, were required to change the de facto pattern of Jim Crow in northern school districts or to undo the legacy of discrimination in slum societies. As Claude Brown wrote of Harlem in *Manchild in the Promised Land,* "There were too many people full of hate and bitterness crowded into a dirty, stinky, uncared-for closet-size section of a great city." To some, Detroit and Los Angeles may have seemed model communities, but Watts suffered from a dreadful transportation system and even worse police-black relations, and Detroit had a nonwhite unemployment rate triple that for whites. Anti-poverty programs raised expectations and dashed them. And though the income of Negroes had been steadily rising, the economic gap between the races remained wide, at the very time when TV commercials were rubbing noses in the disparity between the two worlds.

When blacks in the ghettos erupted, they lashed out at the institutions of the consumer culture that they felt denied them a fair share. Dynamite charges blew up supermarkets, and Molotov cocktails burned out shopping centers. The consumer culture provided adaptable weapons in the form of empty Coca Cola bottles which were filled with gasoline and rags and lit. *"Things go better with coke,"* Lester wrote sardonically. One participant in the Detroit uprising explained: "On Twelfth Street everybody was out, the whole family, Mama, Papa, the kids, it was like an outing. . . . The rebellion —it was all caused by the commercials. I mean you saw all those things you'd never been able to get—go out and get 'em. Men's clothing, furniture, appliances, color TV. All that crummy TV glamour just hanging out there." Many whites were disturbed by the way the noble aspirations of Dr. King were demeaned by the sacking of liquor stores. However, Paul Jacobs observed:

Looting in the cities can be just as much an act of politics as it is a desire for goods. It is a way in which the poor can make a representation to the society, for they have no other kind of representation; it is a way in which the black poor can express their hate of the white world for not giving them their chance to share in the goodies.

Hatred of whites became a cardinal principle of SNCC, which had been founded as a vehicle for interracial amity. When Stokely Carmichael, a twenty-five-year-old West Indian–born graduate of the Bronx High School of Science and Howard University, became chairman of SNCC in May 1966, he set about to establish black control of the organization. He insisted that blacks develop their own indigenous leadership, likened the role of whites in the movement to that of colonial administrators, and suggested that if white liberals wanted to be helpful they should work not in black communities but to eliminate racism in white communities. "If we are to proceed toward true liberation, we must cut ourselves off from white people," said a SNCC document that Carmichael played a prominent part in drafting. "We must form our own institutions, credit unions, co-ops, political parties, write our own histories." Still, in the summer of 1966 SNCC's attitude was not extreme. It credited white volunteers with gaining for Mississippi Negroes the right to vote and to demonstrate and stated, "The reason that whites must be excluded is not that one is anti-white, but because the efforts that one is trying to achieve cannot succeed because whites have an intimidating effect." However, with his lieutenant, H. Rap Brown, Carmichael was soon advancing slogans like "Off the Pigs" and "Kill the Honkies." After Brown, who took over from Carmichael in 1967, urged a black audience in Cambridge, Maryland, to "get your guns" and "burn this town down," fire consumed a large section of the community, and a similar incendiary harangue in Dayton preceded arson in that Ohio city. In 1967 too the Chicago office of SNCC asserted, "We must fill ourselves with hate for all white things." "Black traitors" were to be ostracized and, if necessary, exterminated. The Chicago faction emphasized, "We have to hate and disrupt and destroy and blackmail and lie and steal and become blood-brothers like the Mau-Mau." So far did SNCC depart from its original character that it lobbied against civil rights legislation and dropped the word "nonviolent" from its name.

By the beginning of 1967, the civil rights movement, at its greatest vantage only seventeen months before, lay on its deathbed. In January, President Johnson gave just forty-five words to civil rights in his State of the Union message, and *Harper's* published an article by C. Vann Woodward pronouncing the demise of the cause and finding "disturbing parallels" to the end of Reconstruction. The following month *The New York Times* reported:

The civil rights movement has collapsed in broad areas of the South, and is fighting what seems to be a last-ditch battle for survival in its few remaining spheres of influence. . . . Civil rights headquarters have been abandoned in many communities, and street demonstrations are now only a memory in all except a handful of Southern communities.

Soon members of the black Revolutionary Action Movement would be plotting the murder of Roy Wilkins, leader of the NAACP, and Whitney Young, executive director of the National Urban League. Carmichael enrolled in the paramilitary Black Panther Party, founded in Oakland in 1966, only to be subsequently expelled and denounced as a CIA agent by the party's Minister of Defense Huey P. Newton. Inflamed and badly schismatized by black power tactics, black militants had turned to devouring one another.

However, if in its extreme forms "black power" served to frighten whites and disjoin Negroes, the cultural emphases of black nationalism yielded a richer harvest. The demand for recognition of black culture was sometimes carried to regrettable lengths such as jerry-built curricula and exclusionist dormitories, but it also called attention to shamefully neglected areas of history. As late as 1963 the Fuller Products Company had grossed better than $10 million in the sales of bleaches and hair-straighteners to make Negroes over in the image of whites. Young blacks of the late 1960's, sporting Afros and sometimes dashikis, made clear they did not want to be alchemized into plasticized whites. The rejection of King's teachings had pernicious results, but it was evident in retrospect that white liberals had often been paternalistic and that the efforts of Negroes to suppress rage in the cause of nonviolence had been psychologically disabling. James Brown's song hit spoke for a whole generation, "Say It Loud—I'm Black and I'm Proud."

The current of cultural nationalism also coursed through other communities. Puerto Ricans demanded the incorporation of the history of the island in high school and college syllabi, and the paramilitary Young Lords seemed a duplicate of the Black Panthers. Indians advanced similar claims for attention to their heritage as well as to their economic needs, especially the problem of alienated lands. They wrote books with titles like *Custer Died for Your Sins,* succeeded in banishing offensive symbols such as Dartmouth's "Indian" football mascot, and startled the country by maneuvers such as seizing Alcatraz island, which they proposed to develop as a cultural center. (They offered to buy it from the national government for $24—"in glass beads and red cloth.") "Even the name Indian is not ours," protested a Sioux who was a candidate for the Ph.D. at Berkeley. "It was given to us by some dumb honky who got lost and thought he'd landed in India." In November 1970, two hundred Indians came to Plymouth Rock to proclaim Thanksgiving a day of national mourning. "That damned rock," said a young Mohawk. "I'd like to blow it up. It was the start of everything bad that has happened to the American Indian." But it was Mexican-Americans who, save for the Negroes, mounted the most broad-gauged campaign for recognition.

Although the word was a generation old, "Chicano" first exploded on the national consciousness as a result of strikes of migrant *obreros* in the lettuce fields and vineyards of California organized by Cesar Chavez after the founding of the National Farm Workers Association in 1963. Young militants used the term to signify that Mexican-Americans (or even all Spanish-Americans) were not a hyphenated people defined by their relationship to the Anglo world but constituted a unified nation with its own traditions and cultural identity. While separatists proclaimed the need to build a discrete society for *La Raza,* Chavez chose to work within the system with allies like Robert Kennedy and the national AFL-CIO and to appeal to a liberal public. He made clever use of the political potentialities of a consumption society by encouraging a national boycott that left grapes the forbidden fruit of college dining rooms and, after protracted struggles, he won out over the corporation farmers. The consumer culture figured in a different way in Chicano strategy when protests were mounted against the debased image of the Spanish-American projected by Frito Bandito purloining corn "cheeps" on TV commercials and, in the movie type associated with Leo Carrillo, obligingly holding John Wayne's reins as he doffs his sombrero. The cultural separatist wing of *La Causa* appealed for bilingual education in the public schools, Chicano courses and degree programs in southwestern universities, the use of *Pocho* dialect, community control in cities (where most Hispanic Americans were concentrated), and acceptance of a distinctive value system. As Ysidro Ramon Macias explained, "Rejecting the Puritan ethic of self-improvement above all else, the Chicano . . . recognizes that he is part of a brotherhood, that he has an obligation to work for the betterment of his people in whatever way he can."

While the exponents of brown power, red power, and black power captured the headlines, they met resistance among their own people. Older Mexican-Americans rejected the term "Chicano," while San Antonio's Congressman, Henry B. Gonzales, denounced "hate sheets" that threatened gringos with death and added: "I cannot accept the belief that racism in reverse is the answer for racism and discrimination; I cannot accept the belief that simple, blind, and stupid hatred is an adequate response to simple, blind, and stupid hatred." The overwhelming preponderance of black Americans honored not Eldridge Cleaver but Martin Luther King, and polls showed that integration remained the goal of most of them. There was a growing tide of black nationalism even within groups like the

The embattled Indian. The former site of the federal penitentiary on Alcatraz Island in San Francisco Bay is seized for "Indian land." In an ironic commentary on the consumer culture, the Indian stands by an "Apache" Chevrolet.

Paul Fusco, Magnum

The Chicano leader Cesar Chavez appears center forward at this rally of the National Farm Workers Association (NFWA). "Huelga," the Spanish word for strike, is a clue to the Spanish-speaking origins of the NFWA which united migrant field hands from Mexico. Robert Kennedy called Chavez "one of the heroic figures of our time."

SCLC. But prominent leaders, including Wilkins, Young, and A. Philip Randolph, reaffirmed their commitment to integration and announced, "We repudiate any strategies of violence, reprisal or vigilantism, and we condemn both rioting and the demagoguery that feeds it." Wilkins castigated black power as a "reverse Mississippi," "the father of hatred and the mother of violence," and Negro strategists pointed out that blacks had been the main victims of riots and that, as a minority group, they needed white allies. Bayard Rustin scolded the militants as conservatives masquerading as revolutionaries and as defeatists too indolent to tackle the difficult job of uniting with white workingmen. Above all, Martin Luther King, who said that "black supremacy would be equally as evil as white supremacy," continued to serve as a bridge between the races and the best hope for achieving an integrated society.

On April 4, 1968, in Memphis, that hope was tragically extinguished. Dr. King had come to the Tennessee city to lend support to a strike of predominantly black garbage workers. Criticized for staying at an expensive Holiday Inn, he checked into the cinderblock Lorraine Motel; at dusk on a balcony of that motel he fell mortally wounded, the victim of a shot fired by a disreputable drifter and ex-convict, James Earl Ray, another homicidal American loner. Within minutes after the news was flashed over transistor radios, angry blacks were on the streets. Rioters burned out twenty blocks of West Madison Street in Chicago, where Mayor Richard J. Daley ordered police, should another outbreak occur, to "shoot to kill" arsonists, "shoot to maim" looters. In Cincinnati a gang of young Negroes grabbed a white graduate student from his car and stabbed him to death; in Jacksonville white teen-agers wantonly shot a black cyclist. The worst pillaging took place in Washington, D.C., where more than seven hundred fires created an incendiary spectacle not seen since the British ignited the capital in 1814.

In the smoking ruins of the gutted cities little remained of the sanguine expectations of liberalism. At his desk in the White House, President Johnson could hear the sounds of racial turmoil that reached within two blocks of the executive mansion. He had come to office dedicated to building a national consensus, but from the steps of the Capitol a machinegun emplacement eyed the approaches to Congress. His allies in the civil rights movement, Negro and white, were appalled by the bloodshed and sickened by the looting. "Martin's memory is being desecrated," said Roy Wilkins. King's death was all but unbearable. On an Indianapolis street corner, where he broke the news to a crowd of Negroes, Robert Kennedy told the grief-stricken gathering that he understood how they felt, for he too had lost a brother at the hands of a white assassin, and, as the weeping subsided, he quoted Aeschylus: "Even in our sleep, pain which cannot forget falls drop by drop upon the heart until in despair, against our own will, comes wisdom through the awful grace of God."

The Violent Society

One month before the assassination of Dr. King and the ensuing commotion, the National Advisory Commission on Civil Disorders issued a 250,000-word report that became a critical document in the national self-examination into the causes of race riots and the pre-

Burk Uzzle, Magnum

After the assassination of Martin Luther King, Coretta King, her right hand clasped to her
fatherless son's, leads a march in Memphis where the Negro leader was slain.
In the light coat is King's successor as head of the Southern Christian
Leadership Conference, Rev. Ralph Abernathy, and next to him,
Rev. Andrew Young, who would subsequently be appointed ambassador to the
United Nations. Behind King's widow stands Rev. Jesse Jackson, who later promoted
the interests of urban blacks through PUSH (People United to Save Humanity.)

valence of violence. The report gave no comfort to those who placed
the chief onus for the disturbances on black conspirators. "What
white Americans have never fully understood—but what the Negro
can never forget—is that white society is deeply implicated in the
ghetto," the commission stated. "White institutions created it, white
institutions maintain it, and white society condones it."

The commission, which recommended vigorous measures to heal
the festering sores of the slums, expressed alarm that the predominant
reaction of the white community had been to acquire more armament.
"In several cities," the commission found, "the principal official
response has been to train and equip the police with more sophisticated weapons." In Newark and other communities, white vigilante

bands sprang up, and the deputy editor of *The Economist,* having been told by Washingtonians that they had acquired rifles, was reminded of a passage in Gibbon about another capital: "At such a time . . . when none could trust their lives or properties to the impotence of the law, the powerful citizens were armed for safety, or offence, against the domestic enemies whom they feared or hated." Unless the spiral of neglect, outbreak, and retaliation was broken, the commission warned, it "could quite conceivably lead to a kind of urban apartheid with semi-martial law in many cities." Liberals hoped that a different lesson would be learned from the explosions. Federal Communications Commissioner Nicholas Johnson said, "A riot is somebody talking. A riot is a man crying out, 'Listen to me, mister. There's something I've been trying to tell you and you're not listening.' "

Congress acknowledged the crisis in the ghettos ambiguously. It struck out punitively, imposing stringent penalties for crossing state lines with the intent of inciting disorders, action (according to its sponsor) aimed at firebrands such as Stokely Carmichael, a "freelance insurrectionist." However, Congress attached this provision to a statute that marked another significant leap forward. The "open housing" law of 1968 banned discrimination in the sale of some 80 percent of United States housing. Furthermore, Congress approved an ambitious housing and urban development bill to expedite slum clearance and riot insurance.

Although the new legislation suggested an enduring commitment to civil rights, liberals no longer basked in the euphoria of the March on Washington era. Civil rights romantics had learned with innocent surprise that not only whites harbored prejudices or were guilty of cupidity, and they were unsure of how to cope with demands not for equity but for revenge. Confidence faltered when it became evident that the community action programs were fraught with difficulty and that meliorism would not suffice to overcome decades of neglect in the slums.

In 1965 the Johnson government circulated a memorandum, known after its author as "the Moynihan report," which angered blacks and depressed whites. In *Beyond the Melting Pot,* Daniel P. Moynihan and Nathan Glazer had argued that white racism was not the total explanation of the Negro's plight and that civil rights legislation could not expect to solve one critical problem — the pathology of black family structure and communal life. Moynihan's government study, *The Negro Family,* expounded further on how the "deterioration of the fabric of Negro society" resulted from the "deterioration of the Negro family." Although the matriarchal family structure of lower-class blacks had earlier been dissected in the classic monograph by the Negro sociologist E. Franklin Frazier and although Moynihan was sympathetic to civil rights goals, his appraisal vexed black leaders because it was understood to imply that until Negroes corrected their faults they could not claim equal treatment. White liberals were no less dismayed, for the report indicated that, in the very year of the Watts riots, "the Negro problem" was more intractable than they had thought.

Moynihan and other analysts traced the infirmity of the family structure of lower-class Negroes both to desertion by fathers and to illegitimacy, but the latter attracted the greater attention. In 1961, according to a federal government estimate, 22 percent of black infants were born out of wedlock (some 1.8 million), compared to 2.5 percent of white infants, and in 1970 the illegitimacy rate for young black girls was said to be running almost ten times that among whites, figures some blacks disputed. In "Love Child," the number 1 record of late 1968, Diana Ross and the Supremes sang of the shame of being raised with the stigma of illegitimacy and of having been abandoned by one's father. As a result, President Johnson pointed out in a speech at Howard University, "Only a minority — less than half — of all Negro children reach the age of 18 having lived all their lives with both of their parents." Blacks responded hotly that since middle-class Negro families proved as stable as white families, the predicament lay not with the shortcomings of blacks but in the failure of a white-dominated society to provide the economic opportunities that would permit Negro fathers to build secure households. Many whites, however, found it disconcerting that despite the rise in black family income since 1950, the proportion of nonwhite families headed by women had risen from 18 percent in that year to 29 percent in 1971.

If some were disheartened by the obduracy of the black ghetto, others saw in the riots and in the assassinations mortifying confirmation of their conviction that the United States was a peculiarly violent society. After the assassination of King, Senator Frank Church cried, "We are steeped in violence. It is the curse of the land." A numbing series of murders had taken the lives of so many leaders that it seemed, as Bruce Jay Friedman wrote, that "a new, Jack Rubyesque chord of absurdity has been struck in the land." "God, we even got to the point where we compared the style of the funerals," observed

David Halberstam. "We could make a calendar of the decade by marking where we were at the hours of those violent deaths." The casualty lists numbered too all those nameless unfortunates who were killed or mugged or raped. From 1960 to 1968 "offenses against persons" more than doubled, and in the large cities apartment dwellers immured themselves in buildings scrutinized by closed-circuit television and guarded by doormen and platoons of vigilantes. Yet neither violent crime nor the wave of assassinations could persuade Congress, cowed by the National Rifle Association, to enact an effective gun control law, although the gun-homicide rate in the United States was forty times that of the British Isles, the Netherlands, and Japan.

The consumer economy and popular culture thrived on the merchandising of violence. Mod audiences made a box office smash of Arthur Penn's movie *Bonnie and Clyde*, which transmogrified brutal killers into unconscious folk revolutionaries and tarried lovingly over the riddling of Bonnie's body by machine-gun bullets. The appeal of Jimi Hendrix owed much to acid rock's pulverizing volume and pitiless rhythm; Janis Joplin was described as a "volatile vial of nitroglycerine"; Bob Dylan, noted one critic, "tends to snarl his songs rather than sing them." Children were schooled in violence from their first shoot-out with toy guns to comic book gougings and mayhem. In 1966 New York's leading toy emporium announced, "On Valentine's Day nothing says 'I Love You' more heartily than a Valentine from F. A. O. Schwarz Children's World," the lead-in for a child's Valentine that unfolded to reveal a "swept-wing jet fighter . . . machine guns blazing." In the six weeks following one assassination, a survey discovered that at the times when most children were watching, TV showed 372 threats or acts of violence including 84 killings in eighty-five and a half hours. "Television," observed Alfred Hitchcock, "has brought back murder into the home where it belongs." TV cameras made a household event of the death of their favorite son, John F. Kennedy, who had won the presidency as a result of televised debates; born on the tube, he would die on the tube. And his slayer, who had but a moment's exposure to a national video audience, in turn met death in the camera's eye. Moreover, the technique of the "instant replay," indispensable for conveying "the violent world of Sam Huff," was first employed in televising a football game in December 1963, after being proved useful a few weeks earlier in filming the murder of Lee Oswald by Jack Ruby.

To be sure, the United States in the 1960's held no monopoly on

Characteristics of Major Types of Civil Strife in the United States, June 1963–May 1968[a]

Type of event	Number of events identified	Estimated number of participants	Reported number of casualties	Reported arrests
Civil rights demonstrations	369	1,117,600	389	15,379
Antiwar demonstrations	104	680,000	400	3,258
Student protests on campus issues	91	102,035	122	1,914
Anti–school integration demonstrations	24	34,720	0	164
Segregationist clashes and counter-demonstrations	54	31,200	163	643
Negro riots and disturbances	239	(200,000)	8,133	49,607
White terrorism against Negroes and rights workers	213	(2,000)	112	97

Source: Hugh Davis Graham and Ted Robert Gurr, *Violence in America: Historical and Comparative Perspectives,* a report submitted to the National Commission on the Causes and Prevention of Violence (New York: Bantam Books, 1969), p. 576.

[a] The data in the table include many estimates, all imprecise. Figures in parentheses are especially tentative.

violence, and some of the national lamentation about it reflected little more than the affinity of intellectuals for self-flagellation. As Richard Hofstadter observed, "The United States, even with its considerable record of violence, appears not as some mutant monster among the peoples of the world but rather as a full-fledged and somewhat boisterous member of the fellowship of human frailty." The death rate from civil strife in the United States ran well below the figures for the rest of the world, and violence in America did not begin to approximate that of Stalinist Russia or the more recent fratricide in Indonesia or Nigeria or Colombia. Furthermore, despite manifestations of violence, the United States enjoyed remarkable political stability. Nor was violence a new phenomenon in this country. Civil strife was actually greater in late-nineteenth-century America than in the 1960's, and, as Richard Maxwell Brown pointed out, "Violence has formed a seamless web with the most positive episodes in American history."

Nonetheless, contemporary America offered grounds enough for concern. A task force report by Hugh Davis Graham and Ted Robert Gurr for the National Commission on the Causes and Prevention of Violence concluded that, compared with other nations, "acts of collective violence by private citizens in the United States in the last 20 years have been extraordinarily numerous" and "in numbers of political assassinations, riots, politically relevant armed group attacks, and demonstrations, the United States since 1948 has been among the half-dozen most tumultuous nations in the world." While in the past violence in America had been inflicted by the powerful, in the 1960's it assumed a much more volatile mode in action by dissidents against persons or symbols of authority. And most ominous of all, month by month the violence of the Vietnam War was imperiling public safety by leading more and more Americans to question the very legitimacy of the national government.

By 1968 the conflict in Southeast Asia had become the longest war in the country's history, one of the bloodiest, and certainly the least popular. To be sure, most Americans, however much they disliked the slaughter, could not bring themselves to accept defeat. In the fall of 1965, two out of every three students supported the administration's war policy, and even in 1968, contrary to the impression given by the press, those under thirty were more hawkish than those over fifty. But to a significant minority, especially on campuses, United States intervention with all its consequences — the death and maiming of young Americans, the napalm-scarred bodies of Vietnamese children, the pulverization of villages, and the defoliation of the countryside — seemed a gross betrayal of humane, democratic values. The Vietnamese carnage, said Senator Fulbright, was "poisoning and brutalizing our domestic life. . . . The 'Great Society' has become the sick society."

To a rapidly radicalized segment of students, the hostilities demonstrated that American liberalism led inevitably to war and repression. It had been liberal Presidents who had lofted the bomb-laden planes and liberal advisers like the Rhodes Scholar Dean Rusk and ex-Harvard and MIT teachers such as McGeorge Bundy, Robert McNamara, and Walt Rostow who had egged them on. More than this, the very rationale for the commitment in Southeast Asia derived from the Wilson-FDR tradition of globalism. In truth, well before 1968 most liberals stoutly opposed the war. But radicals jeered that when orthodox methods had clearly failed (who, they asked, could any longer believe in the democratic process after Johnson's election as a peace candidate in 1964 and his subsequent betrayal?) liberals flinched from joining them in bolder acts.

Although most of the young continued to work within the system, ever-growing numbers, soured on liberalism and incensed by the war, felt alienated from the government and indeed from American society. The conflict, radicals charged, exposed the real priorities of Kennedy-Johnson progressivism, for social welfare programs were slashed in order to fund armaments. When General Hershey authorized draft boards to punish dissidents, when President Johnson dismissed thoughtful critics as "nervous Nellies," when disc jockeys seemed never to tire of spinning records in tribute to the Green Berets, it appeared to the radicals that "Amerika" had become a repressive, war-mad nation, even, in the words of James Baldwin, "the fourth Reich." A few young Americans chose prison to war, many more renounced their native land for Canada or, like Yossarian on his rubber raft in *Catch-22*, Sweden.

By word and by deed, numerous foes of the bloodletting in Vietnam and of the social order embraced violence. In an unconscious parody of the Wilsonian rhetoric of a war to end all wars, the Progressive Labor faction of Students for a Democratic Society (SDS) claimed that "to get rid of the gun it is necessary to take up the gun." H. Rap Brown, who called violence "as American as cherry pie," suggested shooting the President and his wife. Underground newspapers printed instructions on how to make Molotov cocktails, hailed motorcycle gangs such as Hell's Angels because they terrorized the Establishment, and apotheosized assassins at home and abroad. Eldridge Cleaver, who felt remorse for his deeds, wrote, "I became a rapist. . . . It seemed to me that the act of rape was an insurrectionary act. It delighted me that I was defying and trampling upon the white man's law, upon his system of values, and that I was defiling his women." In a destructive acting-out of the animus toward men in the women's liberation movement, one flower child organized SCUM (the Society for Cutting Up Men) and took the first step toward creating "a swinging groovy, out-of-sight female world" by shooting Andy Warhol, an improbable symbol of male supremacy.

Abusive discourse contravened the most elementary canons of fair play and civility, and slogans became truncheons. When war opponents created such a din that defenders of the administration's Asia policy could not be heard at a Harvard meeting, one professor exculpated them by claiming the right to shout down speakers as a fundamental civil liberty, and at the March on the Pentagon in 1967, a sign read, "Where is Oswald now that we need him?" Paul Goodman, one of the gurus of the young, regretted that instead of "*Satyagraha,* soul force, we have seen plenty of hate" in which "the confronted are *not* taken as human beings, but as pigs." Staughton Lynd, a dedicated agitator against the war, declared, "I am ashamed of a movement which calls policemen pigs. . . . I feel deeply troubled by the attitude that, since we are right, we can take away civil liberties from others which we insist on for ourselves." "Don't Trust Anyone Over Thirty" was lauded as preternatural wisdom, but Saul Bellow remarked pointedly, "In the way the young declare the obsolescence of the old, there's a kind of totalitarian cruelty, like Hitler's attitude toward Jews, or Stalin's toward kulaks."

The disposition of the young to resort to force took vivid form in April 1968, the tumultuous month of the riots following the murder of Dr. King, when militants at Columbia University seized five buildings, held three officials captive for twenty-six hours, took over the president's office, which they befouled, and, after a six-day occupation had been ended by club-swinging police, compelled the university to shut down. During that spring and over the next two years, Columbia was beset by a series of outrages including the deliberate destruction of one professor's notes on years of historical research, the burning of library books, the disruption of lectures, and the roughing-up of faculty and staff. The paroxysm in Manhattan had a forerunner in the Free Speech Movement led by Mario Savio at Berkeley in 1964, but while the melees in California were followed by a period of relatively small-scale outbreaks, the Columbia eruptions proved to be harbingers of explosions that would rock hundreds of other campuses. On some, black rebels were the main agents, notably at Cornell, where blacks brandishing guns wrung concessions from an administration that for months had seemed to be motivated by a death wish. At Cornell and at Yale, prominent faculty found it necessary to evacuate their families. Violence did not always stop with the terrorizing of students and teachers or the vandalizing of libraries. Bombs killed a faculty club custodian at the University of California, Santa Barbara, blinded a secretary at Pomona, and snuffed out a student's life at the University of Wisconsin.

Constantine Manos, Magnum

As the placards at this demonstration in Harvard Yard indicate, two of the big demands at Harvard and on other campuses were a termination of Reserve Officers' Training Corps (ROTC) programs and a halt to the expansion of the university into the neighborhood.

The uprisings had contradictory results. They led to the creation of new institutions of academic governance with greater student representation, the abatement of parietal rules and *in loco parentis*, more intensive recruitment from minority groups, a diminution of the military presence on campus, and keener social responsibility on the part of administrators and trustees. But they also left a patrimony of bitterness and dangerously speeded up the politicization of the academic world. Furthermore, they had the ironic consequence of strengthening the political power of the right, which was able to exploit the disgust that many Americans felt with faculty and administrators wanting in minimal self-respect and students who cried out against repression but practiced intimidation. The combination of Berkeley and Watts cemented Governor Ronald Reagan's tenure in California, and the Columbia and Cornell fracases helped raise the Conservatives, under James Buckley, to prominence in New York.

Analysts attributed much of the campus unrest to the climate of affluence. Years before the first disturbances, David Potter had written: "Today the economy of abundance can afford to maintain a substantial proportion of the population in nonproductive status, and it assigns this role, sometimes against their will, to its younger and its elder members. It protracts the years of schooling, and it defers responsibilities for an unusually long span." Bruno Bettelheim found it "unnatural to keep a young person in dependence for some 20 years attending school" and traced the spirit of rebelliousness to "the waiting for things—for the real life to come." Affluence made possible not only a huge increase in the numbers of those consigned to the period of waiting but also the rise of the multiversity. Only two institutions had more than twenty thousand students in 1941; thirty-nine did in 1969. Although this expansion was the envy of other countries, it made the university more impersonal and bureaucratic and added to the undergraduate ranks many who had small interest in intellectual pursuits. Even the radicals recognized that they were a different breed. The Port Huron statement of the SDS, mostly written by Tom Hayden, began: "We are the people of this generation, bred in at least modest comfort, housed now in universities, looking uncomfortably to the world we inherit."

Still, if the campus tumult derived from general socioeconomic circumstances, it also ensued from particular political challenges, responses, and perceptions. Much of the resentment was aroused by specific issues, notably the Vietnam War and the draft, and the university made a vulnerable target, even when its complicity in military affairs was minor. The campus served as a base, too, for sorties on behalf of black nationalism. Shrewdly, the confrontationists sensed the recruitment value of provoking counterviolence by agents of the establishment, who proved all too willing to fall into the trap. As John W. Gardner wrote, "The student with an inclination toward violent or coercive action and the policeman with a taste for brutality are waiting for each other." But it was neither the pursuit of such exemplary goals as an end to war and racism nor the tactics of confrontation that gave the campus outbreaks their special character, but rather the way in which both were mingled with new-fashioned attitudes toward institutions and mores. The aroma of pot in the corridors of occupied buildings, the up-against-the-wall obscenity, the rhetoric of generational war, the guerrilla theater, the casual sex, the anti-privacy etiquette of communal toilets, the organization of "free universities" and "counter courses," the rebellion against grades, the emphasis on participatory democracy and "doing your own thing," all suggested the way in which the "counter culture" had permeated student activism, and this inter-relationship between violence-prone radicalism and the icon-breaking counter culture (and the indignant opposition it incited) imbued the late 1960's with their distinctive spirit.

The Greening of America

In the mid-1960's, during the same years that violence was rocking the country, there erupted that remarkable concatenation of phenomena that social analysts have denominated the "counter culture." Upper middle class white youth, and some of their elders, advanced ideas and behaved in ways that ran "counter" to much that was cherished not only by Eisenhower's America but by Kennedy-Johnson liberalism—affluence, economic growth, technology, and the institutions and value systems associated with the Protestant ethic of self-denial and sexual repression and the more modern premises of the consumer culture and the meritocracy. The situation, wrote Paul Goodman, was "very like 1510, when Luther went to Rome, the eve of the Reformation. There is everywhere protest, revaluation, attack on the Establishment."

Although the counter culture of the 1960's bore resemblances to earlier enthusiasms on the Continent like the Bohemianism of the Left Bank and the Burschenschaften of nineteenth-century Germany, no precursor in the United States ever permeated so broadly or so intensively. To be sure, the counter culture was foreshadowed by the "revolution in morals" and the critique of Puritanism and materialism in America of the 1920's and, more recently, by the beats in the 1950's. But to produce a movement of this particular nature demanded the special circumstances of the 'sixties—the emergence of a generation of young people endowed with a superabundance of worldly goods, locked into an educational system for two decades or more, cordoned off in multiversities, roiled by the draft and the Vietnam War, troubled by its prospects in a world that seemed increasingly bureaucratized and technologically driven.

The counter culture raised a challenge not just to entrenched institutions but to the whole way of thinking that had prevailed in the West since the eighteenth century. "Nothing less is required than the subversion of the scientific world view with its entrenched commitment to an egocentric and cerebral mode of consciousness," wrote Theodore Roszak. "In its place, there must be a new culture in which the non-intellective capacities of personality—those capacities that take fire from visionary splendor and the experiences of human communion—become the arbiters of the true, the good and the beautiful."

The counter culture rejected systematized knowledge, Aristotelian logic, and, at times, even reason itself. The few who bothered to consider the claims of traditional processes of cognition intimated that rules of evidence were snares devised by the power structure to trap the unwary, or advanced the curious notion of "radical truth," or touted the superior insights gained from intuition. "The sensibility epitomized by the Enlightenment," concluded the historian J. Meredith Neil in 1971, "has now become so embattled that it is very possible that its requiem has already been sung."

In spurning Western emphases on rationality, some explored the ancient mysteries of Asian or African creeds or found solace in the occult. Skinheaded, orange-garmented young people debouched on downtown streets chanting the Hare Krishna. Students pored over Tarot cards or perused the I Ching or shared Roszak's appreciation of shamanism, and in the Age of Aquarius, astrology won legions of devotees. Others became preoccupied with witchcraft and demonology, and even soap operas like "Dark Shadows" and movies such as *Rosemary's Baby* gave the devil his due. Women's lib publicists viewed the Salem witches as kindred political deviationists, and in Chicago coeds claimed to have put a curse on professors. In New York the Civil Liberties Union came to the aid of an organization that had been denied a permit to hold a witch-in in Central Park on Halloween, and when the city relented, the coven hailed the reversal as "the first Civil Rights victory for true witches ever won in modern times."

Frequently the interest in mysticism and the quest for communion found expression not in new cults but within the Christian church. The young, who had once scorned theological questions, ruminated about the death of God and the theology of hope and sought artless communication through "speaking in tongues." At church services Bach yielded to rock, when, to the accompaniment of electric guitars, mod liturgies made "a joyful noise unto the Lord." As William L. O'Neill observed:

Hare Krishna. On a street in San Francisco, a young Buddhist chants while bemused spectators look on. Buddhist teachings affected a small number of writers like Allen Ginsberg in the 1950's, but they did not make a mark on the public consciousness until the 1960's, when young converts, their heads shaven, appeared on city sidewalks.

American religious life was probably more fertile and diverse in the sixties than at any time since the nineteenth century. If all this did not quite amount to an age of faith, it certainly seemed so compared with the 1950's which now looked like merely an age of churchgoing. The old religious revival declined; religion itself did not. The established churches became more secular, unchurched youths more religious. Anti-communism excepted, the 1950's was a time when rational, scientific, and secular ideas dominated. In the sixties romantic, millennial, chiliastic, and utopian impulses undermined them.

Some of the same impulses, as well as the desire to escape the rigidities of a work-oriented society and to expand sense perception, led millions of Americans to experiment with drugs. "Tune in, turn on, drop out," urged the advance man of the drug culture, Timothy Leary, whom one writer called "the Johnny Appleseed of LSD." Frequently, drugs were associated with performing or listening to rock music, especially after San Francisco's light and sound shows gave birth to the "acid rock" of groups such as Big Brother and the Holding Company billeted in strobe-lit bivouacs like Bill Graham's Fillmore West. It required little special knowledge to understand that "Magic Carpet Ride" referred to a drug trip or that the Beatles' "Lucy in the Sky with Diamonds" spelled out LSD. Drugs penetrated deeply, too, into the literary world. Ken Kesey's *One Flew Over the Cuckoo's Nest* was partly written under the influence of LSD, and the undergraduate cult of Hermann Hesse got official sanction when Dr. Leary recommended: "Before your LSD session, read *Siddhartha* and *Steppenwolf*. The last part of *Steppenwolf* is a priceless manual." While psychedelic potions like LSD spread slowly, marijuana became increasingly commonplace at high school and college parties, and the question of whether it was harmful produced one of the less rewarding debates of modern times, in large part because it was not really about pharmacological properties but about clashing life styles. Drug use, said the Yippie leader, Jerry Rubin, "signifies the total end of the Protestant ethic: screw work, we want to know ourselves. But of course the goal is to free oneself from American society's sick notion of work, success, reward, and status and to find and establish oneself through one's own discipline, hard work, and introspection."

"Leaving the straight life behind," many people sought alternative ways of living. "Crash pads" accommodated nomads in the big cities, while communes in the New England hills or the deserts of the Southwest attempted to create enclaves hived off from the bustle of bourgeois striving. In the mid-1960's, thousands of "hippies" set up house in the Haight-Ashbury district of San Francisco or in New York's East Village. The hippie communes were but one of a number of free-form institutions aimed at breaking the barriers that isolated people from one another, themes of Paul Simon's "The Sound of Silence" and "The Dangling Conversation." To learn how to communicate and to become reacquainted with themselves, people joined encounter and sensitivity groups and spent weekends at Esalen. Rock concerts offered another way of achieving communion, for, as Benjamin DeMott wrote, "the rock experience at its most intense is an intimation of engulfment and merger, a route to a flowing, ego-transcending oneness."

The hegira of the young to Hashbury heightened concern about a widening "generation gap." The older generation was bewildered by the ragamuffin army of disheveled, unkempt "potheads" who dropped out of school and drifted from pad to pad with no visible ambition or direction, cadging handouts in Harvard Square or at Sather Gate, and the discontented young felt alienated from the conformity of their "uptight" parents. By the middle of the decade, more than half of the nation was under the critical age of thirty, and many had a keen sense of belonging to their own subculture. "From Los Angeles on down the California coast, this is an era of age segregation," wrote Tom Wolfe in "The Pump House Gang." "Surfers, not to mention rock and roll kids and the hot rodders . . . don't merely hang around together. They establish whole little societies for themselves." Apartment houses like the Sheri Plaza in Hollywood were restricted to tenants between twenty and thirty. Sometimes the generation gap took curious forms. In Duluth, the Zimmermans, a Jewish merchant family, encouraged their son's musical talent, purchased a piano on which he began to pick out songs, and supported him in college. But hardly had Robert arrived at the University of Minnesota than he insisted that he had no parents, was partly Indian, had lived a bleak childhood bouncing between foster homes and orphanages—and that his name was Bob Dylan.

Probably no dispute between the generations provoked more angry words than one that might have been thought to be trivial—hair. It gave a name to a raucous, impertinent "tribal love-rock musical," and law journals soberly discussed "Long Hair and Judicial Clippers: Can Welfare Officials Constitutionally Require Applicants to Trim Their Locks to Enhance Their Employability?" Fathers who could not be certain whether a passing pedestrian was a boy or a girl were profoundly shaken, and their demeanor was not improved by awareness that there was an irrational element in this response. For the young, long hair expressed withdrawal from the crewcut, repressed world of their parents, at least at the outset before it became a vogue. Some of the young took a covert pleasure in the discomfort they were causing; "We are the people our parents warned us against," read a sentence on a subway billboard.

The "now generation" judged little in man's history usable or even worthy of notice. The "now culture" pronounced the past irrelevant, observed Hazel W. Hertzberg in *Social Education,* because it appeared to be altogether different. "We seem to be producing a new generation every three or four years characterized by a sense of estrangement from the generations above and below it," she noted, and "in the now culture's intense focus on youth there is little conception of a life cycle which includes the very young or the 'mature' or 'old.'" Inevitably, many of the young turned away from the study of history to such ostensibly "time-free" disciplines as sociology. Artists often had a similar temporal perception. When an experimental music group referred to a "historical piece," it meant a 1965 opus. John Barth's *The Sot-Weed Factor* burlesqued the historical method, and Norman Mailer wrote, "We're in a time that's divorced from the past. There's utterly no tradition anymore."

The counter culture fostered a rebellion against almost every accepted personage and institution, some of them of ancient lineage. Neither army officers nor college administrators nor party officials nor cardinals could any longer count on the traditional patterns of deference. In Vietnam some soldiers refused assignments, and at stateside training camps underground newspapers and cabarets flourished. Even the professional competence of the military came into question. To accept the advice of the Pentagon in Southeast Asia, said Senator George McGovern, would be like asking "General Custer how to fight Indians." On college campuses the "disestablishmentarians" set up free universities that gave podiums to "existentialists without portfolio." So volatile did party identification become that in 1968 most of the electorate split tickets. Protestant churchmen wrestled with such disturbing works as Thomas J. J. Altizer's *The Gospel of Christian Atheism,* while the Catholic hierarchy confronted priests who revolted against celibacy and nuns who wore short skirts.

Some Americans departed so far from traditional beliefs that they advocated a heresy, which, far more than free love or Bolshevism, ran counter to the national creed—no growth. To stabilize population, young people wore buttons saying "Stop at 2" and suggested that the Mother of the Year was one who kept her IUD in place and adopted a child. An expanding gross national product "may, after a certain level, serve more as a sign of social deterioration than improvement," Professor Richard A. Falk of Princeton told a congressional committee. "If the United States were to double its GNP, I would think it would be a much less livable society than it is today."

Only a "no-growth economy," it was reasoned, could save man from making the earth uninhabitable by polluting his environment. John Gardner gave warning that Americans would get "richer and richer in filthier communities until we reach a final state of affluent misery—Croesus on a garbage heap." To achieve a high GNP, industry gouged the earth for raw materials, spewed its wastes into the air, and defiled rivers with its excrement. The achievements of the consumer culture seemed mixed boons. Shopping centers defaced the countryside; automobiles, the pride of the land of Henry Ford, were denounced, in Lewis Mumford's words, as "insolent chariots"; and detergents, previously acclaimed as household miracles, proved to be lethal contaminators. "The good earth, once golden, has begun to run out, as any neglected field, and we are discovering, a bit late, the consequences of fouling the only nest we have," wrote E. B. White. "To grow the perfect lawn we destroy the perfect bird. To kill the ultimate gnat we load the liver of the final fish. Even our national bird fights for survival and lays eggs that don't hatch."

Critics of the doctrine of economic growth cast an especially skeptical eye at twentieth-century technology. Some deprecated the sacrifice of technological efficiency to consumer culture trumpery — gorgeously colored telephones that did not yield a dial tone, rakishly styled automobiles that turned out to be death cars. Others objected that technological gains had unanticipated and unwelcome social consequences, as when life-saving medical advances helped bring on the population crisis. But most broadly articulated of all was the complaint that technology was dehumanizing. The protagonist of Saul Bellow's *Herzog* concluded that the modern world had drastically altered

what it means to be a man. In a city. In a century. In a mass. Transformed by science. Under organized power. Subject to tremendous controls. In a condition caused by mechanization. After the late failure of radical hopes. In a society that was no community and devalued the person. Owing to the multiplied power of numbers which made the self negligible. Which spent military billions against foreign enemies but would not pay for order at home. Which permitted savagery and barbarism in its own great cities.

Creative artists, radicals, and expositors of the counter culture all remonstrated against the imperatives of technology. In John Barth's *Giles Goat-Boy,* computers warred for control of the world, and in Stanley Kubrick's film *2001: A Space Odyssey,* Hal, the menacing computer, was lobotomized, to the applause of cinema audiences. Malcontents at Berkeley alleged that students at their multiversity were shuffled like IBM cards by administrators under Clark Kerr, who was essentially a systems manager. Radicals charged, too, that systems managers in Washington were sending men to their death in Vietnam at the behest of Pentagon computers. "The time has come," Mario Savio cried, "to put our bodies on the machine and to stop it."

Tom Wicker of *The New York Times,* who wrote that "we now have to turn away from the gods of production," warned:

Already these modern Americans submit to being sealed into gigantic toothpaste tubes and hurled through the skies at incredible speeds, literally peas in a pod, and already, for reasons no one can explain, the speed is being whipped up to supersonic levels. Already creatures of shrinking dimensions drive to work on swarming eight-lane highways, where metal monsters reduce human drivers to dollsize; and someday, if electronics prosper as predicted, the highway itself will drive the cars. Everywhere man turns, from the classroom to the supermarket to Mission Control, he is being dwarfed by his own handiwork—hapless and driven in his zip-code world, among his reactors and data banks, breathing his canned or polluted air and eating his frozen foods, even his physical security dependent—he is assured —upon the reaction time and judgment of an ABM computer. How typical and pathetic it was that when the great power failure of 1965 deprived urban Americans for a night of their greatest technological prop, human nature instinctively asserted itself in the darkness, and more children were conceived in and out of wedlock than on any other single occasion of which we have records on our ubiquitous punch cards.

In the 1960's the consumer culture underwent the most relentless criticism it had ever experienced. The value system of the consumer society, detractors asserted, was anti-human, a way of "making things nobody needs so they can afford to buy things nobody needs." FCC Commissioner Nicholas Johnson, who offered the heretical counsel that "you can easily ignore most of the products in your supermarket," denounced the view "that the primary measure of an individual's worth is his consumption of products, his sexuality, his measuring up to ideals found in packages mass-produced and distributed by corporate America." *Hair* mocked the consumer who pasted King Korn trading stamps in books one by one, and hippies rebelled against the "moneytheism" of an acquisitive society.

By rejecting the bourgeois catechism, the counter culture rediscovered the pleasures of ritual and rejoiced in festivals, from the "happenings" at the end of the 1950's to "love-ins" on the grass of Golden Gate Park to the grand *fête champêtre* at Woodstock. Allen Ginsberg wrote *How to Make a March / Spectacle,* and Harvey Cox began his book *A Feast of Fools* by quoting W. H. Auden:

> I know nothing, except what everyone knows—
> if there when Grace dances, I should dance.

To theologians like Cox, the recovery of festivity had a religious connotation, for Western culture, they believed, had robbed man of the sense of wonder and the joy of playfulness. "In losing our capacity for play and in devaluing our imaginations, we have in a very important sense lost ourselves," explained Marcia Cavell:

The death of God in our world is a death of our capacity to experience the world in a godlike way: with the full release of our creative powers, valuing our experience of people and of things for their own sakes, with that sense of ease and timelessness we have when for the moment we are set free from anxiety and self-preoccupation.

In August 1969, at Max Yasgur's farm in the Catskills, the counter culture reached a joyous climax. The Woodstock Music and Art Fair convened not in Woodstock, the Hudson Valley village that was Dylan's retreat, but at Bethel, which became a magnet for from 300,000 to 400,000 young people, "moving steadily down Route 17-B, like a busy day on the Ho Chi Minh Trail." The ostensible attraction was the music: Joan Baez, Jimi Hendrix, Crosby, Stills, Nash & Young, Country Joe & the Fish. But more remarked was the ready availability of sex and drugs. Unmolested by the police, hawkers called out "acid, mesc, hash," and for three days, sprawled on blankets in a sea of mud, merged in oceanic communion, the counter culture generation blew its mind. "No one in this country in this century had ever seen a 'society' so free of repression," wrote Andrew Kopkind. "Everyone swam nude in the lake, balling was easier than getting breakfast, and the 'pigs' just smiled and passed out the oats."

Much of the country considered the promiscuity and nudity of the Woodstock Nation peculiar to hippiedom, but in truth new attitudes toward sex antedated the rise of the counter culture and were by no means confined to the young. The postwar years witnessed a veritable revolution in public acceptance of forms of sexual depiction and vocabulary that had hitherto been proscribed. In 1948 Norman Mailer had been compelled to resort to the euphemism "fuggin" in *The Naked and the Dead,* and as late as 1953 Otto Preminger's movie *The Moon Is Blue* was denied a seal of approval because it employed the word "virgin." But by 1966, the bitchy language Elizabeth Taylor spoke in the film of Edward Albee's *Who's Afraid of Virginia Woolf?* was becoming conventional, and downtown movie houses would soon be screening fetishism, autoeroticism, and fellatio. In 1969 *Time* commented that "writers bandy four-letter words as if they had just completed a deep-immersion Berlitz course in

The new Dionysians. In the spirit of the Greek god, these revelers strip down to let joy
be unconfined. Nudity, a common feature of "happenings" at urban parks
and of rock festivals in the 1960's, implied both
greater sexual freedom and, as this picture suggests,
a desire for more direct communion with nature.

Anglo-Saxon" and observed that "today, the corner drugstore sells
Fanny Hill along with Fannie Farmer."

The turning point had come in 1959, and once again the Warren
Court stood front stage center. In voiding the censorship of *Lady
Chatterley's Lover*, the Court, in the words of Mr. Justice Stewart,
maintained that the First Amendment "protects advocacy of the

opinion that adultery may sometimes be proper, no less than advocacy of socialism or the single tax." The film was based on D. H. Lawrence's novel of anal eroticism, published in its unexpurgated form by Grove Press that same year. Heartened by the Court's latitudinarianism, Grove Press in 1961 brought out Henry Miller's *Tropic of Cancer*, another under-the-counter item; it sold two and a half million copies and also won the benison of the Supreme Court. The Court did indicate there were still some constraints when in 1966 it sustained the conviction of Ralph Ginzburg, publisher of *Eros*, for promoting the circulation of his magazine in a pandering fashion; he had even applied for a mail permit from Intercourse, Pennsylvania. But the much-criticized Ginzburg decision proved to be an exception rather than a guideline.

In the 1960's almost every barrier came down. That bourgeois standby, *Cosmopolitan*, ran an article on "Low-Fidelity Wives" and printed instructions for its female readers on how to achieve an orgasm. Manufacturers turned out dolls with sexual organs, and in Jeane-Claude van Itallie's *America Hurrah* giant dolls fornicated on stage. "Billy the Kid" and "Jean Harlow" simulated an act of oral intercourse before audiences for *The Beard*, while in *Dionysus 69* a troupe invited members of the audience to disrobe and take part in a mock orgy. Some did. Bacchantic rock stars like Janis Joplin sang with a raw, sexual urgency, and at a Miami concert Jim Morrison of the Doors enticed female "groupies" by exposing himself. In 1970 the Federal Commission on Obscenity and Pornography brought the new era to a culmination by recommending wiping out all legal restrictions on the acquisition by adults of hard-core pornography.

The falling away of taboos on expression appeared to be accompanied by a radical change in sexual activity. Affluence and mobility encouraged experimentation and slackened the hold of folkways, and technology contributed the Pill, which virtually eliminated the fear of conception in premarital intercourse. Colleges made birth control devices available to single coeds; young unmarried mothers cited the model of Mia Farrow; and *Select*, a periodical for swingers, claimed a readership of one hundred thousand among a swiftly growing movement that was said to number perhaps 2 million middle-class citizens engaged in transient trysts. Sex, wrote David Riesman, had become America's last frontier. In a society where many groped for identity, "sex provides a kind of defense against the threat of total apathy," and the other-directed person "looks to it for reassurance that he is alive."

Scholars contributed to the fostering of this "erotic renaissance," and the modified value system in turn made possible a warmer welcome for advanced ideas. By the 1960's there was a more hospitable audience for the precepts of earlier sages like Wilhelm Reich and Henry Miller as well as for such latter-day evangelists as Norman O. Brown, who in *Life Against Death* celebrated the "resurrection of the body" and "erotic exuberance." In 1956 Dr. William H. Masters and Mrs. Virginia E. Johnson of Washington University in St. Louis began an eleven-year study in which they observed nearly seven hundred men and women masturbating and copulating and measured the intensity of their orgasms. "The '60's," Dr. Masters declared, "will be called the decade of orgasmic preoccupation." It was widely thought that the Pill accounted for the permutation in mood, but Edward Grossman reasoned that it was rather the altered perceptions that made the Pill possible. "The grants to set up the labs would not have been awarded, the talent to synthesize the chemistry would not have been collected, if there had not been an agreement . . . too deep to be put into words," he wrote, "a state of mind, in which sex would be separated—as far as science, will and conscience could separate it —from duty, pain and fear, from everything but pleasure."

Yet sexual liberation seems not to have been as seismic a development as some thought, or to have had all the consequences its earlier exponents claimed for it. Dr. Kinsey's successor as director of the Institute for Sex Research at Indiana University explained:

People talk more freely about sex nowadays, and young people are far more tolerant and permissive regarding sex. But we don't think there have been changes that we could truly call revolutionary. Our studies indicate that there has just been a continuation of pre-existing trends, rather than any sudden revolutionary changes. For instance, premarital intercourse has increased, but it hasn't shot up in any inflationary way; it has been on the rise ever since the turn of the century.

Moreover, the Dionysian spirit proved less emancipating than the oracles had foretold. The campus liaisons of the "unmarried marrieds," noted one report, were "familiar, predictable and slightly boring," and a student of group sex found that swingers "have now gone from Puritanism into promiscuity without passing through sensuality." So much did libertinism resemble babbittry that in the summer of 1970 in Chicago 184 couples congregated at the First National Swingers Convention. As the French critic Raoul de Roussy de Sales once remarked, "America appears to be the only country in the world where love is a national problem."

Furthermore, the uninhibited displays in book stores and on movie marquees obscured the fact that there was no national concordance on sexual mores. An opinion survey in 1969 learned that 76 percent of respondents wanted pornography outlawed, and a minority report of the President's commission protested that hardcore materials had "an eroding effect on society, on public morality, on respect for human worth, on attitudes toward family love, on culture." Reverend Dr. Billy James Hargis, leader of the Christian Crusade, charged that the new morality was "part of a gigantic conspiracy to bring down America from within." "I don't want any kid under 12 to hear about lesbians, homosexuals, and sexual intercourse," the evangelist said. "They should be concerned with tops, yo-yos and hide and seek." The division in the country revealed, as *Newsweek* wrote, "a society that has lost its consensus on such crucial issues as premarital sex and clerical celibacy, marriage, birth control and sex education; a society that cannot agree on standards of conduct, language and manners."

The lost consensus on sexual roles derived not just from the counter culture but also from the women's liberation movement, which combined new emancipationist convictions with old-fashioned reformism. In much of its program, "women's lib" requested simply the accomplishment of traditional and unexceptionable feminist objectives such as equality of opportunity. Spokesmen pointed out that for all the gains that had been achieved women comprised a smaller percentage of the college population in the 1950's than in the 1920's. Moreover, those with degrees earned only half of the median income of men with the same training. Although most women college graduates found ready employment, they continued to be consigned, disproportionately, to occupations defined as "female" like clerical work, and they encountered difficulty in rising to higher grades, in part because they had to assume nearly full responsibility for child-rearing. To put women on a par with men in the job market, feminists asked for statutes barring discrimination on the basis of sex and for the funding of child-care centers, which would make it possible for mothers to hold full-time positions and compete for advancement on an equal basis with men.

However, women's lib partisans pushed well beyond familiar goals like wage parity to demand an end to the exploitation of women as sexual objects. Opposed to having their roles defined exclusively by gender, they had been dismayed by the treatment accorded to their sex in the protest movements. When they joined their male

The women's liberation movement. This 1970 rally of Woman's Strike for Equality is addressed by Gloria Steinem, called "probably the most persuasive publicist for the growing feminist movement in the United States." In 1972, she was one of the founders of *MS.*, of which she became the first editor.

comrades in taking over buildings at Columbia, they were peremptorily assigned the food preparation chores, a practice in keeping with Che Guevara's manual, which pointed out that women could be useful to a guerrilla movement as cooks. Even more exasperating had been Stokely Carmichael's dictum: "The position of women in our movement should be prone." They resented, too, the way in which the consumer culture presented women, and they struck back by scribbling graffiti on offending billboards, writing letters against TV commercials, picketing the Miss America contest in Atlantic City, and burning their bras. Above all, they insisted on sovereignty over their own bodies. They regarded rape as a political act (and to cope with assailants took courses in karate) and campaigned strenuously for reform of anti-abortion laws.

Yet the latter-day sisters attracted attention less because they voiced these demands than because they threatened to rend the social fabric by destroying such stabilizing institutions as marriage, the home, and the nuclear family. Ti-Grace Atkinson staged a sit-in at a city marriage license bureau, and Susan Brownmiller remarked that it was "hard to find a woman's liberationist who is not in some way disaffected by the sound of wedding bells." Some of the feminists were frankly hostile to men. Refusing any longer to be "breeders," they spurned sexual intercourse, denounced the penis as a weapon of male imperialism, and insisted women could find fulfillment by concentrating their attention on the true center of sexual gratification, the clitoris. Anne Koedt discounted "the myth of the vaginal orgasm," Kate Millett announced she was bisexual, and Roxanne Dunbar advocated masturbation as preferable to the tyranny of heterosexuality. Nanette Rainone, producer of a liberationist radio program, said that a housewife's life was "nothingness, total nothingness," and even more moderate leaders like Betty Friedan, founder of the National Organization of Women (NOW), expressed contempt for homemaking. In her runaway best seller, *The Feminine Mystique*, she called the American home a "comfortable concentration camp."

Such conceptions encountered resistance from women as well as from men. Many wives found satisfaction in child nurture and conjugality, and a Gallup poll in 1970 revealed that two-thirds of American women thought they were fairly treated. Feminists were forced to concede that they spoke for only a minority (and these largely upper class). They attributed this to the fact that women had been brainwashed, and they sought through consciousness-raising sessions ("Do you pretend to have an orgasm?") to produce a sense of grievance. "There are few Noras in contemporary society," commented Alice Rossi, "because women have deluded themselves that a doll's house is large enough to find complete fulfillment within it." However, one woman writer protested: "You might have to go back to the Children's Crusade in 1212 A.D. to find as unfortunate and fatuous an attempt at manipulated hysteria as the Women's Liberation movement. . . . Where do they get the lunatic idea that women had rather work for a boss than stay home and run their own domain?" Other observers pointed out that women already wielded tremendous power. They owned most of the country's economic resources, spent most of its money, outlived men, and, as a tradition from the old comic strip of Maggie and Jiggs in "Bringing Up

Father" to TV programs like "The Donna Reed Show" suggested, were perceived to be the decision makers in the household. Dr. Benjamin Spock, not normally thought of as a spokesman for reaction, said with measured imagery: "If you liberate women in America one more inch, man will be completely subjugated."

Still, however ill regarded some of their contentions may have been, the women liberationists began to have an impact. In the same year that Betty Friedan's book appeared, the Civil Rights Act of 1964 forbade discrimination in employment on the basis of sex, and in 1970 the House of Representatives gave emphatic approval to the Equal Rights Amendment, which had been incarcerated in committee for nearly half a century. The long-term shift of women into the employment market made further headway too. Women took almost two-thirds of the new jobs in the 1960's, so that by 1970 over 43 percent of female adults were employed (up from 34 percent in 1950, and almost twice the figure for 1920), and the proportion of married women in the labor force was greater even than in Sweden. A number of states legalized abortion, and in New York during 1970 one child was legally aborted for every two born alive. The liberationists claimed, too, that women no longer experienced guilt over not meeting the consumer culture's expectations. The movement, asserted Mrs. Friedan, "has stopped women from feeling like freaks for not having that orgiastic bliss while waxing the floor."

Women's lib and the transit of wives from home to office had a more subtle influence in the blending of sexual roles. Social scientists concluded that when women added a second income to the family they could not continue to assume all their usual household obligations and husbands had to share in "female" tasks. This "increased overlapping of sexual spheres," William H. Chafe has noted, "represented perhaps the most significant by-product of the growth in women's economic activity." "Today we may be on the verge of a new phase in American family history," wrote the sociologist Robert Blood. "The classic differences between masculinity and femininity are disappearing as both sexes in the adult generation take on the same roles in the labor market."

The distinction between "male" and "female" blurred. Robert Oldenwald, who coined the word "unisex," wrote of *The Disappearing Sexes,* and Faubion Bowers insisted, "The time is long overdue to face what is by now a truism—the psychically androgynous nature of man." The media showed a morbid fascination with transsexuals like Christine Jorgensen and Gore Vidal's *Myra Brecken-*

ridge. Couples wore identical clothing, and when the *National Observer* assayed trends for the 1970's, it forecast, "The look will be natural, the sex indeterminate." While some women had long been wearing "mannish" garb (in the early 1930's Marlene Dietrich had shocked Hollywood by strolling Vine Street in slacks), the change in male plumage was startling. The "Peacock Revolution" saw shirts and ties take on the colors of the rainbow, and even the gray flannel suit set switched to epicene Nehru jackets. Leaders of the women's liberation movement noted with approval that gorgeously garmented, long-maned males were rejecting "the masculine mystique." "How can any man live up to that Ernest Hemingway *machismo* concept of masculinity?" Betty Friedan asked.

The new-type professional athlete indicated that *machismo* was no longer a universal ideal. The life style of the athletic performer had traditionally been that of the tobacco-spitting, no-quarter-given plug-uglies of John McGraw or St. Louis' spikes-flying, belly-sliding Gas House Gang. Now Yogi Berra huckstered hair sprays for men, Ron Swoboda wore beads, and Spider Lockhart donned a blue crushed velvet suit from Neiman-Marcus. The athlete was reflecting a change in the definition of "male," which by the mid-1960's made possible a thriving business in men's beauty salons. "The embrace of the hairnet, the whisper of the hair dryer, the provocative aroma of hair spray, all are now as routine as shaving lotion for thousands of men who only a few years ago would have recoiled in disgust at such vanities," noted *The New York Times.* Joe Pepitone grew bangs, and Jim Bouton curried a Clara Bow fringe. In a tribute to "The Frankly Beautiful New Young Gentleman," *Harper's Bazaar* admired its hero's "long, extremely tossable hair," which he brushed "with absorption," and reported that he "chooses his shampoos with the gravity of a connoisseur, and scents himself with enormous care."

This mitigation of sex differences sometimes took the form of an open avowal of homosexuality. In the 1960's the "closet queens" came out of hiding. Male homosexuals who had formerly feared ostracism or blackmail identified themselves publicly with groups like the Mattachine Society and the Pink Panthers, and the University of Minnesota was only one of a number of institutions that accorded recognition to a student homosexual association. In June 1970, militant homosexuals organized in the Gay Liberation Front marched boldly from Sheridan Square in Greenwich Village through the heart of midtown Manhattan to the Sheep Meadow in Central Park where

they held a "gay-in." Flaunting brilliantly hued silk banners, the
paraders, whose ranks extended fifteen blocks long, chanted, "Say
it loud, gay is proud." Movie audiences hailed the tragicomic *The
Boys in the Band,* which centered on a homosexual gathering, and
John Schlesinger's less explicit *Midnight Cowboy.* To some, these
occurrences represented a stride toward freedom for another per-
secuted group. Others, however, deplored the flight from heterosexuality said to be occasioned by growing female aggressiveness
and regretted that the attenuation of sexual distinctions further
accelerated the homogenization of American society.

The counter culture and radical politics frequently merged, and one
convention in Philadelphia, called to write a new Constitution,
united the gay liberation movement and the Black Panthers, Weathermen and Yippies. Conservatives preferred to treat the two phenomena as one, and, in truth, the two movements did find occasion to

Lesbians take part in a gay liberation demonstration in New York City. At times members of both sexes
participated in homosexual protests and in campus homosexual organizations. Americans were familiarized with lesbianism by movies like *The Fox* and *The Killing of Sister George.*

Leonard Freed, Magnum

join forces against "the power structure." "Make love, not war" harmonized the aims of peace and sexual freedom, and in *On Liberation,* Herbert Marcuse wrote, "The new society will be one where the hatred of the young bursts into laughter and song, mixing the barricade and the dance floor, love play and heroism."

But frequently the two tendencies diverged or even conflicted. Peter and Brigitte Berger wrote of the counter culture: "The rhetoric is Rousseauean rather than Jacobin, the imagery of salvation is intensely bucolic, the troops of the revolution are not the toiling masses of the Marxist prophecy but naked children of nature dancing to the tune of primitive drums." There was a deep-seated contradiction between the privatism of doing one's own thing (especially by tripping) and a commitment to political engagement. After observing the Woodstock festival, a *Newsweek* reporter conceded that the hippie population was far larger than anyone had thought but added, "They form a new constituency whose views go beyond the anger that produces picket lines and reform drives in Congress to the turned-on indifference that sets them questing after tangerine trees and marmalade skies."

Black nationalists, radicals, and other advocates of social change found increasingly that they had essentially different perceptions from many in the counter culture. Eldridge Cleaver denounced drugs as a way of avoiding confrontation with the system and disowned the counter culture as "harmful to our cause," and the Viet Cong foreign minister, Madame Nguyen Thi Binh, complained that antiwar students in America were protracting United States involvement in Vietnam by antagonizing their elders with their bizarre life style. When homosexuals at Columbia requested a gay lounge similar to the exclusively black lounge, the Students' Afro-American Society belittled them as "social misfits," adding that blacks "don't have time to wallow in the mud with people who cannot decide if they are men or women." While the counter culture spurned work-oriented America, women's lib believed that a woman's place was in the office. It was shocked, too, by the way rock degraded women, especially the debased groupies. The name of Dr. Spock, a hero of the peace movement, was hissed at women's lib gatherings. If the counter culture often parted company with radicalism, conservatism showed some of its effects. Reporters were surprised to observe a conservative youth convention attended by long-haired, bearded delegates, and a survey learned that a good number of pot smokers backed Barry Goldwater and William Buckley.

Far more than it was ready to acknowledge, the counter culture blended with the consumer culture. While bemoaning the material-ism of suburban America, the young rebels acquired expensive stereo sets, amplified the sound of electric guitars, and drove Triumphs decorated with psychedelic butterflies. Psychedelicates-sens catered to the needs of drug addicts; the forty-six-store chain, Jeans West, profited from the sale of hippie clothing; and other merchants retailed accessories like love beads and Benjamin Franklin eyeglasses. One participant in the Woodstock festival, Tom Smucker, recalled:

We awoke to hear the U.S. Committee to Aid the National Liberation Front announcing over their loudspeaker: "Get Your Dry Che Guevara T-Shirts. Only Two Dollars."

The T-shirts had cost them, so I heard, about 5 or 10 per cent of that maybe, and were silk-screened earlier in New York.

"The slogan of Dr. Leary's medicine show, 'Tune in, turn on, drop out,' is fundamentally the same make-it lyric as 'There's a Ford in your future,'" wrote Frederic Morton. "Yesterday the young mar-rieds from Yonkers motored to the country club in their de luxe hardtop for a cocktail with prestigious friends. Today they split for the Electric Circus in their (American Motors) Rebel to freak out with fellow swingers." Arlo Guthrie's "Alice's Restaurant" may have impaled bourgeois America, but the actual Alice, who provided the locale for the song and the movie, wound up commissioning a chain of Alice's Restaurants.

The ideology of the counter culture, set forth in works such as Charles Reich's *The Greening of America* and Theodore Roszak's *The Making of a Counter Culture,* drew heavy flak. Some intellectuals were offended by the soggy ratiocination. One reviewer called Reich's best seller "a colloidal suspension of William Buckley, Wil-liam Blake and Herbert Marcuse in pure applesauce." Others pointed out that in celebrating the natural, these writers were demeaning man. Reich, said Samuel McCracken, was "a humanist at odds with humanity" who held "stricter standards for man than for nature, blaming him for the bomb, excusing her of such peccadilloes as anthrax and the typhoon." Most of all, critics decried the counter culture's rejection of technology because it made no allowance for technologically dependent necessities such as modern surgery and the requirement of disciplined training to achieve surgical skills. Moreover, the counter culture was "profoundly parasitic" and in-trinsically elitist. As Kenneth Keniston observed:

Historically, the Byronic romanticism characteristic of Roszak's counter culture has arisen only among the privileged classes of prosperous societies. People who *really* live in organic, tribal, symbiotic and shamanistic cultures generally can't wait to escape into the world of affluence, science and technology. It is only *after* technology has triumphed, and only for those whose lives are glutted with the goodies it provides, that the young can begin to look wistfully at the delights of shamanism.

Even intellectuals who were well disposed toward the counter culture were perturbed by its more egregious manifestations. Paul Goodman, who had done so much to encourage the young to question shibboleths, recoiled from the realization that some had carried antinomianism to the point of denying that there were any professional standards at all. Toward the end of the decade he wrote:

Suddenly I realized that they did not really believe that there was a nature of things. Somehow all functions could be reduced to interpersonal relations and power. There was no knowledge, but only the sociology of knowledge. They had so well learned that physical and sociological research is subsidized and conducted for the benefit of the ruling class that they did not believe there was such a thing as the simple truth. To be required to learn something was a trap by which the young were put down and co-opted. Then I knew that I could not get through to them. I had imagined that the world-wide student protest had to do with changing political and moral institutions, to which I was sympathetic, but I now saw that we had to do with a religious crisis of the magnitude of the Reformation in the fifteen hundreds, when not only all institutions but all learning had been corrupted by the Whore of Babylon.

Much more important than the second thoughts of intellectuals was the repugnance millions of their countrymen felt to the counter culture and the radical persuasion. The most bitter resistance to both the counter culture and the New Left came not from Wall Street but from the "hardhats." A 1969 study by Daniel Yankelovich found that the generation gap between the young and their parents was not nearly so wide as the gulf separating the attitudes of college students from young people not in college. While suburban youth was queuing up to see *The Graduate,* the sons of factory hands crowded drive-in movies to cheer John Wayne in *The Green Berets.* Campus *sans culottes* scoffed at split-level respectability, but workers who had scrimped to achieve lower middle class status and the appurtenances of the consumer culture felt a fierce protectiveness about their achievements. Admirers of the Vince Lombardi regimen of hard work and discipline, they were driven to fury by the sight of indolent hippies strung out on drugs and panhandling for their next fix. They were even more incensed by the burning of the American flag. To show their own colors, they pasted decals of Old Glory on their car windows alongside "Support Your Local Police." The tremors of the 1960's, especially war, violence, and the counter culture, were wrenching the axes of controversy away from the old simplicities of economic interest and aligning them instead with the disturbing new polarities of cultural politics.

Crescendo: The 1968 Campaign

The 1968 presidential campaign encapsulated the strains of cultural politics and violence of the mid-1960's, and raised profound concern over the viability of the American political system. As early as the summer of 1967, the cover of *United States News and World Report* had asked: "IS THE U.S. ABLE TO GOVERN ITSELF?" By February 1968, Robert F. Kennedy, noting the turn of the young from public commitment to "lives of disengagement and despair," was writing, "We seem to fulfill the vision of Yeats: 'Things fall apart, the center cannot hold; / mere anarchy is loosed upon the world.'" In the following month James Reston commented, "The main crisis is not Vietnam itself, or in the cities, but in the feeling that the political system for dealing with these things has broken down."

In 1968, the sores that had been rapidly spreading on the body politic abcessed and burst. The war in Vietnam, the breeding place of much of the infection, refused to respond to poultices, and during those twelve months 16,511 more Americans died, leaving critics of the bloodletting in a feverish rage. Unnerving, too, was the sickness at home, for race riots came unseasonably early and hard upon them the mayhem at Columbia and other universities. Only two men had the ears of both whites and blacks, both campus and ghetto, and before 1968 was half over, Martin Luther King and Robert Kennedy would be gone. By the time the fever had run its course, a President had been toppled, a presidential candidate murdered, a party convention stained with blood.

The new year had hardly begun when on January 3, 1968, Eugene McCarthy, a fervent critic of the administration's Vietnam policy, announced that he was launching an insurrection to wrest the Democratic presidential nomination from his party's chieftain, Lyndon Johnson. As the first move in this patently quixotic endeavor, he would enter New Hampshire's primary. Few took the gambit seriously. Almost everyone understood that it was impossible to deny renomination to a President who wanted to run again, let alone to an incumbent who had been elected by the biggest margin in modern history. Furthermore, McCarthy had never cut much of a figure in the Senate. Liberal colleagues complained that he was frequently missing when the going got rough, and no important legislation bore his name. To be sure, the Vietnam War had eroded much of Johnson's popularity. But Johnson appeared to have a firm grip on the party apparatus, and reports from Saigon were encouraging. On January 17, exactly two weeks after McCarthy's announcement, the President boasted that "the enemy had been defeated in battle after battle" and "the number of South Vietnamese living in areas under government protection tonight has grown by more than a million since January of last year." Small wonder that early polls gave McCarthy as little as 8 percent of the primary ballots in New Hampshire.

On the final day of January, the situation changed dramatically. Exploiting the distracted mood of the Tet (lunar new year) festivities, the Viet Cong attacked innumerable villages, sixty-four district towns, over four-fifths of the provincial capitals, a dozen United States bases, and, brazenly, the American embassy in Saigon. A bazooka blew a hole in the embassy compound, and for several hours V.C. commandos put the custody of this "impregnable" bastion in doubt. The Pentagon claimed that the enemy had suffered a devastating defeat, and in a military sense it had, for it failed to capture a single capital and it sustained terrible losses. But that was beside the point. By demonstrating that it could invade the very grounds of the United States embassy, the Viet Cong shattered confidence in the Johnson administration's claims. As McCarthy said to a gathering in Manchester, New Hampshire: "Only a few months ago we were told sixty-five percent of the population was secure. Now we know that even the American Embassy is not secure."

The Tet offensive gave a big lift to McCarthy's campaign because from the outset his strength lay in opposition to the war. He cheered anti-militarist elements by stating that, if elected, he would go to the Pentagon: "I would at least try to get diplomatic representation there." McCarthy offered himself, too, as the champion of a "new politics." "Whatever is morally necessary must be made politically possible," he declared.

As the evangel of a renascence that would foster spiritual values and innovative ideas in American politics, McCarthy had an unusual background and exceptional attributes. A devout Catholic, he had spent a nine-month novitiate at a monastery and had contemplated taking the vows of a monk. Subsequently he had taught at a Catholic college. He was close to Robert Lowell, read difficult poets like Wallace Stevens and Charles Peguy, and wrote passable verse himself. Appropriately, his favorite writer was the author of *Utopia,* Sir Thomas More. McCarthy salted his speeches and conversation with literary and historical imagery. In an address to a political gathering he alluded to the Punic Wars, and on another occasion he told a British reporter, "One of the things I object to about the

On the night of March 21, 1968, Senator Eugene McCarthy of Minnesota celebrates with young admirers his strong showing in the New Hampshire presidential primary. College students played an important role in his campaign against Lyndon Johnson, which culminated in the President's withdrawal from the race less than three weeks later.

Charles Harbutt, Archive, from *Crisis in America,*
published by Ridge Press and Holt, Rinehart and Winston

Kennedys is that they are trying to turn the Presidency into the Wars of the Roses." If introspection led him to self-doubt, it was not because he overvalued his rivals. In 1960 he had said, only half in jest, that he thought of making a run for the White House because "I'm twice as liberal as Hubert Humphrey, and twice as intelligent as Stuart Symington, and twice as Catholic as Jack Kennedy."

McCarthy's wit and learning, conjoined with his stand against the war and his moral preachments, attracted legions of young volunteers. To New Hampshire flocked over ten thousand students from more than a hundred campuses. Sensitive to the fact that counter culture styles of hair and dress might alienate New Englanders, they resolved to be "Neat and Clean for Gene." Hair trimmed, shirts laundered, chinos pressed, they went door to door in towns from Keene to Berlin, politely soliciting votes for the Senator. "What is happening," reported the Washington correspondent Mary McGrory, "is that violet-eyed damsels from Smith are pinning McCarthy buttons on tattooed mill-workers, and Ph.D.s from Cornell, shaven and shorn for world peace, are deferentially bowing to middle-aged Manchester housewives and importuning them to consider a change of Commander-in-Chief." To appeal to the Granite State's hundred thousand people of French-Canadian descent, an Amherst student translated McCarthy pamphlets into French, and two score sons of Eli went house-to-house in Berlin's factory districts speaking Yale French and distributing leaflets with titles like *"McCarthy au sujet de Vietnam"* and *"McCarthy parle des citoyens âgés."* Buoyed by the reaction to the Tet raids, reinforced by the student volunteers, McCarthy's campaign, once a forlorn gesture, reached formidable proportions. On March 12, New Hampshire Democrats gave McCarthy 42.4 percent to LBJ's 49.5 percent, and when Republican write-ins were added, Johnson's margin in "hawkish" New Hampshire fell to less than 1 percent.

The tidings from New Hampshire reached a President already sore beset. Two weeks earlier the military command in Saigon had sent him a request for 206,000 more United States troops, and even this huge increment could not assure success. When Johnson called for a full-scale policy review, he was told that victory was unachievable save at unacceptable risks. Staggered by this intelligence, he realized that if he decided to push for negotiations, the fact that he was a candidate for reelection meant any action he took would be discounted as a campaign ploy. Moreover, he could not help but recognize that he had become a divisive force in a dangerously fragmented nation. There were political considerations too. Advisers warned the President that McCarthy would trounce him in the April 2 primary in Wisconsin, where eight thousand students were in the field, fanning out from the University of Wisconsin in Dane County. One of LBJ's deputies reported, "We sent a man into Dane County to recruit for Johnson and all we've heard from him since is a few faint beeps, like the last radio signals from the beach of the Bay of Pigs." Even more ominously, four days after the New Hampshire primary Robert Kennedy had entered the race.

On the night of March 31, Johnson sounded retreat. At the end of a nationally televised address in which he announced initiatives toward a Vietnam settlement, the President raised his right arm as a signal to his wife that he would add a postcript. "I have concluded that I should not permit the Presidency to become involved in the partisan divisions that are developing in this political year," he said. "Accordingly, I shall not seek, and I will not accept, the nomination of my party for another term as your President." The McCarthy forces were jubilant. It had taken less than three months to bring down a President. Two days later, as predicted, McCarthy shellacked Johnson in the Wisconsin primary.

However, for McCarthy, the fruits of victory had soured. He had eliminated Johnson only to confront a new challenge from Robert Kennedy (as well as from the President's surrogate, Hubert Humphrey). Critics of the junior Senator from New York who had earlier taunted him for hesitating to oppose the President (placards read "BOBBY KENNEDY: HAWK, DOVE, OR CHICKEN?") reviled him as a ruthless opportunist for waiting until McCarthy's courage had shown the way. Yet if his belated candidacy incensed McCarthy's acolytes, Kennedy had a constituency that McCarthy could not reach — among admirers who viewed him as a prince of the blood, among white workingmen tempted by George Wallace, in black ghettos and Mexican-American *barrios,* in Appalachian hamlets and on Indian reservations. Such coalitions carried Kennedy to a string of primary victories. But in Oregon on May 28 McCarthy snapped the skein by chalking up the first defeat for a Kennedy after twenty-seven consecutive triumphs. The duel headed toward the moment of truth in the California primary on June 4 and Robert Kennedy toward his appointment at Samarra.

Kennedy's campaign had aroused ecstasy bordering on the dangerous, and in California the frenzy reached a peak. In Los Angeles, especially in areas of Mexican-American concentration, his motorcade could barely get through the crowded streets loud with cries of "Viva Kennedy." For weeks, clutching mobs had bloodied his hands, had stripped him of laces and cuff links; here even his shoes were removed. McCarthy hoped to counter this appeal by getting the same intense effort from young people he had elicited in New Hampshire. His daughter Mary told California students, "We do not want to go to the beach with an uneasy conscience." But abetted by his advantage in Los Angeles County, Kennedy won a clear-cut victory. On primary election night, as he prepared to leave his suite at the Ambassador Hotel in Los Angeles to go downstairs to greet his exultant campaign workers, Kennedy received word of another big success that same day in South Dakota. Indians, he was told, had voted 811 for him, 11 for McCarthy, 4 for Humphrey. "That's marvelous," he replied. "I just wish we hadn't taken Oregon away from them." To his volunteers, he remarked with quiet restraint, "I think we can end the division within the United States, the violence." Moments later, as he walked through a kitchen corridor, Kennedy was shot and mortally wounded by Sirhan Bishara Sirhan, a twenty-four-year-old Jordanian immigrant. "Not *again!*" screamed a spectator. On the wall a few feet from where he lay someone scribbled in crayon, "THE ONCE AND FUTURE KING."

As a result of the assassination, McCarthy became the legatee of the hopes of most anti-war Democrats, but not all were reconciled. In Negro neighborhoods, Samuel Lubell found a sense of irreparable loss. "I won't vote," a New Yorker said. "Every good man we get they kill." Some Kennedy Democrats tried to scrape together a candidacy for Senator McGovern as an alternative to McCarthy. Even a number of early enthusiasts found McCarthy exasperatingly aloof and indecisive. In "The Lament of an Aging Politician," McCarthy had written:

> I have left Act I, for involution
> And Act II. There mired in complexity
> I cannot write Act III.

"You know the old rules," he elaborated. "Act I states the problem. Act II deals with the complications. And Act III resolves them. I'm an Act II man. That's where I live—involution and complexity." As the day of the Democratic convention approached, he immured himself in a Benedictine retreat and seemed indifferent to the ardor of his followers. "No one doubted that Eugene McCarthy bore love in his heart—but it was an abstract love, a love for youth, a love for

At a Chicago rally, a grim Humphrey contrasts with the projected image of the usually smiling, ebullient Hubert as Chicago's Mayor Richard Daley looks on. When, in Salt Lake City on September 30, 1968, Humphrey modified his support of Johnson's war policies, the lectern was no longer adorned with the vice-presidential emblem, signifying that he spoke not for the administration but on his own.

beauty, a love for vistas and hills and song," observed Theodore White. "All through the year, one's admiration of the man grew — and one's affection lessened."

Neither McCarthy nor the anti-war cause fared well at the convention. Vice-President Hubert Humphrey won the presidential nomination handily by accumulating more than twice the number of votes for McCarthy and McGovern. The peace forces did somewhat better in corraling support for a minority plank calling for "an unconditional end to all bombing in North Vietnam," but by a 3 to 2 margin the administration's plank prevailed. After the tally, the band played "Off We Go into the Wild Blue Yonder." Still, as the

Foreign Policy Association observed, "Never before in time of war against a foreign foe had so large a minority of a presidential nominating convention signified its readiness to repudiate its own leadership on so critical a question." However, to many of the disgruntled delegates, the outcome proved that America was a repressive society and that the political system no longer worked. McCarthy, the choice of the people, they claimed, had been passed over for a Johnson toady who was bulldozed through by party bosses, and the platform had turned a deaf ear to the nation's cry for peace.

In truth, the process of choosing delegates left much to be desired, although the Chicago convention had more democratic features than its critics acknowledged. It outraged the conservative Texas governor, John B. Connally, by abolishing the ancient unit rule, initiated a pathbreaking democratization of delegate selection for 1972, and refused to seat the segregationist Mississippi regulars. When half

A tune for Mars. A flutist taunts national guardsmen at the Democratic convention in Chicago in 1968. Some foes of the war used less peaceful means, but even critics of the demonstrators conceded that the violence perpetrated by the Chicago police was inexcusable.

Roger Malloch, Magnum

of the Georgia vote was allotted to insurgents led by the Negro legislator Julian Bond, Governor Lester Maddox went home in a fit of pique. The peace element had ample opportunity to state its case at Platform Committee hearings, where their spokesmen included Senators McGovern and Fulbright, and in a full-dress debate on the convention floor. The final vote may have been a rough representation of the actual divisions within the party, for although many wanted to get out of the war, fewer wished to lose it. Polls in the early spring revealed that most Americans opposed halting the bombing and that a preponderance of those interviewed opted for an invasion of North Vietnam. Those who recalled McCarthy's "victory" in New Hampshire forgot that he actually lost the state, and to a write-in candidate; moreover, a substantial portion of McCarthy's ballots came from people who wanted to escalate the fighting and who later voted for George Wallace. Humphrey never underwent the trial by combat of party primaries, but polls showed that he was the favorite of registered Democrats.

Anti-war delegates objected, too, to the "police state" atmosphere of the convention — the barbed-wire and chain-link fences cordoning off the amphitheater, Mayor Daley's ubiquitous bluecoats. Yet given the events of that spring — the carnival of violence, the assassinations of King and Kennedy — it would have been irresponsible not to have taken thorough precautions. Apprehension about the vulnerability of public men was extensive and deeply felt. Mourners alongside the tracks of Robert Kennedy's funeral train bore hand-lettered signs reading "Who Will Be The Next One?" (as well as "The Gebharts Are Sad"). To be sure, the call for a national mobilization of radicals in Chicago brought only a small turnout. Blacks were noticeably absent, and most young people drawn to the city were Gene McCarthy volunteers working within the system. But to Chicago had also come a cadre bent on savaging "the pigs" and provoking a violent incident. A subsequent investigation, the Walker Report, found that the police "were the targets of mounting provocations by both word and act" and that they "had been put on edge by widely published threats of attempts to disrupt both the city and the Convention."

However, none of these extenuating circumstances justified the sadistic behavior of the Chicago police. Even sympathetic journalists certified that Daley's minions went "berserk," and the Walker Report later described a preliminary episode at Lincoln Park as a "police riot." "The cops had one thing on their mind," wrote Jimmy Breslin.

"Club and then gas, club and then gas, club and then gas." A memorandum from a British journalist from the crack staff of the *Sunday Times* recounted:

Then at 8 p.m. it happened. Cohorts of police began to charge the crowd from a street north of the Hilton, Balbo. The kids screamed and were beaten to the ground by cops who had completely lost their cool. Some tried to surrender by putting their hands on their heads. As they were marched to vans to be arrested, they were rapped in the genitals by the cops' swinging billies.

The Walker Report concluded that there had been "unrestrained and indiscriminate police violence" and added:

That violence was made all the more shocking by the fact that it was inflicted upon persons who had broken no law, disobeyed no order, made no threat. These included peaceful demonstrators, onlookers, and a large number of residents who were simply passing through, or happened to live in, the areas where confrontations were occurring.

(The disorders had a shameful aftermath in the trial of Bobby Seale, Abbie Hoffman, and others, in which judge and defendants seemed bent on outdoing one another in making a travesty of a court of justice.)

The imbroglio left Hubert Humphrey the nominee of a party many of whose followers blamed him both for the wanton harassment in Chicago and for the prolonged conflict in Vietnam. Garrulous but ineffective, he cut a sorry figure in the first weeks of the campaign, a dreadful comedown for a man who had been the helmsman of civil rights legislation, the initiator of the Peace Corps, the sponsor of a host of social welfare measures for two decades. His very achievements led him to be too complacent about his credentials as a reformer, insufficiently alert to the needs of a new day. "People say to me, 'Whatever happened to that liberal program you stood for?' " Humphrey related. "I say to them, 'We passed it. Does that upset you?' " As the number 2 man in the Johnson administration, he wore around his neck the albatross of LBJ's Vietnam policies. Although he had developed misgivings about the war, he feared that if he advocated a different course Johnson, who held him in contempt, would punish him and that others would accuse him of disloyalty. For weeks Humphrey waffled, despite the clamor of antiwar dissidents. In Boston left-wing students howled him down, and in Seattle they jeered him noisily. No endorsement was forthcoming from Senator McCarthy, and party activists rusticated. In early

October the Vice-President had only twenty-eight sure electoral votes.

The divisive war and the disastrous Democratic convention permitted the Republicans, like Lazarus, to rise from the dead. In 1964 the GOP had been devastated, and some doubted that this party of lace curtain respectability could recover. If it did, it would not be for a long time to come, and certainly not under Richard Nixon. Two years earlier, his political career palpably finished, the former Vice-President had ranted at reporters, "You won't have Nixon to kick around any more, because, gentlemen, this is my last press conference." That week ABC televised the "Political Obituary of Richard Nixon," with Alger Hiss as one of the pallbearers. But with a tough animal instinct for survival, Nixon earned the confidence of party professionals through his faithful service in the 1966 campaign, and when the Republicans picked up forty-seven seats in the House, he received the lion's share of the credit. By the time the 1968 Republican convention got underway in Miami, a location that signified that the GOP had become an all-section party, Nixon was the front runner. At Miami, Nixon, through quieting the doubts of Senator Strom Thurmond of South Carolina and other southerners, out-pointed California's Governor Ronald Reagan so skillfully that he made his hard-fought victory look easy. Russell Baker said the convention had been "planned in advance by six bores and a sadist," but the Democratic donnybrook in Chicago put the relative calm of Miami in a favorable light.

Nixon, who had won notoriety as a divider, campaigned in 1968 as a unifier. The change reflected in part his own maturation in the 1960's, for as a New York attorney he had become more self-assured and self-controlled. But it also represented his conviction that a "silent majority" of the nation desired surcease from civil discord. In his acceptance speech, Nixon showed that his talent for pathos had lost none of its fine edge. As Eisenhower lay dying, Nixon urged, "Let's win this one for Ike." But he also struck the chord that would find a sympathetic vibration in the weeks to come. Nixon stated:

As we look at America, we see cities enveloped in smoke and flame. We hear sirens in the night. We see Americans hating each other; killing each other at home.

And as we see and hear these things, millions of Americans cry out in anguish: Did we come all this way for this? Did American boys die in Normandy and Korea and in Valley Forge for this?

Listen to the answers to these questions.

It is another voice, it is a quiet voice in the tumult and the shouting. It is the voice of the great majority of Americans, the forgotten Americans, the nonshouters, the nondemonstrators.

In capitalizing upon the yearning for domestic tranquility, Nixon's "low-profile" campaign singularly suited the public mood in 1968. The Republicans sensed that the country had heard more than enough about its shortcomings (at Miami John Wayne delivered "an inspirational reading" of "Why I Am Proud to Be an American") and of the need to smash the State. By making Nixon a present of the law and order issue, the zealots of the New Politics committed a grave tactical error. Robert Kennedy had understood the advisability of presenting himself as the former "chief law-enforcement officer of the United States," a tough Eliot Ness who had cracked down on the Mafia and put Jimmy Hoffa behind bars and who would "bring an end to this violence." But many insurgents viewed the demand for "law and order" as nothing but a code phrase for racism. Often it was. Yet most of those who wanted an end to burning cities did not wish to halt gains for blacks, and the anxiety about the destruction and disunity had to be spoken to. In the end the conviction that a healing emollient was required determined the outcome of the election, for millions shared the sentiment on the sign held aloft by an Ohio girl in the closing days of the campaign: "BRING US TOGETHER AGAIN."

While Nixon sought to take advantage of what political analysts called the "social issue" by offering himself as a harmonizer, the American Independence Party candidate, George Wallace, made headway by catering to the resentments of his followers. "If any demonstrator ever lays down in front of my car," Wallace cried, "it'll be the last car he'll ever lay down in front of." A Harris poll learned that more than half of the nation shared Wallace's view that "liberals, intellectuals, and long-hairs have run the country for too long." Attacking the "pointy-head," bearded "intellectual morons" who "don't know how to park a bicycle straight," the Alabama governor promised, "When I get to Washington I'll throw all these phonies and their briefcases into the Potomac." He rallied, too, those who believed, as one conservative said, that as a result of the Social Security Act "breeding children as a cash crop has become a way of life for many women." New York City alone had a million on its welfare rolls by the end of 1968, and indignation at the tax burden and at what was thought to be a mendicant style of life was mounting. Merle Haggard's "Welfare Cadilac," aimed at cheaters who thrived on government checks, became a big hit, as did his "Okie from Muskogee" on pot smokers and long-hairs, and "The Fightin' Side of Me," which chewed out "squirrely guys who don't believe in fightin'" for their native land. When Nixon invited endorsements from Nashville's Silent Majority singers, he found that almost everyone was for Wallace.

Wallace profited from the disapproval of demonstrators, the counter culture, and the Welfare State, but his audiences identified him chiefly as the most prominent opponent of racial integration. In his inaugural address in 1963, Governor Wallace had said, "I draw the line in the dust and toss the gauntlet before the feet of tyranny, and I say, 'Segregation now . . . segregation tomorrow . . . and segregation forever.'" President Kennedy soon forced him to back down, but his state remained a bastion of white supremacy. When in September 1963 a bomb blasted a Negro church, Martin Luther King wired him: "The blood of four little children . . . is on your hands. Your irresponsible and misguided actions have created in Birmingham and Alabama the atmosphere that has induced continued violence and now murder." But in 1964 Wallace aroused alarm over the power of "white backlash" by rolling up 34 percent of the vote in the Wisconsin Democratic primary, 30 percent in Indiana, 43 percent in Maryland. He did especially well in working-class districts that had been the mortar of the Roosevelt coalition; in Gary, he took every white precinct. Wallace's strong run challenged the liberal expectation that as politics became increasingly nationalized the South would become more like the North and suggested instead that the North was becoming more like the South. The correspondent Douglas Kiker wrote: "It is as if somewhere, sometime a while back, George Wallace had been awakened by a white, blinding vision: they all hate black people, all of them. They're all afraid, all of them. Great God! That's it! They're all Southern! The whole United States is *Southern!*"

As Wallace invaded the North in 1968 to test the assumption that it shared the predilections of the former Confederacy, he found white working-class neighborhoods, particularly those bordering on black ones, markedly hospitable. He appealed to transplanted Appalachian hilljacks, to Polish and other "newer" ethnic groups, and generally to blue collar laborers who believed that blacks were getting away with murder—like the Brooklyn members of SPONGE, the Society for the Prevention of Negroes Getting Everything. To the dismay of

UAW leaders, key locals reported Wallace had the edge on the major party candidates. Some were drawn as much by his pugnacious style as by his content. He was attractive, said the political scientist David Derge, to the "kind of guy the Tuesday night bowling league might choose to represent them with a group of unfriendlies." Although many of his ideas were conservative, Wallace, who won Tom Watson's millworker ward in Augusta, frequently sounded a Populist note. He asserted that the major parties were "owned by the Eastern Establishment" and in a jab at Nixon remarked, "I can't afford to sun myself on Key Biscayne." "On November 5," he declared, "they're going to find out there are a lot of rednecks in this country."

Well before the November 5 election, it had become clear that the Governor would have to be reckoned with. Wallace moved steadily upward in the polls from 9 percent in the spring to 16 percent in June to 21 percent by mid-September. If he had maintained that rate of increase until November 5, he would have denied any candidate a majority in the Electoral College, and the nerve-fraying year of 1968 would have ended with the presidential succession in doubt for weeks, even months. At that pace he would have finished ahead of Humphrey, who would have suffered the humiliation of coming in third. In late September Humphrey was running fifteen points behind Nixon in the Gallup survey and was only seven points ahead of Wallace.

However, at precisely that juncture Humphrey's fortunes took a decided turn for the better. He advanced his own cause when on September 30 in Salt Lake City he indicated he would no longer be LBJ's vassal. His lectern divested of the vice-presidential seal, Humphrey announced that he would "stop the bombing of North Vietnam as an acceptable risk for peace." It was a guarded speech, with conditions attached, but he made it without the President's approval, and the address heartened anti-war Democrats. By late October, even Gene McCarthy managed a feeble endorsement: "I believe the Vice-President is a man who can be relied upon to tell the difference between the pale horse of death and the white horse of victory. I am not sure that Mr. Nixon can make that distinction."

Humphrey also benefited from the contrast between his running mate, Senator Edmund Muskie of Maine, who exuded quiet good sense, and the vice-presidential nominees of his rivals. Wallace's most damaging blunder was his choice of General Curtis LeMay, former air force chief of staff and Warfare State potentate as chairman of the board of Networks Electronic, to fill out his ticket. LeMay, who had launched the fire raids against Japan in World War II and who favored bombing North Vietnam "back to the Stone Age," was held to be the model for the general in *Dr. Strangelove*. At a disastrous press conference, he stated, "We seem to have a phobia about nuclear weapons." Such indiscretions permitted Humphrey to tag Wallace and LeMay the "bombsy twins." Nixon's teammate, Governor Spiro Agnew, reinforced the image of the Republicans as the party of well-to-do WASPs. He even said, "We the Establishment." Agnew made artless ethnic allusions to a "fat Jap" and to "Polacks," aroused recollections of McCarthyism by calling Humphrey "squishy-soft" on communism, and illustrated the callousness of the Old Guard by remarking that "if you've seen one city slum, you've seen them all." So often did he goof that at one stop he was greeted by a sign: "APOLOGIZE NOW, SPIRO. IT WILL SAVE TIME LATER."

By mid-October, Democratic voters were flocking back to FDR's party like the swallows returning to Capistrano. More Americans regarded themselves as Democrats than as Republicans, and, with Agnew to rekindle memories of Herbert Hoover and Joe McCarthy, the old pulls of party identification began to reassert themselves. Unions did such a herculean job of counteracting the Wallace temptation and of mobilizing their members behind Humphrey that the Alabama governor eventually received only 15 to 18 percent of the votes of unionists. But the biggest boost came on October 31, less than a week before election day, when Johnson announced, "I have now ordered that all air, naval, and artillery bombardment of North Vietnam cease." For a brief interval it seemed that peace was in the offing, and the shift of voters, especially women, to Humphrey picked up speed. Over the final weekend of the campaign, the Vice-President pulled even. However, when the South Vietnamese spiked the understanding, the movement reversed, and Humphrey's remarkable upsurge fell just short of success.

Nixon scored a 301 to 191 victory over Humphrey in the Electoral College, but his edge in pivotal states was razor-thin and his popular margin less than seven-tenths of 1 percent. His 43.4 percent of the popular vote was the smallest share for a winner since Wilson's in 1912. Despite an increment in the electorate of over 4 million, he received 2.3 million fewer ballots than he had in 1960. The Democrats also demonstrated their residual strength by retaining control of both houses of Congress. Wallace polled 9.9 million, 4.1 million from the North and West, and 46 electoral votes. His 13.5 percent of the popular vote was the best showing for a third party in forty-·

Election of 1968

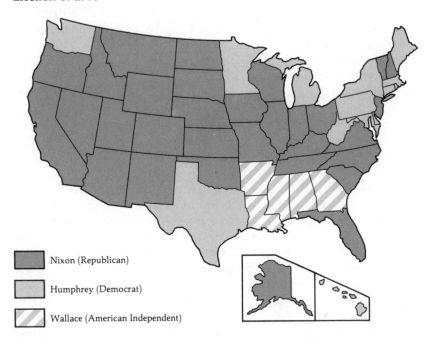

Nixon (Republican)

Humphrey (Democrat)

Wallace (American Independent)

four years, but it netted him only five states, all in the South (plus the ballot of a Nixon elector in North Carolina who defected to him).

Every four years pundits proclaimed the death of the Roosevelt coalition, but in 1968 the Democrats once again ran most strongly in the great cities, none of which went Republican, and among less well-to-do workers, unionists, and blacks, albeit in diminished proportions. Income cleavages remained the most salient determinants of voting, but with reduced force. Humphrey prevailed over Nixon among manual laborers by only a 50 to 35 ratio. The Democratic component of the nonwhite vote also fell off from the spectacular 94 percent of 1964, but it still totaled an impressive 85 percent. Petersburg, Virginia's black third ward, gave Humphrey 1,092, Nixon 17, Wallace 3. Nixon, who got 32 percent of the Negro vote in 1960, received only 12 percent in 1968. However, a smaller proportion of blacks in the North and West went to the polls, and this falloff proved critical. The erosion of the Roosevelt coalition was just large enough to cost Humphrey the victory.

Roosevelt had been able to take for granted one large electoral cluster—the South—but 1968 made clear how far the "Solid South" had disintegrated in presidential politics. Humphrey carried only a single state in the ex-Confederacy, LBJ's Texas, and this narrowly, with an increased turnout by Mexican-Americans and blacks tipping the balance. Of his meager 31 percent of the popular vote in Jefferson Davis' old realm, over two-thirds came from Negroes. (Nixon and Wallace divided the remainder of Dixie's ballots almost evenly.) Although the South was no longer a one-party preserve, sectionalism persisted, for Humphrey's domain lay almost wholly in the Northeast, while Nixon fell only four states short of capturing the entire trans-Mississippi West.

So after all the tumult of the 'sixties, Richard Milhous Nixon, the quintessential man of the 'fifties, entered the White House. The forces of radical change had been frustrated, largely because, as Richard Scammon pointed out, most of the electorate was composed of "the unyoung, the unblack, and the unpoor." Thwarted too was George Wallace, for racism failed to sway most white voters, and the deadlock he hoped to precipitate never eventuated. Of all the extraordinary developments of 1968, perhaps least expected was the durability of characters and institutions in the face of defiant challenge.

In the 1968 campaign, the consumer society and pop culture had come into their own. The son of a grocer, Dick Nixon had operated a hamburger stand, Nixon's Snack Shack, while serving in the navy in the South Pacific and, after law school, had tried to launch an enterprise to market packaged orange juice. His main rival for the Republican nomination, the former film star Ronald Reagan, had once been "the voice of the Chicago Cubs." The father of Nixon's campaign manager, John Mitchell, had been part owner of one of the first trading stamp companies. In the 1950's Nixon's running mate, Spiro Agnew, the son of a restaurant proprietor, had managed a supermarket. "The Drugstore Liberal," Hubert Humphrey, who had worked in his father's pharmacy, had begun with a decided disadvantage; appropriately, he had chosen as his first agency the advertising firm that had coined Avis Rent A Car's slogan, "We're only Number Two. We have to try harder." (His chief Democratic opponent, Eugene McCarthy, had been publicized by the same company that huckstered Hertz Rent A Car.) Nixon, the former Whittier College benchwarmer, had taken great pride in winning the endorsement of Bart Starr, quarterback of the Green Bay Packers. Humphrey had called a press conference to announce that he was

The Wallaceites. In the 1960's, the Alabama governor drew audiences that were almost exclusively white. He attracted not only men and women who shared his racist views but also those who believed strongly in the work ethic and distrusted paternalistic government. In the 1970's, Wallace startled some of his followers by catering to black voters.

being backed by Diana Ross of the Supremes. The third-party candidate, Governor Wallace, married to a former dime-store clerk, had enjoyed the ardent support of a young lady who had been imploring TV viewers to join "the Dodge rebellion" and had given consideration to selecting as his vice-presidential nominee "Colonel" Harland Sanders, the "finger-lickin' good" fried chicken impresario.

Foreign journalists, often hypercritical of American society in the 1960's, found themselves impressed by the bloodless transfer of authority. Although there was "dramatic and even melodramatic" violence in the United States in 1968, noted the British observer Henry Fairlie, "it is politically illiterate—ignorant and impatient—to refuse to acknowledge that the American political system took the strain. It may not have produced the result that one wanted. But there was a peaceable change of government." Another British writer, Louis Heren, Washington correspondent of the *Times* of London, concluded:

Some of the onlookers standing in the freezing cold as Nixon was sworn in remembered the bitter divisions, the loss of confidence, and the fear that the country was coming apart. Yet at the end of the year the presidential election was held, and there was no violence as 69 million Americans went to the polls. The enormous power of the presidency passed peacefully from one man to another.

The Center Holds

The inauguration of Richard Nixon as thirty-seventh President brought a decided change in the climate of public affairs. To the White House came a man determined to pursue the kinds of policies associated on the European Continent with Center parties. During the 1968 campaign one of his more conservative speech writers, Richard Whalen, had been distressed to find that Nixon was not interested in right-wing ideology, or indeed in the validity of any ideas; rather he wanted to position himself "athwart the technically determined 'center' of the electorate." In office he proved no less preoccupied with "the pragmatic splitting of differences along a line drawn through the middle of the electorate." To further this end and to take advantage of the revulsion against the excesses of the mid-'sixties, he sought also to lower the temperature of political controversy. As Eisenhower incarnated much of the 1950's, as Kennedy quickened concern in the 1960's, so Nixon fostered the spirit of moderation of the 1970's.

The new President began his administration in a temperate manner that deliberately contrasted with the frenetic mood of the Johnson era. In his inaugural address, he stated:

America has suffered from a fever of words; from inflated rhetoric that promises more than it can deliver; from angry rhetoric that fans discontents into hatreds; from bombastic rhetoric that postures instead of persuading.

We cannot learn from one another until we stop shouting at one another — until we speak quietly enough so that our words can be heard as well as our voices.

Nixon's centrist politics and muted style seemed particularly well suited to winning the allegiance of "Middle America." The columnist

The inauguration of Richard Nixon. The incoming President is sworn into office by Chief Justice Earl Warren, a man whom he had been roundly criticizing. Between them stands the new First Lady, Thelma "Pat" Nixon. The second person to the right of the Chief Justice in the photograph is Vice-President Spiro Agnew.

Joseph Kovacs from Stock, Boston

Joseph Kraft coined the phrase to describe "the great mass of some 40,000,000 persons who have recently moved from just above the poverty line to just below the level of affluence," but it came to connote something else, the vast United States interior that provided a ballast of common sense not to be found on either seaboard. The phrase thus incorporated three different notions, none precisely defined—an income group, a geographic location (although "Middle Americans" could also be found in Baltimore and Oakland), and a state of mind. Middle America was where the white petite bourgeoisie lived, people who went to 8 A.M. mass or to vespers, enlisted in the army, boosted their town, and were "damned sick and tired of listening to all this nonsense about how awful America is." To its denigrators in the universe of *The New York Review of Books*, Middle America suggested what George Babbitt's Zenith conveyed to intellectuals in the 1920's or Squaresville to the 1950's. But Nixon understood that "as the champion of the good, God-fearing burghers of Heartland U.S.A.," as *Newsweek* called him, he could count on a large following among those who looked back on the 'sixties with dismay.

Neither a politics of the center nor a state of tranquility came easily. In his attitudes on civil rights, in his Supreme Court appointments, and in forging an economic program, Nixon swerved in a conservative direction, although in each area he was brought back closer to the middle of the road. Some of his initiatives in Asia were sharply divisive, and his Vice-President polarized sentiment. The Nixon administration felt the impact of a politicized counter culture and was shaken by spasms of violence. Yet Nixon partly offset his rightward lurches with more unorthodox policies. Before his first three years were over, he had become the champion of costly welfare programs, had frozen prices and wages, and had shaken hands with Mao in Peking. The persistence of turmoil proved less characteristic than a condition of relative quiescence. By preempting Democratic positions and by bringing a respite from the tumultuous 1960's, Nixon appropriated so much center ground that he left his opposition in disarray.

The electoral and legislative situation also worked toward moderation. Having been elected by so narrow a margin, Nixon could claim no mandate and was well advised to tread lightly. Since he had received less than 44 percent of the vote, he knew he would have to find substantial additional support to gain reelection if the 1972 contest turned out to be a two-way race. Sometimes this inclined him to the right to pick off followers of George Wallace, although he had to keep in mind that the Wallace movement contained a populistic element. At other times he gravitated to the left to attract independents and progressive Democrats. The thorny situation on Capitol Hill made the latter course especially prudent. Not since the disputed election of 1876 had a presidential candidate won for the first time while the opposition party gained control of the House of Representatives. The Senate, also under Democratic dominance, was in an ornery mood. Having been badgered by Lyndon Johnson as majority leader and President over a long period, that august body was determined to assert its independence. To chalk up a record of legislative achievement, Nixon needed to adjust to the disposition of the Democratic majority in both houses.

Nixon contributed rather unexpectedly to the politics of moderation by advancing propositions and employing language that indicated he held larger views than adversaries had credited to him. Under the tutelage of his adviser on urban affairs, Daniel Patrick Moynihan, who gave him a copy of Lord Blake's biography of Disraeli, he persuaded himself for a time that like the Victorian Prime Minister he could achieve social reforms where a liberal Democrat would fail. After a hardline campaign in 1970 yielded indifferent returns in the midterm congressional elections, he blossomed forth in his January 1971 State of the Union message as the leader of a "New American Revolution" that, in a catchphrase of the Left, would give "power to the people," "a revolution as profound, as far-reaching, as exciting as that first revolution 200 years ago." Some of his White House aides were embarrassed by the President's overblown rhetoric, and not much came of most of his specific recommendations, but liberals were agreeably surprised by his stance.

The President created the biggest stir by proposing a sweeping overhaul of the welfare system through guaranteeing a national minimal level of support. In place of the controversial Aid to Dependent Children program, the Family Assistance Plan would give a family of four with no income $1600 a year ($2460 when food stamps were added), a big rise from Mississippi's $468 and more than welfare families were receiving in nineteen other states, predominantly Southern. In addition the plan might double the total of eligible beneficiaries through helping the "working poor." To allay conservative misgivings, Nixon insisted that every head of household on the welfare rolls, save for mothers with preschool children, work or register for job training. "There is no reason why

one person should be taxed so that another can choose to live idly,"
he asserted. Critics objected to forcing welfare recipients to labor
at substandard pay and protested that the FAP minimum was too
low; the congressional Black Caucus demanded $6500. When Con-
gress adjourned in the fall of 1972, it still had not approved the program. Yet Nixon's "great leap forward," as Moynihan, one of its
chief authors, called it, markedly shifted the fulcrum of debate. As a
putative Disraeli, the President claimed, "Tory men with liberal
principles are what has enlarged democracy in this world."

The movement to preserve the environment could count substantial
gains, only partly due to Nixon's influence. Of all his appointments,
none seemed so regrettable as that of Walter J. Hickel to be secretary
of the interior. A loud outcry greeted news of the choice, for the
self-made millionaire governor of Alaska was alleged to be close to
oil interests and said he opposed "conservation for conservation's
sake." But Hickel rapidly won over his assailants. He joined in a
successful effort to preserve the Everglades from a destructive jet-
port, halted oil drilling in the Santa Barbara Channel after a devastating blowout, persuaded the Justice Department to prosecute the
Chevron Oil Company for befouling the Gulf of Mexico, encouraged
suits against corporations charged with poisoning waters with mer-
cury, banned billboards on United States government lands, helped
defend whales and alligators from predators, and held up construction of the trans-Alaska oil pipeline that jeopardized the tundra of
his state. Nixon approved, or at least tolerated, Hickel's actions and
he included in his 1970 State of the Union message an environmental
protection program.

However, on the main ecological issue of Nixon's first two years —
the supersonic transport plane — the environmentalists scored a
notable victory over the President's opposition. Nixon was one of
many who thought that American prestige was at stake in the construction of the mammoth conveyance that might dominate air
traffic in the future. Opponents objected that the expensive project
was an example of distorted priorities and threatened the quality of
life on earth and in the upper atmosphere. At first their cause seemed
hopeless. In 1969 when the Wisconsin Democrat, Senator William
Proxmire, sought to kill government funding for the SST, the administration had no trouble in overwhelming him, 58 to 22. Yet so
rapidly did the tide of opinion change that in December 1970 the
Senate, under Proxmire's leadership, voted down the SST, a heart-
ening performance to those who believed it was possible to work
within the system.

Liberal Democrats like Proxmire accounted for much of the modest legislative portfolio of Nixon's first term, but the administration had a hand too. Few of the Great Society arrangements were scrapped, and new schemes were undertaken. Congress increased social security benefits, voted nearly $3 billion for medical training, and enacted the first comprehensive regulation of campaign spending since the Corrupt Practices Act of 1925. It balanced accounts on the era of McCarthyism by repealing the part of the McCarran Internal Security Act of 1950 that authorized setting up detention camps for subversives in times of national emergency. Legislation granting eighteen-year-olds the right to vote in federal elections was followed by the Twenty-sixth Amendment, ratified in June 1971, extending the privilege to state and local elections; the two measures enfranchised 11.5 million youths. The assumption that advertisers could manipulate the consumer culture at will received a setback when Congress banned cigarette advertising on television and radio. On January 1, 1971, viewers of the bowl games got their last glimpse of Marlboro Country. Nixon's "Second American Revolution" fell far short of fulfillment, but on the eve of the 1972 election Congress approved a path-breaking revenue-sharing plan that allotted funds to the fifty states. Although the legislative record in the four years after Nixon's 1968 victory did not approach that of Lyndon Johnson's "fabulous 89th," Congress was productive enough to give some substance to Nixon's claims for a centrist emphasis.

When he tried to cope with the unruly economy, however, Nixon's policy of moderation foundered, largely because the President inherited difficulties that were not amenable to middling measures. Lyndon Johnson bequeathed his successor not only an ugly war but rampant inflation that was a by-product of that war. Liberal economists had been proud of the fact that they had achieved expansion without cheapening the dollar, for, as Paul Samuelson said, "Creeping inflation is the malaria of the modern mixed economy." But after Johnson abruptly escalated Vietnam expenditures without calling for a tax rise to siphon off purchasing power, he came to grief. The injection of war spending into an already booming economy shot prices up—3 percent in 1967, 5 percent in 1968. As a consequence, real earnings of industrial workers, which had soared in the first half of the decade, slowed to a halt. His predecessor's policies left Nixon unpalatable alternatives: permit inflation to continue or take action to curb it but at the cost of rising unemployment. Shortly before Nixon's inauguration, his choice for chairman of the Council of Economic Advisers, Paul W. McCracken, remarked, "There is some kind of malevolent law about the rhythm of political life that puts some of us here when it is hard to be a hero."

In shaping economic policy, as in other aspects of his administration, the new President set out on what to him was a centrist course but to others was a veer to the right. While putting the economy through "slowing pains," as he phrased it, Nixon tried to avoid a full-blown recession with a high rate of joblessness, for he remembered that the final downturn under Eisenhower had cost him the election in 1960. However, Nixon was no less determined to arrest inflation, in part because he believed that by penalizing thrift it sapped the nation's character. And to check rising prices he was prepared to bring about a higher level of unemployment than Johnson had been willing to tolerate.

The President's "game plan," as the anti-inflation program of the country's Number 1 football fan was labeled, proposed to keep government intervention to a minimum. During World War II Nixon had worked for ten months as a small-fry bureaucrat for the Office of Price Administration in a shabby Washington building left over from the first world war, and he had come out of that lonely experience with a deep distaste for the New Dealers and their ways. When it was suggested in 1969 that he clamp a lid on prices, he said, "Controls. Oh my God, no! I was a lawyer for the OPA during the war and I know all about controls. They mean rationing, black markets, inequitable administration. We'll never go for controls." Nor would he sanction more modest approaches. He rejected both an "incomes policy" of federal guideposts on wages and prices and "jawboning" to use the prestige of his office to shame corporations and unions into line, since neither met the fundamental problem of excess demand. Instead, Nixon resorted to two-pronged action— fiscal and monetary. He pruned the federal budget, and he encouraged the Federal Reserve System to act in accordance with the theory of the University of Chicago economist, Milton Friedman, who claimed that prices could be leveled by adjusting the money supply. Convinced that fine tuning would be sufficient to contain inflation, he carried out both activities in a spirit of "gradualism."

Nixon's strategy plunged the country into the recession he had hoped to escape. After the Federal Reserve tightened the money supply in the last half of 1969, interest rates reached their highest peaks in at least a century, and investors staggered under the worst bear market since the Great Depression. The Dow-Jones average, at 985 on December 3, 1968, a month after Nixon's election, tumbled to 631 on May 26, 1970 — the biggest decline in more than three decades. In June 1970 the country saw the worst business failure in its history when the Penn Central Railroad went bankrupt. Real gross national product declined in 1970 for the first time since 1958, and as the recession ate into tax receipts the government began to run an unanticipated deficit. Unemployment, at a low 3.3 percent when Nixon took office, climbed to 6 percent by the end of 1970, and each point sacrificed another 800,000 jobs, including positions in prestige industries such as aerospace.

In spite of the slowdown, prices kept going up. The 5.3 percent rise in 1970 was the most precipitous since the Korean War year of 1951. In a society of highly organized economic units, policies based on the assumption of a free market miscarried. Walter Heller gave the name "Nixonomics" to this unhappy compound of lagging output and soaring prices. "Nixonomics," explained the chairman of the Democratic National Committee, Lawrence O'Brien, "means that all the things that should go up — the stock market, corporate profits, real spendable income, productivity — go down, and all the things that should go down — unemployment, prices, interest rates — go up."

His game plan a bust, Nixon decided to revamp it before the whistle blew for the second half. Especially after Arthur F. Burns took over as chairman of the Federal Reserve Board, the tight money emphasis was scuttled, although some thought Burns should have been even more unrestrained. "Gradualism" and voluntarism having failed, Nixon began "jawboning" the steel industry and took to task the construction unions, thereby alienating hardhats who supported him on the war. Concluding that economic decline was a greater evil than inflation, the President turned cautiously to fiscal policies that would stimulate employment. On January 4, 1971 he told the ABC news correspondent, Howard K. Smith, "I am now a Keynesian." (For such a longtime foe of liberal economic doctrine to take up this heresy was, said Smith, "a little like a Christian crusader saying, 'All things considered, I think Mohammed was right.'") Yet the administration still would not countenance wage-price guideposts, let alone controls, and as late as June 1971, when top-level policy makers held a weekend "summit conference" at the President's retreat in Camp David, Maryland, the anti-control faction prevailed.

Despite the new tactics, Nixon lost ground. Unemployment reached 6.2 percent in May 1971 and hovered at about that point for months thereafter. Prices rose another 4 percent in 1971, only a small improvement on the previous year. To Nixon's distress, the United States ran an acutely adverse trade deficit; in 1971 imports exceeded exports for the first time since 1893. Confidence in the President's program buckled, in Washington and in the nation. When administration experts predicted that the country would soon turn the corner, a union leader responded, "Paul McCracken on the economy is getting to sound more and more like General Westmoreland on Vietnam." The President's new secretary of the treasury, the handsome Texas Democrat John Connally, decided a more aggressive policy was required, and other advisers agreed. In July, shortly after Nixon made the startling announcement that he would visit China, McCracken said, "There may come a time for an economic 'trip to Peking.'" When the President's counselors met again at Camp David in mid-August, the activists carried the day.

On the night of August 15, 1971, a month after he divulged that he would call on Mao, Nixon performed another somersault. He announced he was freezing wages, prices, and rents for ninety days. In addition he asked for tax cuts to stimulate business, slapped a surcharge on most imports, and paved the way for the devaluation of the dollar, which took place in December. All of the President's original game plan—gradualism, resistance to an incomes policy, objection to intruding into the private sector, hostility to controls—had been jettisoned. He even referred to his turnabout as a "new economic plan," terminology resembling that hitherto associated with Leninist Russia. An Office of Emergency Preparedness issued edicts that recalled OPA directives, although its docket included unfamiliar items such as a complaint against a marijuana dealer who kited prices.

In mid-November the emergency freeze gave way to long-term thaw. Phase II aimed to hold annual price rises to 2.5 percent and aggregate wage increases to 5.5 percent, although exceptions were made for special cases like the sensational Oakland pitcher Vida Blue. Critics of the administration protested that the controls were manifestly unfair since neither profits nor dividends were restrained and the worker had to stretch his paycheck to meet items that were not controlled—taxes, credit, and supermarket produce like fruits and vegetables. In March 1972 the AFL-CIO walked out of the Pay Board in protest. Unemployment continued at a high rate, and industrial capacity was one-quarter unused. But Nixon could claim somewhat better results from braking inflationary expectations. In July 1972 the administration reported an encouraging decline in the rate of price rises coupled with the biggest gain in real GNP for any quarter since late 1965. Nixon had still not discovered how to combine stable price levels with full employment, but he had succeeded in reducing the political penalties for his earlier failures and in disclosing himself to be both flexible and forceful.

The "new, new Nixon" confounded some of his persistent critics. He exhibited a skill in foreign affairs that to many was a revelation, and if his performance on domestic matters was less imposing, he showed greater hospitality to novel ideas than had been anticipated. In a curious way his reputation as "Tricky Dick," the low-level politician who had never accomplished much beyond getting Alger Hiss, helped him. "Everybody is saying that Mr. Nixon is doing better than they expected," wrote James Reston, "which proves the success of past failures." As President, this "shy, lonely, much-wounded, ambitious, courageous and deeply patriotic man," in Allen Drury's words, seemed a bigger man than he had before. He gave an impression of self-confidence and composure that had been missing in the tense, scowling Cold Warrior of the 1950's.

Yet some expressed skepticism about the President's serene demeanor, for it was achieved by such an effort at self-control that he almost seemed programmed. "There is an extraordinary lack of affect about Nixon," observed Bruce Mazlish in his "psychohistorical" study of the President. "If Nixon did visit Dr. Arnold Hutschnecker as a 'psychotherapist,' I suspect the going must have been very tough for the doctor. Nixon's opaque quality becomes in itself a subject for investigation; it directs our attention to the time when the young Nixon must have 'switched off' his emotions (or was he born with the tendency?)." The President recognized that he constantly kept himself in check, never let himself out of his sight. "I have a fetish about disciplining myself," he acknowledged.

This self-command helped Nixon dissipate much of the animus against him, but it did not inspire a great deal of affection. "The Presidency makes some men father figures," commented a Washington correspondent. "But not Richard Nixon. He is a brother-in-law figure." When he used expressions like "the lift of a driving dream," as he had during the campaign, he moved out of character, and when he tried to establish easy relationships, he stumbled. The man the country saw on its television screens was rigid, his face jowly, his eyes hooded, his gestures mechanical, his smile wooden. Reclusive, solitary, wary, he walled himself off even from his Cabinet and appeared remote from the concerns of ordinary citizens, especially those who had not made it and never would. To be sure, fewer liberals continued to think of him, as Philip Roth did in *Our Gang*, as

Hiroji Kubota, Magnum, from *Crisis in America*,
published by Ridge Press and Holt, Rinehart and Winston

The President gestures in the mechanical manner that encouraged speculation about whether there was a "real" Nixon. The political scientist James Barber wrote that he was an "active-negative type" with an "unclear and discontinuous self-image" engaged in "continual self-examination and effort to construct a Richard Nixon."

"Trick E. Dixon." "He is no longer viscerally hated," said a Democratic Congressman, but neither was he "viscerally loved." His foes held this against him too. One liberal journalist, Paul Hoffman, complained, "He has re-made himself into someone so bland, so colorless, so devoid of passion that even those who disagree with him most cannot rouse enough emotion to hate him."

People who cherished the Camelot era feared that Nixon would usher in "four years of Lawrence Welk," and from the outset his administration was analyzed for its cultural as well as its political significance. Indeed, to the President's critics the two had a symbiotic relationship. A chief executive who put catsup on his cottage cheese and listened to Mantovani and Kostelanetz records would naturally shape his political appeal to Middle America. As Vice-President Agnew told a banquet audience after the inauguration, "We're all middlebrows here." At the inauguration ceremonies the Reverend Billy Graham offered a prayer, and the evangelist, whom I. F. Stone called Nixon's "smoother Rasputin," led off the White House series of religious services. "It's a measure of the capital's social life under the Nixons," noted a disgruntled reporter, "that the one 'in' invitation is to the White House Sunday prayer meetings."

The President's family brought back memories of the bland 1950's. As First Lady, Pat Nixon exhibited few of the impulses of her predecessors to beautify the national estate or to aid the disadvantaged. Their daughters, Tricia and Julie, seemed to come out of a stylized magazine ad from the age of Eisenhower. In Gore Vidal's *An Evening with Richard Nixon,* "the two daughters are rolled into view; large cutie-pie dolls on wheels." When Julie married the cleancut, boyish David Eisenhower, the former President's grandson, it was inevitable that the ceremonies would be performed by the Reverend Norman Vincent Peale, the representative clerical figure of the 'fifties.

"The marketing managers of Nixon, Inc.," in Richard Whalen's phrase, also derived from the consumer culture of the Eisenhower period. One disenchanted aide, who dismissed the "suburban cronies" on the White House staff as "the Hot Shoppes vote," pointed out that Nixon's press officer had earlier wielded a pole to fend off the hippopotamus on the Jungle Ride at Disneyland. Predominantly good gray technicians, the President's associates well suited a government that aimed less to solve problems than to manage them. The key responsibility for running the domestic policy operation fell to Harry R. Haldeman and John Ehrlichman, two former "advance men." Eagle Scouts, Christian Scientists, total abstainers from alcohol and tobacco, these college roommates were so indistinguishable that they were called the "Rosencrantz and Guildenstern" of the administration. Nixon's original Cabinet, all white, all male, all Republican, "suggests cool competence rather than passion or brilliance," wrote *Time.* "There are no blooded patricians in the lot, just strivers who have acted out the middle-class dream."

Nixon's accession to office signaled a shift in the public mood toward retrenchment and tranquility. After the spring of 1968, riots in black ghettos tapered off. No one fully understood why the long hot summers ended (at least for a time), but black leaders apparently concluded that burning their own neighborhoods was self-destructive and fighting beefed-up police forces foolhardy. In the strife-torn universities, too, the high tide of violence had ebbed. The fall semester of 1970 opened quietly. At Columbia's Low Plaza, political placards had vanished, and Berkeley's Sproul Hall reported all quiet on the Western front. In the spring of 1970 the peace of the Yale campus was shattered by outcries over the trial in New Haven of Black Panthers accused of torture and murder. But that fall a Saturday afternoon political rally drew a small turnout because most of Yale's undergraduates were more interested in cheering their football team on against Dartmouth; Bobby Seale had given way to Boola Boola. Early in 1971 Mel Elfin, Washington Bureau Chief of *Newsweek,* commented:

Today, the sirens in the night no longer wail as urgently as they once did. An uneasy but palpable calm has settled over the cities and the campuses. Voices have been lowered and, if the President has not succeeded in bringing us together, at least things are no longer falling apart. The center has held.

The President played an important part in promoting domestic tranquility. Even some of his liberal opponents found his low-key manner an agreeable relief from LBJ's bombast. In contrast to his Democratic forerunners in the 1960's, he promised neither a New Frontier nor a Great Society, and since little was expected of him there was less possibility of disappointment. Furthermore, the President made one notable contribution to peace in America — winding down the war in Vietnam. He reduced troop levels there, which at their peak had reached 543,000, to 39,000 by September 1, 1972. Reform of selective service greatly lessened anxiety for young men with higher numbers in the lottery. The peace movement approved his decision to terminate production of biological weapons and his role in carrying on the Strategic Arms Limitation Talks (SALT) with Soviet Russia and in negotiating the historic treaty limiting land- and sea-based missiles. Nixon's journeys to Peking and Moscow, a far cry from his former image of Cold Warrior extraordinary, encouraged hopes for a détente.

The campus stillness resulted from such external causes but also from internal reexaminations. Nixon's policies helped to defuse the war issue, and a slowdown in the economy, which sharply diminished employment opportunities, turned energies toward job seeking and professional training. Some students were inactive not because they accepted the system but because they felt exhausted and disillusioned after a period of hyperactivity. But the calm also emanated from second thoughts about many of the assumptions of the 1960's, especially with respect to the efficacy of violence. The

U.S. Troops in South Vietnam, 1965-1972

Source: © 1972 by The New York Times Company. Reprinted by permission.

conduct of radicals encountered increasing criticism from those who had long favored fundamental social change. Supreme Court Justice William O. Douglas, whose tolerance of iconoclasm had brought calls for his impeachment, denounced "radicals of the left" for employing disruptive courtroom tactics that struck "at the very heart of Constitutional government." Students who had sanctioned the resort to violence recoiled when a bomb factory in a Greenwich Village townhouse exploded in March 1970, killing three Weathermen, including one of the leaders of the 1968 Columbia uprising, and when the bombing of the Army Mathematics Research Center at the University of Wisconsin five months later resulted in the death of a graduate student. Even some of the conspirators reconsidered. In the manifesto "New Morning—Changing Weather," Bernadine Dohrn asserted that the Greenwich Village disaster "forever destroyed our belief that armed struggle is the only real revolutionary struggle. It is time for the movement to go out into the air, to . . . risk calling rallies and demonstrations."

After the nerve-jangling dissonance of the 1960's, young Americans in the early 1970's reached back toward the 1950's, which, to the surprise of some who had lived through that decade, were perceived as a time of innocent pleasure. The 'sixties had written off the 'fifties as moribund, but at least a few in the 'seventies thought of the age of Eisenhower as a lively era before it became fashionable to take dope, look cool, and dig groups like the Grateful Dead. "Everybody in the sixties was into a death trip," said one girl. In the spring of 1971 a wave of nostalgia for the 1950's swept the campuses. Students packed auditoriums to join Buffalo Bob in singing "It's Howdy Doody Time," watched kinescopes of "Hopalong Cassidy" and "Sergeant Preston of the Yukon," and staged "sock hops" at which greased-haired young men in pegged pants danced with pony-tailed coeds to "golden oldies" like "Teen Angel" and "Sealed with a Kiss." Nostalgia often fused with romanticism. Acid rock made way for the sweet sounds of James Taylor and Neil Young, and groups like Creedence Clearwater Revival identified with the pristine countryside. In a return to the never-never land of Sigmund Romberg, the White House even dressed its police force in Graustarkian regalia. Whereas the romantics of the counter culture wanted to refashion the world, romanticism in the 1970's implied a sentimental attachment to the past and a deliberate rejection of the politicized adolescence of the 'sixties.

The *Mein Kampf* of the new romanticism was Erich Segal's teary novella, *Love Story,* which by the late spring of 1971 had sold 450,000 hardback and 9 million paperback copies, and as a motion picture had already grossed more than any production since *Gone with the Wind.* In campus bookstores it climbed past *The Greening of America* to take over the Number 2 spot on the best seller list; Number 1 was David Reuben's *Everything You Always Wanted to Know About Sex (But Were Afraid to Ask).* To the true believers of the counter culture, the success of *Love Story* heralded the arrival of Thermidor, and they responded by abusing Segal as "the Lawrence Welk of literature" and a "venal reactionary" who turned out "garbage." The film, grumbled a reviewer, was an "exploitation movie, cashing in on crying the way other movies cash in on sex." To Segal's detractors, *Love Story* not only raised questions of aesthetic sensibility but was a political event. "Segal's not the point," one of his critics explained. "It's what he stands for. He stands for a return to Eisenhower morality, commercialized emotion, political insensitivity, the whole Middle America schmeer." Segal, under such heavy fire that he was counseled to take a leave of absence from his teaching position at Yale, said, "God, it's crazy! If I were a homosexual or wanted by the FBI, the same people who attack me would protect me. They're killing me because I'm straight."

In this circumambience of nostalgia and romanticism, the counter culture lost much of its exuberance. Campus bookstores found themselves overstocked with volumes by Marcuse and Jerry Rubin. Bob Dylan, a married man with children, accepted an honorary degree from Princeton and aged visibly on his thirtieth birthday. At thirty-five, Abbie Hoffman got a haircut. Hippie society had actually come to grief before the Nixon era. Haight-Ashbury began to disintegrate when "speed" (methedrine) took over in 1967, the same year that Linda Rea Fitzpatrick, a runaway from a suburban Connecticut home, was raped and murdered in the East Village. In both Hashbury and Manhattan, there were too many scary trips, too many cases of hepatitis, too many foul-ups in communal living. Some in the counter culture blamed the collapse on a repressive society, but others accepted the onus. *Easy Rider* concluded: "We blew it."

Experimentation in consciousness expansion had become a bad scene. More than a few grammar school pupils were taking barbiturates, and numbers of highschoolers were mainlining. "With the same openness that some students hurl Frisbees and do homework on the major lawn of the City College campus," reported *The New York Times*, "others congregate there to buy and use heroin." London worried about its enormous drug problem, but there were only about three thousand known addicts in all of Great Britain, compared to one hundred thousand in New York City alone, concentrated in the Harlem slums but spreading to more prosperous sections. To finance their habit, drug users resorted to muggings, which became a rising threat even in college dorms. The State University of New York at Buffalo was compelled to close down the recreation area of the student union, a center of drug traffic. Communities were horrified by the mounting casualty lists of teenagers who had "OD'd," and the rock world was shaken by the deaths from narcotics of Janis Joplin and Jimi Hendrix, both at the age of 27.

Only four months after the celebration of the Age of Aquarius at Woodstock in August 1969, the world of rock festivals turned sour. At the Altamont Speedway near San Francisco, where three hundred thousand were drawn to a free concert by Mick Jagger and the Rolling Stones, hundreds required treatment for bad trips, including one stoned youth who injured himself by jumping off a freeway overpass. Hired to keep order (for $500 in beer), the Hell's Angels went amok; they struck people with weighted pool cues and, to the horror of onlookers, stabbed and stomped to death a gun-wielding black eighteen-year-old from Berkeley, one of four deaths that day. Despite the lesson of Altamont, Louisiana's "Celebration of Life," which in July 1971 endeavored to offer "a living example of an alternative life style," employed as security guards members of New Orleans motorcycle gangs, who chain-whipped festival goers. That same month, just as Dionne Warwick had concluded singing "What the World Needs Now Is Love, Sweet Love," rock fans, many of them high on drugs, brought the Newport Jazz Festival to a halt by a four-hour rampage that resulted in three hundred being treated at a hospital. Within an astonishingly short period, the exhilaration of the rock culture had been subdued—Joplin, Hendrix, Jim Morrison gone, the Beatles splintered. In New York in the spring of 1971, Fillmore East and the Electric Circus closed down, and, bitter irony, in San Francisco Fillmore West was sold to the consumer culture anaconda, Howard Johnson's.

To the dismay of the Woodstock Nation, the consumer culture prevailed, often by co-opting or absorbing its opponents. General Motors, manufacturers of the Olds, responded to the generation gap by advertising its cars as "Youngmobiles," and soft drink vendors announced that the young were part of "the Pepsi generation." "Every time I turn on the television I see movie stars with long hair—Peter Fonda, Dennis Hopper," said Abbie Hoffman. "The youth cult has been taken over by Warner Brothers." The music of the 1960's found its way into singing commercials when Opel promised to "light your fire," and, with consummate gall, Amoco gasoline used folk rhythms to claim that its product advanced the cause of ecology. Women's lib also served the purposes of the consumer culture. Department stores hired female Santas (as well as black ones), and by advancing the slogan, "You've come a long way, baby, to get where you've got to today," Virginia Slims sold billions of cigarettes. Even the religiosity of the "Jesus freaks" proved marketable. Tin Pan Alley hailed "Jesus Christ Superstar," and a radio blurb announced: "Hi kids, it's me, Jesus. Look what I'm wearing on my wrist. It's a wristwatch with a five-color picture of me on the dial and hands attached to a crimson heart."

Nor had the counter culture persuaded most Americans to abandon traditional values. A University of Michigan psychologist pointed out that most of the younger generation of the 1970's had not experienced directly the "youth rebellion" of the previous decade. "The majority have not gone to college, have not smoked pot, have not demonstrated against the war, and probably still stick to the main principles of the old morality," he noted. Despite the "sexual revolu-

Photographs like this one (of Nixon and Chou En-lai eating with chopsticks in Shanghai in February 1972) had an impact on the United States. The President's visit encouraged chopstick-wielding in Chinese restaurants in America and led to a fad of $130 "people's suits" so that Fifth Avenue dowagers could look like Chinese peasants.

tion" of the 1960's, half of the country's newlyweds in the early 'seventies had not engaged in premarital relations, and for all the interest in alternatives to monogamy, marriage continued to be a thriving institution. A four-year study of suburban adolescents by a team of Chicago psychiatrists "found more of a bridge than a gap between the generations," a 1969 summary reported. "The typical American boy still seems to have more in common with Penrod than with Holden Caulfield or Alexander Portnoy." In 1970, the people of Muncie, Indiana (the "Middletown" dissected by the sociologists Robert and Helen Lynd), had not wavered in their belief in "the Calvinist notion of the virtue of work," a writer stated, and a sociologist concluded that the community's credo was "the importance of work, of enterprise, of upward mobility, of material rewards."

In the summer of Nixon's first term came a climactic event that thrilled Americans who retained their faith in such qualities and that captivated much of the world. On July 16, 1969, Apollo 11 blasted off for the moon. Four days later Neil A. Armstrong and Colonel Edwin E. Aldrin, Jr., set their lunar module down on the Sea of Tranquility while Lieutenant Colonel Michael Collins maneuvered the command vessel. "The Eagle has landed," Armstrong told Mission Control Center in Houston, a report that, as one writer commented, "sounded like a message in a Resistance broadcast from London." At 10:56 P.M. EDT, Sunday, July 20, 1969, Neil Armstrong became the first earthling to set foot on the moon. "That's one small step for [a] man, one giant leap for mankind," he said. "Buzz" Aldrin soon joined him in gathering moon rocks and other scientific data, and the two frolicked about like schoolboys let out of class. Together they unveiled a plaque, signed by the Apollo 11 crew and President Nixon, that proclaimed: "HERE MEN FROM THE PLANET EARTH FIRST SET FOOT UPON THE MOON JULY 1969, A.D. WE CAME IN PEACE FOR ALL MANKIND." A few minutes later, the White House put a telephone call through to the moon, and as the world's television screens showed Nixon's visage with those of the two astronauts on the moon's surface, the President said, "For one priceless moment in the whole history of man, all the people on this earth are truly one — one in their pride in what you have done and in our prayers that you will return safely to earth."

Not everyone joined in the applause for the great odyssey. The Nobel laureate Harold Urey asserted that the endeavor was not a scientific undertaking but pyramid-building. Critics pointed out that the astronauts were returning to an earth plagued by festering social ills, and argued that the vast sums Apollo 11 cost would have been better spent in solving terrestrial problems. Some doubted that twentieth-century civilization ought to be exported to other parts of the universe. "If there are people up there," said one teenage girl, "I hope they can stand us." Still others saw the lunar landing not as a triumph for "all mankind" but as a delayed consequence of the cold war, beginning with President Kennedy's resolve to outrace the Russians and ending with the flagstaff of the Stars and Stripes planted on the resistant surface of the moon.

Even the fantastic achievement of televising live color pictures of the moon walk to one billion viewers 240,000 miles away found nay-

Tranquility Base, the Moon. During the Apollo 11 mission, Neil Armstrong snapped this shot of his fellow astronaut, Buzz Aldrin, alongside the solar wind instrument before the lunar module as they walked on the surface of the moon. The American flag leaves no doubt about which nation was winning this phase of the space race.

sayers. Admirers marveled both at the advanced technology and at the openness of a society that was willing to permit the world to witness an experiment in which the possibility of tragic failure was highly conceivable. But the telecast, it was said, added to the public relations nature of the proceedings. In the *Saturday Review,* Robert Lewis Shayon wrote:

Wherever explorers go in the future accompanied by television cameras, they will be actors, making their nebulous exits and entrances for the benefit of multi-planetary audiences. Nowhere will there ever again be pure events (if ever there were); everything hereafter will be stage-managed for cosmic Nielsens, in the interest of national or universal establishments.

Many, perhaps most, in Nixon's America had few such doubts, for the voyage to the moon offered reassurance that the institutions and the beliefs the counter culture had mocked were essential to worthy achievements. Apollo 11, said Eric Hoffer, marked the "triumph of the squares." Although the leader of the expedition bore the same surname as the hero of the 1930's radio serial, "Jack Armstrong, All-American Boy," he emphasized that he was not an adventurer but an organization man. "I think if historians are fair, they won't see this flight like Lindbergh's," Armstrong commented. "They'll recognize that the landing is only one small part of a large program." *Time* concluded:

The astronauts themselves were paragons of Middle American aspiration. Redolent of charcoal cookouts, their vocabularies an engaging mix of space jargon and "gee whiz," the space explorers gave back to Middle America a victory of its own values. It was little noted, except in Middle America where such things still matter, that among Neil Armstrong's extraterrestrial baggage was a special badge of his college fraternity, Phi Delta Theta.

For Nixon, the successful moon expedition provided otherworldly assistance to his strategy of offering himself as the exponent of middle-class ideals. He had shared in the glory through his transspatial phone call, and when the returning astronauts were plucked out of the Pacific and set down aboard the *Hornet,* Richard Nixon was on the deck of the carrier waiting to greet them. Even though he had contributed nothing to the exploit, the trip to the moon made more credible his claims for a stable social order that rewarded men of energy and perseverance. Like the astronauts, he would guide the ship of state through the perils of a dangerous universe to a safe destination on a sea of tranquility.

However, if Nixon's emphases helped turn America away from violence, political extremism, and the counter culture, much of the spirit of the 1960's persisted, at least in attenuated forms. Even Neil Armstrong indulged in hippie lingo; his move into lunar orbit "was like perfect." George Wallace sported sideburns, and a week after J. Edgar Hoover was buried, the acting director of the FBI announced that his agents could grow beards and wear colored shirts and that he would try to recruit women, blacks, and Indians. Most important, the country came to accept a level of violence that hitherto would have seemed intolerable. Authorities described as "peaceful" an academic year in which institutions such as Kansas University were rocked by explosions and others like Rutgers were nearly paralyzed by false bomb threats.

Not even crime could be relied upon to maintain the pristine character of the American way of life. Murder, arson, banditry, once the domain of a reporter on the police beat, moved into the political and cultural commentary. When mass slayings were uncovered near Yuba City, California, a nationally syndicated columnist lost little time in comparing them to the Mylai massacre in Vietnam. In another California mass murder, the killer left a note identifying himself with Tarot, ecology, and radical politics. A message signed "Knight of Wands, Knight of Cups, Knight of Pentacles, Knight of Swords" warned: "Today World War 3 will begin as brought to you by the People of the Free Universe. From this day forward anyone and/or company of persons who misuses the natural environment or destroys same will suffer the penalty of death." Whereas a bank holdup by a Jesse James or a John Dillinger had been triggered by a straightforward desire for loot, similar heists in contemporary America were sometimes motivated by eagerness to advance the Revolution. The savage ritual murder of the actress Sharon Tate and her jet set companions by a band of young people associated with the hippie pads of Hashbury, desert communes, drugs, rock, sex, hints of race war, and hatred of sybaritic society suggested the degree to which crime had become connected with a complex cultural politics, even if a Weatherman leader had not confirmed the relationship by applauding the deed. It was symptomatic that San Quentin's death row housed simultaneously Charles Manson and Sirhan Sirhan.

Nixon and his circle tended to exploit the more conservative aspects of cultural politics. The administration's policies, predominantly centrist and temperate, gravitated in a more rightward direction to take advantage of certain characteristics of the middle of the electorate. Since the ranks of Middle America were swelled by unionists and ethnic groups who had benefited from the New Deal, Nixon sometimes adapted by offering social reforms that approximated the orientation of the Democrats rather than the position of Barry Goldwater. Yet the middle range of the voting public included not a few who were receptive to the argument that the Democrats were friends of the blacks but not of the white blue collar worker, of Chicanos but not of Polish-Americans, were indulgent toward campus violence, soft on crime, profligate with welfare funds, and indifferent to the expansion of communism overseas. To win voters like those in Minneapolis who elected a police detective as their mayor, the Republicans frequently concentrated not on moving toward the center with regard to social issues but on stressing the themes of law and order and national honor. Democrats like Adlai E. Stevenson III might respond by wearing American flags in their lapels, but Republicans knew that when the Archie Bunkers drove to work their cars often bore bumper stickers reading "SPIRO IS MY HERO."

While Nixon played the part of the Grand Unifier who counseled a lowering of voices, his Vice-President took on the rowdy role of "the Great Polarizer." In the spring of 1970 he declared, "I intend to be heard above the din even if it means raising my voice." No one doubted him after his performance of the preceding year. To a commencement audience at Ohio State in June 1969 he said:

A society which comes to fear its children is effete. A sniveling, hand-wringing power structure deserves the violent rebellion it encourages. If my generation doesn't stop cringing, yours will inherit a lawless society where emotion and muscle displace reason.

That fall, at a time when protests against the Vietnam war were being organized in Washington, he railed against the "spirit of national masochism . . . encouraged by an effete corps of impudent snobs who characterize themselves as intellectuals," and he denounced political leaders who promoted peace demonstrations as "ideological eunuchs." In Las Vegas he leveled his sights at *Easy Rider* and the Jefferson Airplane. But he created the greatest uproar when he attacked network television commentators as "a tiny and closed fraternity of privileged men" who reflected the biases of the Eastern seaboard. "Gresham's Law seems to be operating in the network news," he observed. "Bad news drives out good news. . . . One minute of Eldridge Cleaver is worth ten minutes of Roy Wilkins."

Agnew's invective nettled liberals, delighted the Old Guard, and disconcerted Republican moderates. Liberals professed to regard him as a dim-witted bumbler and joked about the appearance of the Vice-President's face on Mickey Mouse wristwatches. They belittled his addiction to pretentious alliteration—"pusillanimous pussyfooting," "vicars of vacillation," "nattering nabobs of negativism"—and noted that he had been a faithful reader of the "Increase Your Word Power" section of *Reader's Digest*. But Agnew was no dunce. He had an instinctive touch for the spot that would make his critics cry with rage, and he revealed an unexpected talent for self-mockery. ("I told the President I was appearing here, and he said I could only give my name, rank and serial number." Or: "The President has just ordered that I be issued my own plane. It's Air Force Thirteen . . . and it's a glider.") Agnew was invaluable for attracting southerners; Senator Strom Thurmond of South Carolina praised him as "next to John C. Calhoun, the greatest Vice President in the history of America." Even so, some GOP leaders were troubled by Agnew's hardshell conservatism and his divisive style and doubted that their party would benefit from his activities in the long run. Republicans should not try to "polarize anything," confided one party chieftain. "We want to broaden the base of the party, not narrow it." Still, Agnew's sharp-tongued sallies threw Democrats on the defensive and had the considerable advantage of permitting Nixon, who had once served a similar purpose for Eisenhower, to seem by contrast a dignified, self-composed statesman.

Occasionally, however, Nixon joined Agnew in focusing political debate on the newer cultural questions of disparate life styles. Even the nurture of children became politicized. Nixon scoffed at the "Spock-marked" generation, and Agnew fulminated against the progeny of "affluent, permissive, upper-middle class parents who learned their Dr. Spock and threw discipline out the windows." He told guests at a Fort Lauderdale fund-raising dinner:

They are the children dropped off by their parents at Sunday school to hear the modern gospel from a "progressive" preacher more interested in fighting pollution than fighting evil—one of those pleasant clergymen who lifts his weekly sermons out of old newsletters from a National Council of Churches that has cast morality and theology aside as "not relevant" and set as its goal on earth the recognition of Red China and the preservation of the Florida alligator. Today, by the thousands—without a cultural heritage, without a set of spiritual values, and with a moral code summed up in that idealistic injunction "Do your own thing," Junior—his pot and Portnoy secreted in his knapsack—arrives at college and finds there a smiling and benign faculty even less demanding than his parents.

The administration's views found their way into both political campaigns and public policy. In 1970 the Vice-President reminded his admirers that he had been "travelling the length of this land . . . to help elect men to public office who will lean hard against the trend toward permissiveness." Agnew complained, "The decree that infants should be fed on demand and not on schedule has been elevated to dogma up to age 30." When the President subsequently vetoed a bill for a national system of day care centers, he announced that he was against committing "the vast moral authority of the national government to the side of communal approaches to child-rearing over against the family-centered approach."

The Nixon forces exploited the political potentialities of the sexual revolution too. In 1967 Congress had voted funds to pay a presidential commission to read dirty books and decide what ought to be done about them. When in 1970 the commission issued its report opposing punitive action, Nixon denounced the conclusions as "morally bankrupt" and Agnew assured campaign audiences, "As long as Richard Nixon is President, Main Street is not going to turn into Smut Alley." The following year the President, in placing the question of abortion on military bases under state jurisdiction, seized the occasion to say that he could not square "abortion on demand" with his "personal belief in the sanctity of human life—including the life of the yet unborn." After Republican Senator Charles E. Goodell broke with the Nixon administration over its Vietnam policies, the Vice-President castigated him not as a turncoat but as the "Christine Jorgensen of the Republican party," an allusion to the male nurse whose sex had been transformed by an operation. (Similarly, at Wallace rallies the Alabama governor would reply to long-haired hecklers by feigning confusion as to their sex.) Agnew managed to link the cultural upheaval to political persuasion by charging that the erosion of decency had "been abetted by a political hedonism that permeates the philosophy of the radical liberals." Indeed, he said, "a paralyzing permissive philosophy pervades every policy they espouse."

The President's social and economic policies also often bore a conservative stamp. In appealing to groups in the center who wanted stability, he by-passed those who asserted that the urban crisis required more rapid change. He addressed himself hardly at all to the deterioration of the black ghetto. Nixon's Cabinet overweighted the business interest—it included a Chicago banker, an auto manufacturer, and three men who had profited from construction—and spokesmen for other elements had few friends in court. The leader of the liberal wing of the administration, HEW Secretary Robert Finch, lost out when the President bowed to pressure from the American Medical Association on a crucial appointment; and after Hickel criticized the administration for hostility to the young, Nixon fired him. The President grasped that Disraeli had sponsored social reforms, but he knew even better that the Prime Minister had been a Tory. He vetoed health, education, and welfare legislation, a measure to expand public works, and appropriations for hospital construction. Nor did he make much headway on those proposals he did favor. Nixon seemed to lose interest in projects once he had announced them, and he could never work up the enthusiasm for the "New American Revolution" that he did for the SST. Congress procrastinated on programs like the Family Assistance Plan in part because of the President's preoccupation with foreign policy and near indifference to domestic concerns.

Nixon's conduct of foreign affairs frequently proved inflammatory. Although his phased withdrawal of troops from Vietnam helped to bank the fires of dissent, he earned the animosity of the peace forces by making Lyndon Johnson's war his own, especially after he called Nguyen Van Thieu one of the world's five greatest statesmen. Four years after he claimed that he had a plan for ending the conflict, the fighting was still going on, at a cost in Nixon's first three years of 15,000 additional American lives. Furthermore, he periodically undertook new military initiatives—the Cambodian invasion in 1970, the venture in Laos in 1971, the saturation bombing of North Vietnam in 1972—that excited angry protests.

As early as the fall of Nixon's first year, discontent with his Southeast Asian policies exploded into massive demonstrations. A "moratorium" on October 15, 1969, attracted what was said to be the biggest turnout in the nation's history, with perhaps a million participants across the country, and on November 15 a mobilization in Washington, D.C., drew hundreds of thousands in a witness against the war. One homemade placard read, "all too long i dwelt with those who hate peace," and another sign said simply, "MY FRIEND JIMMY SILVERSTEIN IS DEAD: AUG. 16, 1969 VIETNAM WAR." But the antiwar forces could not maintain the momentum of that autumn. By the beginning of 1970, Nixon's combination of rebuffs to their endeavors and continuing troop withdrawals appeared to have succeeded in deflating his opposition. In mid-April, the Vietnam Moratorium Committee closed its Washington office with the announcement that the age of the large-scale peace rally was at an end.

Less than two weeks later, Nixon destroyed this uneasy equilibrium. On April 29, 1970, United States troops crossed the border of Cambodia. To millions of war-weary Americans, the news that a conflict they thought nearly over had been expanded was shocking enough. But the President's justification in a televised address on April 30 made the situation far worse. In language more appropriate to Armageddon, he asserted:

We will not be humiliated. We will not be defeated. . . . If when the chips are down, the world's most powerful nation . . . acts like a pitiful, helpless giant, the forces of totalitarianism and anarchy will threaten free nations and free institutions throughout the world.

At a time when he was sending young men to their death, he asked pity for his own plight. "I would rather be a one-term president and do what I believe was right than to be a two-term president at the cost of seeing America become a second-rate power," he declared. Before the week was out, infuriated students were on a rampage — from campuses in the big coastal cities to those in small Midwestern towns like Kent, Ohio.

On the night after Nixon's speech, students at Kent State University hurled bottles at police cars and smashed store windows, and on the following night they firebombed the ROTC building. Governor James Rhodes responded by imposing martial law and dispatching units of the national guard to Kent. On Monday, May 4, violence renewed. Students threw rocks and other projectiles at the guardsmen, who replied with barrages of gas. Then suddenly, without warning or any direct provocation, guardsmen opened fire with their M-1 rifles. Four students fell dead; eleven were wounded, one paralyzed by a bullet in his spine. None of the four was a radical: one of the two young men slain ranked second in his ROTC class; the two girls killed were walking to class. A report by the President's Commission on Campus Unrest subsequently condemned the casual issuance of live ammunition to guardsmen and denounced the "indiscriminate firing" as "unnecessary, unwarranted and inexcusable." But it also added, "Those who wreaked havoc on the town of Kent, those who burned the ROTC building, those who attacked and stoned National Guardsmen and all those who urged them on

The avuncular evening newsman Walter Cronkite reports to millions of Americans on yet another shattering development. The map in the background indicates that the story comes from Kent, Ohio, where on May 4, 1970, four college students were slain.

and applauded their deeds share the responsibility for the deaths and injuries of May 4.''

Reports of the massacre at Kent State reached campuses already overheated by Nixon's speech on Cambodia and sent temperatures to the boiling point. Resentment was heightened by word from Mississippi that on May 15 highway patrolmen killed two and wounded eleven black students at Jackson State College. During May the lid blew off on campuses in every part of the nation, including many that had been unscathed in 1968. Students sacked the treasurer's office at the University of South Carolina, scores were injured in riots at the University of Maryland, a half-million-dollar fire blazed at Colorado State, and in a melee at the University of New Mexico three students were stabbed. In what President William J. McGill of Columbia called "the most disastrous month of May in the history of American higher education," hundreds of colleges and universities went on strike for a day or shut down for the rest of the semester.

Faculty members, administrators, and unaffiliated liberals and radicals took part in many demonstrations, and numbers of antiwar protesters once more congregated in Washington. "The country is virtually on the edge of a spiritual—and perhaps even a physical—breakdown," asserted Mayor John Lindsay of New York. The Nixon administration, he said, had so bisected the nation that "for the first time in a century, we are not sure there is a future for America."

Shaken by the realization that he had badly miscalculated, Nixon sought to make amends. He agreed to talk to six Kent State students who had come to Washington, and he conferred with the presidents of eight universities. But he remained disturbed. Before dawn on May 9, unable to sleep, he got out of bed, dressed, and, accompanied only by his valet and Secret Service men, left the White House in a limousine. At 5 A.M., student demonstrators at the Lincoln Memorial were startled to find themselves face-to-face with the President of the United States. "I know you think we are a bunch of sons-of-bitches," he said, but he hoped they would recognize that he and his advisers also wanted peace. In a rambling monologue he urged them to see the world while they were young; among the places he suggested they might visit was Indochina. His desire to communicate, undoubtedly deeply felt, got nowhere because Nixon had come to talk but not to listen and because he did not know how to reach this new generation. When he chatted with students who had come three thousand miles from California to show their concern about the war, he asked them how they liked surfing; and when he spoke to undergraduates from Syracuse, shut down by a strike against his policies, he wanted to know whether the Big Orange would be able to field a powerful football team. Still, his extraordinary caper suggested the extent of his concern and his readiness to be conciliatory.

The President's propitiatory mood reflected awareness that rumblings about his aloofness were rife within his administration as well as on the campuses. A number of highly ranked Republicans had doubted for some time the wisdom of Nixon's calculated display of disdain toward those who advocated a termination of the war. In November 1969, when hundreds of thousands had gathered in Washington for the peace mobilization, the White House had let it be known that the President was preoccupied with the telecast of the Ohio State–Purdue game. Cabinet officers resented the "Berlin Wall" that "the Germans," Ehrlichman and Haldeman, put between them and the chief executive. Both sets of grievances came together in a well-publicized letter Wally Hickel sent to Nixon. The President, his secretary of the interior recommended, ought to make himself more accessible to youth and to members of his Cabinet, while Agnew's abrasive alliteration should be heard less. Nixon was nettled by Hickel's epistle, but for a time he seemed responsive. He asked G. Alexander Heard, the president of Vanderbilt University, to serve as liaison with the universities and appointed a nine-member commission to study campus violence.

Nixon's inclination to placate his critics proved short-lived, in no small part because many Americans applauded his Cambodian policy and thought the Kent State undergraduates had "got what they were asking for." On May 8, when antiwar students from New York City colleges gathered in the financial district, wrench-wielding, helmeted construction workers set upon the long-haired protesters and bludgeoned them while the police looked on. Shouting "All the way, U.S.A.," they marched on City Hall and raised the flag Mayor Lindsay had ordered lowered to half-staff in mourning for the Kent victims.

Bolstered by groups like the hardhats, Nixon resumed a more aggressive stance in the fall 1970 campaign, and periodically thereafter he took steps that provoked further ill feeling. In April 1971, demonstrators were back in Washington, this time because of the invasion of Laos in the first part of the year. On that occasion hundreds of Vietnam veterans, some on crutches, flung away their Purple Hearts, Silver Stars, and campaign ribbons. That month, too, Nixon created bitterness by intervening in the case of First Lieutenant William L. Calley, Jr., convicted of the premeditated murder of unarmed South Vietnamese civilians at the hamlet of Mylai but regarded as a martyr by the Right, especially in the South. This series of actions threatened to impair Nixon's centrist strategy since much of the country wanted to withdraw from Southeast Asia and was sickened by Calley's deed. In fact, Nixon came out of these episodes stronger than before. When in the spring of 1972 he ordered Haiphong harbor mined, there were new outbursts of campus violence but only a small number of antiwar demonstrators turned up in Washington. His willful meddling in the Calley case earned political dividends, for it promoted the Southern strategy devised by John Mitchell, Nixon's 1968 campaign manager and strong man of his administration.

Brusque, self-confident, domineering, Mitchell had been called "El Supremo" by younger Republican workers during the campaign, and in the Nixon government he became top counselor on a

In May 1970 construction workers demonstrate in New York City to show their support of the Nixon administration's policies in Vietnam. The march was organized by the president of the Building and Construction Trades Council, Peter J. Brennan, who in November 1972 was named Secretary of Labor.

wide range of policy questions. A British journalist commented that he "looked like Judge Jeffreys, the hanging judge of the Bloody Assizes, and in his case looks were not altogether misleading." As Nixon's attorney general he alarmed liberals by claiming the right to wiretap without court order and advocating preventive detention for recalcitrant criminal suspects. In 1970 Congress acceded to Mitchell's request to authorize "no-knock" searches and mandatory prison sentences. He initiated a number of prosecutions that critics charged, not always persuasively, were repressive in intent—against "the Chicago Eight" for the 1968 disruptions; against the anti-war priest, Philip Berrigan, and others for allegedly hatching a plot to kidnap Henry Kissinger; and against Daniel Ellsberg, accused of filching the Pentagon papers. An arch-conservative Wall Street lawyer, Mitchell was naturally inclined to push the administration toward the right. But he was also convinced that in such an orientation lay Nixon's best prospects for reelection. Hence he embarked on a Southern strategy to woo Wallace's following below the Mason-Dixon line and those in the North troubled by the breakdown of law and order and especially by black militancy.

One of Mitchell's young aides, Kevin Phillips, spelled out the Administration's battle plan, perhaps indiscreetly, in *The Emerging Republican Majority*. Phillips reasoned that Nixon could win reelection by ignoring those few regions still attracted to liberalism — the Northeast, Minnesota, the Pacific Northwest — and forgetting about black and Latin voters. The Republicans could become the new majority party if they appealed to conservative sentiments in the suburbs, among Catholic ethnic workingmen, and in the increasingly Republican South. The richest rewards would be found in "the Sunbelt," ranging from Nixon's Florida residence in Key Biscayne across the Southwest to his San Clemente compound on the shores of the Pacific.

Mitchell's Southern strategy and Nixon's conservative bent determined their disposition toward the Supreme Court. By promising to put law-and-order judges on the bench, the President appealed to those Wallace enthusiasts who shared his view that *Miranda* and other decisions had "tipped the balance against the peace forces in this country, and strengthened the criminal forces." He soon had four posts to fill, the most open to any first-term president since Harding. President Johnson had nominated Abe Fortas to succeed Earl Warren as Chief Justice, but the attempt miscarried when Fortas' association with a fraudulent stock operator was revealed. (Fortas subsequently resigned from the Court.) Nixon thus gained the opportunity to designate his own choice for Chief Justice, a "strict constructionist." Given the President's determination to reverse the prevailing philosophy of the Court, his selection of Warren Earl Burger to replace Earl Warren was, as Bruce Mazlish suggested, a striking, if perhaps unconscious, play on words. A Minnesotan with long judicial experience, Judge Burger easily won Senate approval.

However, in his effort to put someone in the seat vacated by Fortas, Nixon came to grief, largely because of his relentless pursuit of the

Southern strategy. To repay his campaign obligation to the diehard Republican Senator from South Carolina, Strom Thurmond, Nixon named a conservative South Carolinian, Judge Clement F. Haynsworth, Jr. Labor and civil rights groups mobilized opposition to Haynsworth, and charges of conflict-of-interest improprieties led seventeen Republicans, including the minority leader and assistant minority leader, to join in denying confirmation. On November 21, 1969, the Senate rejected Haynsworth, 55 to 45. He was the first nominee to the Supreme Court to suffer this fate since John J. Parker in 1930, who, oddly, had once been Haynsworth's mentor on the same federal circuit.

The maladroit Mitchell then turned up the name of G. Harrold Carswell of Tallahassee, another Court of Appeals judge from the Deep South. It seemed inconceivable that the President could be humiliated by a second turndown, but the Senate became convinced that Carswell was third-rate. Law school professors, including nine of fifteen at the University of Florida in Carswell's home state, insisted that he was not nearly distinguished enough for a seat once held by Louis Brandeis and Felix Frankfurter. This did not faze the Old Guard Republican Senator from Nebraska, Roman Hruska, who said of Carswell: "Even if he were mediocre, there are lots of mediocre judges and people and lawyers. They are entitled to a little representation, aren't they?" The majority of the Senate, including thirteen Republicans, did not think so, and on April 8, 1970, the nomination failed. Not since Grover Cleveland had a President been rebuffed twice in a row, and Nixon and Mitchell were furious. "I understand the bitter feeling of millions of Americans who live in the South," Nixon declared. "They have my assurance that the day will come when judges like Carswell and Haynsworth can and will sit on the High Court." After his angry outburst against the Senate, Nixon repaired some of the damage he had inflicted upon himself by appointing a respected Northern conservative, Judge Harry Blackmun. So closely did Blackmun's views dovetail with those of his longtime friend, Burger, that he and the Chief Justice were soon being called "the Minnesota Twins."

Neither Nixon nor Mitchell, who professed such concern about the integrity of the Supreme Court, had yet finished showing their contempt for it. Special care was demanded to replace the Court's two most esteemed members, Hugo Black and John Harlan. But the President and the attorney general decided once more on two lackluster nominees, one a California woman with a reputation for toughness, the other a Little Rock attorney known for his role in litigation against desegregation. The American Bar Association's judiciary committee, which had put its stamp of approval on both Haynsworth and Carswell, found neither of the new candidates to be qualified. Recognizing that he faced certain defeat if he persisted with these nominations, Nixon gave up and named instead Lewis F. Powell, Jr., of Virginia, the highly regarded former president of the ABA, and Assistant Attorney General William H. Rehnquist, a Goldwater Republican from Arizona. (Rehnquist had earlier discounted his chances: "I'm not from the South, I'm not a woman, and I'm not mediocre.") In the end, the President wound up with four relatively conservative judges who would shape jurisprudence for many years to come; and, by trying and failing to appoint a Deep South justice, he won the gratitude of loyalists of the Lost Cause.

The Southern strategy also affected Nixon's performance on racial issues, which illuminated the pitfalls in a policy of centrism. "There are those who want instant integration and those who want segregation forever," he said. "I believe that we need to have a middle course between those two extremes." This sounded like a sensible way to strike a happy medium, but in practice it frequently meant that Negroes who had been waiting so long for recognition of their constitutional rights were expected to wait still longer or be viewed as "extreme." Critics feared that blacks would pay the penalty for the administration's desire for quiescence when it was revealed that the President's adviser, Pat Moynihan, had recommended an attitude of "benign neglect" toward the issue of race. Often, too, Nixon's interest in knitting the nation together took shape in obsequiousness toward the mores of the white South.

Mitchell's Southern strategy jolted civil rights advocates when in June 1969 the Department of Justice, in sharp contrast to its position in the Kennedy-Johnson era, came out against extension of the Voting Rights Act of 1965. In the name of sectional equity, the department proposed to eliminate the sanctions that, by placing election procedures in much of the South under federal supervision, had enfranchised nearly a million blacks. Instead it would substitute a uniform national statute. The provisions of Mitchell's bill, protested the Ohio Republican Congressman William McCulloch, "sweep broadly into those areas where the need is least and retreat from those areas where the need is greatest. . . . The Administration creates a remedy for which there is no wrong and leaves grievous wrongs without adequate remedy. I ask you, what kind of civil rights bill is that?" The House went along with Mitchell, but when the Senate balked, the 1965 law was reenacted in essentially its original form.

To the dismay of integrationists, Mitchell's attitude prevailed throughout the government. Talk of encouraging "black capitalism" did not advance much beyond the rhetorical stage. The "Philadelphia Plan" to require construction unions on federal projects to admit blacks was better conceived, but had modest results. So half-hearted was enforcement of civil rights legislation that the United States Civil Rights Commission reprimanded the administration three times in one year. If Mitchell's experience as bond salesman had engendered any empathy for the lot of urban blacks, he never showed it. But he was able to impress his viewpoint even on HEW, although Secretary Robert Finch was regarded as the most liberal figure in the President's circle. Within a year after Nixon entered the White House, mutiny brewed. Half of Mitchell's "line attorneys" in the Justice Department were in a rebellious mood, and HEW functionaries were hopping mad. However, the implacable Mitchell won out, and the top HEW official in charge of enforcing integration guidelines was fired.

The symptomatic episode took place in Mississippi during the first summer of the new administration. In August 1969 Secretary Finch and the head of Mitchell's civil rights division shocked integrationists by asking a federal court to postpone the date scheduled for desegregating Mississippi school districts. Appalled by this turnaround in federal policy, the NAACP's legal arm asked to have the United States switched from plaintiff to defendant on the grounds that it was now in league with white racists. "The United States Government," the NAACP Fund's attorney said, "for the first time has demonstrated that it no longer seeks to represent the rights of Negro children." The Court of Appeals granted the government the reprieve it sought, but that October the Supreme Court in *Alexander* v. *Holmes* ruled unanimously (in Chief Justice Burger's first big decision) that Mississippi schools must be desegregated "at once."

In large part as a result of such stipulations by the federal courts, the Nixon years saw a rapid acceleration in desegregating schools, despite the rhetoric of the Southern strategy. The proportion of Negro students in all-black schools dropped strikingly from 68 percent in 1968 to 18 percent in 1970. Much of the advance represented the culmination of forces set in motion by the courts and by the Johnson administration, especially after HEW established guidelines in 1966. But the Nixon administration made important contributions too. Sometimes it moved aggressively, as when it filed suit against the entire state of Georgia to require an end to dual school systems. More often it acted quietly; the White House refused even to take credit for gains. The achievement of Nixon lay, as John Osborne has written, "in cozening the White South" into thinking he would forestall an inevitable process and thereby lowering resistance to the dismantling of the Jim Crow apparatus, which had finally begun to move at more than deliberate speed.

Moynihan, in a memorandum to the President in March 1970, pointed to the "extraordinary progress" that Negroes had been making in other fields as well. Over the past four years, black enrollment in colleges had increased 85 percent; registration had soared from 27,000 in 1930 to 434,000 in 1968. An American Negro had a better chance of going to college than did a German youth. Median family income for blacks was higher than for British whites. By 1968, 21 percent of nonwhite families were in the above $10,000-a-year bracket (compared to 3 percent in 1947). They were now full-fledged members of the consumer culture, although these increments were frequently due to the fact that families had more than one breadwinner. Over that same 1947–1968 period, the proportion of nonwhite families receiving under $3000 annually (in dollars of the same purchasing power) declined from 60 percent to 23 percent. In many areas integration had moved well beyond tokenism. It was hard to believe that an enterprise like major league baseball had been all-white in 1945; on one occasion in the recent period the Pittsburgh Pirates fielded an all-black nine. Four years after George Wallace stood in the doorway, the University of Alabama had nearly three hundred black students.

In spite of these accomplishments, black Americans viewed the Nixon administration with dismay. "For the first time since Woodrow Wilson," said the chairman of the board of the NAACP, "we have a national administration that can be rightly characterized as anti-Negro." The attainments to which Moynihan and others pointed with pride had largely been consummated in the Johnson years, not under Nixon. In fact, the Nixon recession halted economic improvement and resulted in a rise in black unemployment, especially for inner city youths. Most important, blacks understood that while Nixon would continue to move along some of the paths cleared by his predecessors, he would not run risks to blaze new trails. In particular, he would not act against de facto segregation in housing, North or South, nor would he approve expedients like busing to bring about racial balance in the schools.

Once again, external forces pushed the Nixon administration to a more centrist position, but not for long. In April 1971, in the Charlotte, North Carolina, school case, the Burger Court ruled, again 9 to 0, that cities must bus pupils out of their neighborhoods if this was necessary to bring about greater integration. For a time, the administration went along; HEW included busing provisions in its desegregation guidelines for Austin, Texas, and Nashville, Tennessee. But the busing issue proved to be, quite literally, explosive. So fierce was white resistance in communities like Denver, Colorado, and Pontiac, Michigan, that school buses were firebombed. In March 1972 Nixon startled Congress by asking it to impose a moratorium on busing orders by the federal courts while Congress devised legislation that would sharply restrict busing for purposes of racial balance. (He also asked for $2.5 billion to improve education in impoverished school districts.) The House acceded to Nixon's basic proposal, and it required a determined Senate filibuster led by the Democrat, Walter Mondale of Minnesota, and the Republican, Jacob Javits of New York, to forestall full compliance with the President's anti-busing recommendations.

Nixon's racial policies had one important political aim: to outflank George Wallace. The main threat to the President's election in 1972 lurked in the prospect that Wallace would deprive him of indispensable votes on the right, whether he ran as a third-party candidate or, less likely, as the Democratic nominee. In the 1972 primaries the Alabama governor carried out his promise to "rattle the eye teeth of the Democratic party." He swept through primaries in the South, and ran a strong second in Northern states like Pennsylvania and Indiana. But on May 15, while campaigning in Maryland, Wallace was shot several times at close range by Arthur Bremer, a Milwaukee white described as "a confident loner." Again the consumer culture provided the venue. As Martin Luther King met death on a motel balcony and Robert Kennedy in a hotel kitchen corridor, Wallace was shot at a shopping center in Laurel. However, indicative of the muted violence of the Nixon era, Wallace survived, although the bullets left him paralyzed. On the following day, he demonstrated his political prowess by winning both the Maryland and the Michigan primaries, but he was too ill to continue in the race. Wallace's departure left Nixon with a monopoly of the right. His only concern was the possibility that the Democrats would name a strong candidate who could out-duel him for the crucial center.

To Nixon's relief, the Democrats turned not to the center but to the left, for Wallace's bid inadvertently facilitated the capture of the Democratic presidential nomination by a longshot, the liberal, antiwar Senator from South Dakota, George McGovern. By his powerful showing in the early primaries, Wallace contributed to the elimination of the frontrunner, Senator Edmund Muskie of Maine, who in January had pulled even with Nixon in the polls. With Muskie's popularity put in doubt by Wallace and by a hostile press and with Muskie forced to share middle ground with Humphrey, McGovern was able to win enough votes from the party's left sector to capture a series of contests in divided fields. After the ineffectual Muskie had been removed and Wallace rendered *hors de*

At the 1972 national convention, key figures in the Democratic Party unite. From left to right stand vice-presidential nominee Thomas Eagleton, Senator Hubert Humphrey, Congresswoman Shirley Chisholm, presidential nominee George McGovern, Senator Henry Jackson, Senator Edmund Muskie, and the former governor of North Carolina, Terry Sanford, president of Duke University.

NYT Pictures

combat, McGovern clinched the nomination by surviving a head-on confrontation with Humphrey in California. "Quite frankly, I am not a 'centrist' candidate," McGovern said. His constituency lay among the young veterans of the New Politics who had enlisted under Eugene McCarthy and Robert Kennedy four years earlier, newly enfranchised college students, minorities, and the welfare poor.

Much of the nation had only an indistinct impression of the Democratic nominee. "He appeared something of a hick, from South Dakota — or was it North?" noted his biographer. "Whichever it was, McGovern surely looked the part: a slow-talking, stiff-jointed rube in a shiny Sears Roebuck suit." As a speaker, he rarely electrified audiences. Washington correspondents reported: "His eyes go flat and lifeless on television. His voice struggles for passion and sounds like grace at a Rotary lunch." Yet McGovern had compiled an impressive record — Ph.D. in American history at Northwestern, professor at Dakota Wesleyan, Congressman, director of Food for Peace, United States Senator. A World War II bomber pilot who had earned the Distinguished Flying Cross, he had become one of the first opponents of the Vietnam War, and as an advocate of social reform, he was known as "the Prairie Populist." Above all, he had a reputation for integrity. "George is the most decent man in the Senate," Robert Kennedy once told a visitor. "As a matter of fact, he's the only one."

McGovern conceived of his effort as nothing less than a religious crusade. The son of a "hell-fire, come-to-Jesus" fundamentalist preacher, he modeled himself on the Social Gospel minister Walter Rauschenbusch and for a time had studied for the Methodist ministry. He had begun his campaign by pledging to appeal to "the better angels" of the national spirit, and one of his advisers likened him to Luther and Zwingli. At the Democratic convention, he borrowed a theme from an old hymn to urge, "Come Home, America." Some were moved by these evangelical entreaties. "Saint George will slay the dragon," placards read. But others felt that McGovern did not cope well with issues such as economic controls that could not be framed in scriptural terms and thought that beneath his quiet diffidence they detected an alarming self-righteousness.

Well before the Democratic convention, McGovern's crusade had run into difficulty in his own party. In the California primary, Humphrey riddled McGovern's proposal to give $1000 each year to everyone "from the poorest migrant workers to the Rockefellers," tax it back from the rich, and redistribute it to the needy. Humphrey showed that the proposition had not been thought through and denounced his rival as a radical who would tax the workingman to benefit those on welfare rolls. The former Vice-President also hit out at McGovern's intention to cut $30 billion from the Pentagon budget, a plan that worried large numbers of Americans whose livelihood depended on the Warfare State and upset those who suspected McGovern was an isolationist bent on reducing the United States to a second-class power. After the California primary, a poll found that 40 percent of Democrats who had voted for Humphrey preferred Nixon to McGovern.

The Democratic convention gave much of the nation its first look at McGovern's New Politics, and not all were pleased with what they saw. As chairman of his party's reform commission, McGovern had promoted changes in the rules that required increased representation for the young, women, and minorities, and these innovations paved the way for his nomination. The Miami convention was notably more peaceful than that four years earlier because, it was said, those who had been demonstrating outside in Chicago were now inside the convention as delegates. But many in the party, and in the country, found quota systems menacing and, since quotas were fixed only for a few selected groups, viewed them as elitism masquerading as democracy. Moreover, the reforms resulted in the displacement of many of the party's veteran leaders, notably when Mayor Daley and his contingent were unseated. Union leaders, mainstays of the Roosevelt coalition but vexed by the counter culture and often hawkish on the war, were so outraged that George Meany ordered AFL-CIO unions to be neutral in the forthcoming campaign. As one labor leader grumbled, "There is too much hair and not enough cigars at this convention."

The political neophytes, especially the minority pushing for planks like abortion law reform, reinforced the impression that McGovern was the candidate of the counter culture. In fact, he had been raised with a reverence for the Puritan ethic and preferred small town America to the big city. His views on cultural political issues like abortion, legalized marijuana, and amnesty for draft dodgers and deserters were fairly orthodox. Yet he had written a blurb for *The Greening of America* (which he thought contained nothing he had not learned from his father and in Sunday School forty years before), and his whole campaign was based on the belief that the center would not hold. Three years earlier, Richard Scammon had warned,

In the shadow of the Kennedys. At the Democratic national convention in July, 1972, George McGovern accepts his party's nomination beneath gigantic portraits of the two slain brothers, Robert F. Kennedy and John F. Kennedy. In the ensuing campaign, Senator McGovern sought unsuccessfully to use the Kennedy legacy as a road to the White House.

"If the Democratic image in the 1970s is basically one of a party oriented away from the center, toward beard and sandal rather than toward crew cut and bowling shoe, then it seems very likely that President Nixon and the Republicans will establish a dominant position in American politics."

McGovern capped his predicament by his handling of "the Eagleton affair." At the Miami convention, he appeared to have made a shrewd choice in picking as his running mate the likeable United States Senator from Missouri, Thomas Eagleton, a Catholic with good links to organized labor. But two weeks later, on July 25, Eagleton announced that he had been hospitalized three times for nervous illnesses and had twice received electric-shock therapy. "I am 1000 percent for Tom Eagleton and I have no intention of dropping him from the ticket," McGovern affirmed. Within a week, following an outcry in the press and a malicious column by Jack

Anderson, McGovern had forced Eagleton out. He then began an embarrassing search for a substitute that, after a series of turndowns, resulted in the selection of R. Sargent Shriver, a member of the Kennedy clan who had run the Peace Corps and the War on Poverty and was acceptable to Mayor Daley. McGovern had encountered unusual bad luck, and those who criticized his staff work and blamed him for inconsistency failed to apply the same measuring rod to Nixon. But the episode led to questioning of McGovern's judgment, his fidelity, his decisiveness, and of his most valuable asset, his integrity. Young idealists were disillusioned, and party regulars had added cause to defect. Asked if he would back McGovern, the Rhode Island state chairman replied that he was behind him "1000 percent."

The tribulations of the Democrats and McGovern's posture as a candidate of the left gave Nixon an insurmountable advantage. He became the favorite not just of Republicans but of all those independents and Democrats who had been distressed by the life styles of the 1960's. At their national convention, the Republicans put on display screen stars who embodied the certitudes of an earlier America—John Wayne, Jimmy Stewart, Glenn Ford, and Pat Boone—and the predominantly male gathering adopted a platform that paid tribute to women for their "great contribution . . . as homemakers and mothers." Many in the Roosevelt coalition still approved of social legislation and distrusted the GOP as the party of big business, but they were disturbed even more by the notion that McGovern was associated with runaway change. Eager to terminate American involvement in Vietnam, they were unwilling to accept blame for genocide. Forced to choose, they preferred Julie Eisenhower to Jane Fonda.

McGovern's strength as a candidate for the nomination proved a weakness in his race against Nixon. In the primaries, his uncompromising stands had won him the admiration of the left spectrum of his party. But when he offered undiluted observations during the presidential contest, saying that he would "crawl" to Hanoi and that it was better to "beg than bomb," he alienated the center of the electorate, where most of the votes lay. His attempts to shift direction and move toward the center were also fraught with peril. By wooing Mayor Daley and Lyndon Johnson, he tarnished his reputation as an advocate of party reform and a foe of the war. When he abandoned his scheme for $1000 "Demogrants" and said he would name the conservative Wilbur Mills as Secretary of the Treasury, he raised doubts about the depth of his commitment to income redistribu-

Julie Nixon Eisenhower speaks at a $1000-a-plate fund-raising candlelight dinner at the Alameda Plaza Hotel in Kansas City's Country Club Plaza. Women campaigners played an important part in the 1972 race, but advocates of women's liberation seemed to have less effect on the voters than traditionalists like the President's daughter.

tion. As a consequence, McGovern was thrown on the defensive and the main issue became not Nixon's vulnerable record but McGovern's character. Nixon was even able to run a "noncampaign" in which he almost never appeared at a partisan gathering, a situation admirably tailored to proving that he was the bringer of a politics of tranquility, however ill-suited to educating the public on the principal issues.

To the very end, McGovern persevered in his moral crusade

against Nixonism, but in a losing cause. He received an unexpected boon when intruders were caught red-handed at the Democratic National Committee headquarters in the Watergate, a hotel-apartment-office complex in Washington. Details were murky, but newspapers linked the raiders to the "Disneyland Mafia" of University of Southern California graduates in the White House circle and even to John Mitchell, who had managed Nixon's reelection campaign before his wife compelled him to resign. (Martha feigned innocence about the whole matter. "Why do they keep asking me about the Watergate affair?" she asked. "I never had any Watergate affair.") McGovern said the President headed "the most morally corrupt Administration in the history of the United States," and compared Nixon to Hitler in his conduct of foreign affairs. But since McGovern did not have the nation's confidence, his attacks seemed shrill, especially because the incumbent was no longer perceived as "Tricky Dick" but as "the President." Moreover, two weeks before the election, Henry Kissinger's announcement, "Peace is at hand," served to distract attention from the Watergate controversy. Although some expressed skepticism about Kissinger's statement, Nixon was able to face the electorate as a chief executive who had convinced two-thirds of the American people that he would be "better able to move the world closer to peace."

Nixon won a resounding victory with 45.9 million votes to McGovern's 28.4 million. His 60.8 percent of the popular vote gave him a greater share than that won by any presidential candidate save Lyndon Johnson. He swept to a 521 to 17 electoral triumph, losing only Massachusetts and the largely black District of Columbia; his electoral total came within two votes of matching FDR's all-time high. For Nixon, the results, which reached him on the tenth anniversary of his stormy "last" press conference when he had called an end to his career, climaxed a remarkable comeback. The "Great American Loser," he had twice come close to being dropped from the Eisenhower ticket, had succumbed to Kennedy in 1960, had been beaten in California in 1962, and had narrowly missed defeat in 1968. Now he had run better than Ike or any other nominee in the history of the Republican Party.

On the presidential line, Nixon opened gaping holes in the New Deal coalition. The Southern strategy paid off when the Republican candidate swept the entire region "from the Potomac to the Pedernales," a section that had been solidly Democratic as late as 1944. He took a majority of the urban vote, including cities like Cleveland, of ballots cast by blue collar families, of Catholic voters, and of Italian

Election of 1972

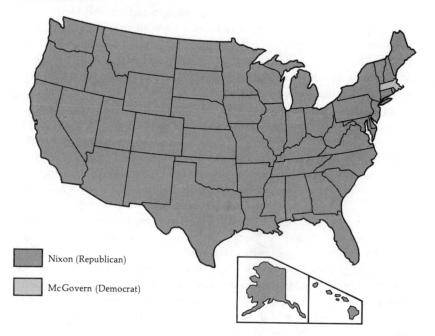

Nixon (Republican)

McGovern (Democrat)

neighborhoods (which had given him just 37 percent in 1968). Only black, low-income, and Jewish voters remained in the FDR alliance, although Nixon doubled his percentage in Jewish precincts in four years. The biggest disappointment for McGovern was the performance of young Americans. They gave almost half their ballots to Nixon and did not go to the polls in nearly the proportion of older voters.

Once again the center had held, in no small degree because Nixon had captured 65 percent of the votes of middle-income Americans who composed more than half of the electorate. The dimensions of the McGovern disaster sent Democratic politicians scurrying back to the center and caused second thoughts about the quota system. Farther to the left, Benjamin Spock's People's Party polled an abysmal 74,000. The candidate of the right, Representative John G. Schmitz, who had accepted the American Party's nomination after Wallace was shot, fared little better. Congressman from Nixon's California district, Schmitz said he had joined the John Birch Society to get the middle-of-the-road vote in Orange County. He castigated

McGovern as the favorite of "Hanoi and the Manson family," but he aimed most of his barbs at Nixon, who had become a Keynesian and had banqueted with Chou. "I'm not opposed to his visiting China," Schmitz remarked. "I'm only opposed to his coming back." Schmitz received a mere 1.1 million ballots and no electoral vote, far below Wallace's 9.9 million ballots and 46 electoral votes in 1968.

Yet for Nixon and the Republicans, the returns also had disquieting aspects. Despite the President's landslide victory, the Democrats maintained control of both houses of Congress; incredibly, they even picked up a net of two seats in the Senate. Nixon became the first President to begin two terms with an opposition Congress. The unprecedented ticket splitting confirmed that the country still was inclined toward the Democrats and supported Nixon less out of enthusiasm for him or his party than from distrust of McGovern. In fact, millions of Americans were so put off by the two candidates that they did not vote; turnout sank to the lowest percentage since 1948. Nixon's success suggested "the emerging Republican majority" that Kevin Phillips had foreseen, and in areas like the upper South it did seem that the Democratic hold had been broken. But in much of the nation the results indicated less a realignment than a transitory rebellion against a candidate who was not thought to be presidential timber. Fittingly, the consumer culture provided the stage for McGovern's final bow. After the defeated candidate checked out of his motel suite in Sioux Falls, South Dakota, on the day after the election, the marquee at the Holiday Inn read, "It's Over."

The verdict of the electorate implied that when the United States celebrated its two-hundredth anniversary in 1976 Richard Nixon would preside over the national stock-taking. For some Americans, especially intellectuals inspired by the departures of the 1960's, this was a dismaying prospect. Henry Adams once observed that contemplating the movement between fixed points in the line of Presidents from Washington to Grant had caused him to lose faith in the conception of inevitable progress; and for reformers the transition from Franklin D. Roosevelt to Nixon vividly highlighted the tribulations of liberalism since 1945. Some had apocalyptic fears —that the Nixon administration would eradicate the First Amendment, that America would become a fascist society, that the United States was doomed to decay as had other civilizations. Nixon himself in his 1972 State of the Union address had said: "I think of what happened to Greece and Rome and you see what is left—only the pillars. . . . The United States is now reaching that point." Such a fate, some felt, was only what the country deserved. "God punishes imperial nations," declared the theologian Harvey Cox, and he would punish America. To critics at home and abroad, Uncle Sam seemed to be on his last legs. In Britain, travel posters urged, "See America While It Lasts."

As Nixon began his second term, he seemed bent on proving that the Jeremiahs were right. Persuaded that what he referred to as his "rather massive majority" was a mandate for conservatism, the President abandoned any pretext of a centrist strategy. In his budget proposals, he slashed funds for medical services, eviscerated New Deal legacies like rural electrification, and liquidated Great Society projects such as community action. "Too much has been going to those who were supposed to help the needy and too little to the needy themselves," he said. He gave up altogether on his own programs for welfare reform and health insurance. The education segment of his budget, declared the veteran Kentucky Congressman Carl D. Perkins, was "an ill-concealed effort to repeal the nineteen-sixties." When Congress passed rural anti-pollution legislation and a "bill of rights for the handicapped," the President vetoed both measures. One of Nixon's first acts after his reelection was to dismiss the outspoken head of the Civil Rights Commission, the Reverend Theodore M. Hesburgh of Notre Dame, and in February 1973 the commission once more judged the President's performance "not adequate or even close to it."

Nixon's economic policies also took a turn to the right. On January 11, 1973, the President terminated most wage and price controls and substituted reliance on "voluntary cooperation." The decision gave a green light to businessmen and farmers to raise prices at a time when the economy was booming. The consumer price index in February 1973 registered the sharpest one-month jump since the Korean War inflation more than two decades before. The initiation of "Phase III" also encouraged new raids on United States currency, leading the President, on February 12, to devalue the dollar. The second devaluation in fourteen months meant that the dollar would buy still less just when the American consumer was running out of patience. In March, housewives began to organize a nationwide boycott of meat, which had risen in cost partly as a consequence of foreign demand. Determined not to pay runaway prices for hamburger, one angry housewife said, "I'd trap starlings first." To forestall the boycott, which proved largely unsuccessful, Nixon imposed price ceilings on beef, pork, and lamb, but not until they had gone sky-high. With inflation exceeding the worst record of the Vietnam War era, *Business Week* rendered its verdict: "Phase III is a failure." Worse was yet to come. In the fall of 1973 the Arab states clamped an embargo on oil while the Organization of Petroleum Exporting Countries (OPEC) was raising oil prices to unprecedented levels. Motorists queued up at gas pumps, fuel bills skyrocketed, and neither Phase IV nor any other Nixon policy assuaged the ire of consumers.

Liberals, admirers of a strong presidency since the age of FDR but unsettled by Lyndon Johnson's reign, developed far darker misgivings over Nixon's style after the 1972 election. No longer captivated by his role as Grand Unifier, the President adopted a pugnacious line. "I believe in the battle," he told a reporter. "I perhaps carry it more than others because that's my way." He warned the country against becoming "weak, soft and self-indulgent," denounced "soft-headed judges" and the "permissive philosophy," and urged Congress to attack crime "without pity." In December 1972, when Kissinger's preelection announcement of imminent peace proved premature, Nixon, exercising control of foreign affairs like an overweening sovereign, ordered the resumption of all-out bombing of North Vietnam and the mining of two North Vietnamese harbors. Commentators outdid themselves in reaching for historical parallels. A British journalist declared that Nixon was asserting "Robespierre's claim to personify the general will," while others favored the example of the imperious Charles de Gaulle. "Le Grand Richard," it was said, resembled France's late ruler in governing from a retreat in Maryland's Catoctin Mountains that suggested Colombey-les-Deux-Églises, in his conviction that history was on his side, and, most of all, in his contempt for legislators.

Conscious of the fact that his foreign policy was losing him friends both at home and abroad, Nixon did another of his about-faces, though it came too late to do much for his reputation as a statesman. A cease-fire agreement, signed in Paris on January 27, 1973, terminated the protracted United States military involvement in Vietnam, and within a month a similar arrangement had been negotiated for Laos. After March 29, no United States combat forces remained in Vietnam. Despite all his talk of "peace with honor," Nixon had acceded to a settlement that left North Vietnamese troops in the South and required the Americans to pull out. On the same day that the cease-fire accord was initialed, Defense Secretary Melvin Laird made another momentous announcement: The draft was at an end. For the first time in a quarter of a century, young men stood out from under the shadow of compulsory military service. However, the fighting among the Vietnamese went on, and American bombers continued to pound Cambodia. Moreover, Nixon repeatedly refused to acknowledge congressional authority either in the realm of foreign relations or in domestic affairs.

Only days after Nixon's second inauguration, Washington reverberated with outcries about a "constitutional crisis." In brazen defiance of congressional authority, the administration began to dismantle the Office of Economic Opportunity, an action that the federal courts subsequently halted. The President aroused still greater furor by impounding billions of dollars appropriated by Congress, though he was not the first chief executive to take such action. "The power of the purse," insisted Senator Sam J. Ervin, Jr., "belongs to Congress, and Congress alone." But the greatest indignation of all arose over the administration's assertion of the doctrine of executive privilege to deny the Senate Judiciary Committee the right to question White House aides like John W. Dean III, the President's counsel, about "the Watergate affair." Attorney General Richard G. Kleindienst affronted lawmakers, Republican as well as Democrat, by postulating that the President could bar any of the 2.5 million employees of the executive branch from testifying before Congress. Unable to sustain this dubious proposition, the administration was forced to back down.

The Watergate episode rapidly assumed the dimensions of the most noisome political scandal of the twentieth century. By April, each morning's headlines blazoned a new revelation. The burglars were quickly convicted, but the matter did not end there. Relentless pressure from newspapers, especially *The Washington Post*, Senators from both parties, and Federal Judge John J. Sirica forced other disclosures that had extensive repercussions. Former Attorney General Mitchell admitted that he had met with some of the conspirators on three occasions prior to the break-in, although he insisted that he had opposed the scheme. L. Patrick Gray III, acting director of the FBI, resigned after it was learned that he had destroyed documents pertaining to the case, reportedly on instructions from White House officials. On that same day the judge in the Pentagon Papers trial announced that two Watergate culprits, with the connivance of White House aides and with bogus identity papers and disguises furnished by the CIA, had burglarized the office of Daniel Ellsberg's psychiatrist, one of several bizarre incidents that would shortly lead to a mistrial and a blunt rebuke to the Nixon administration. A separate transaction to employ *agents provocateurs* to eliminate the strongest Democratic presidential contenders in the 1972 primaries was also traced to the White House. "It's beginning to be like Teapot Dome," said Senator Goldwater.

Throughout the march of events, Nixon cut a sorry figure. Although the crime was discovered on June 17, 1972, the President failed to speak out until April 18, 1973, save to claim that an investigation had cleared everyone presently employed in the White House. During that period, his deputies heaped abuse on those who were trying to ascertain the truth. When after a lapse of ten months Nixon finally condemned "any attempts to cover up in this case," sanctimony no longer sufficed. This "grubby" business, as the Republican national chairman called it, moved in ever-widening circles to encompass the impact of huge campaign contributions on administrative decisions, the activities of giant corporations like International Telephone and Telegraph at home and overseas, and allegations that the President's closest advisers were deeply implicated in illegal activity. On April 30, Nixon yielded to the clamor. Haldeman, Ehrlichman, Dean, and Kleindienst all resigned, Dean, it was made clear, at the President's behest. Yet even at that late date Nixon, in a nationally televised address, offered a self-serving defense remarkable for its lack of candor, its obfuscation, and its self-pity.

On May 17 a special Senate committee opened televised hearings under the chairmanship of the good-natured but tough-minded North Carolina Democrat, Sam Ervin. Over the next several weeks, witnesses from the administration confessed to burglary, bugging, perjury, "dirty tricks," and tampering with judicial proceedings, and told tales of political surveillance, shredded evidence, blackmail, and pledges of executive clemency to buy silence. Increasingly, the chicanery appeared to be much worse than in Teapot Dome, for it involved not simple peculation but the much more fundamental matter of subversion of the democratic process by attempting to rig an election. Yet so bewildering was the welter of charges, counter-charges, and denials that the public found it difficult to sort out the truth, and by early summer it seemed that the wrongdoers might get off scot-free.

In early July, though, came an astonishing development. Inadvertently, a White House official revealed that for the past two years the President's conversations had been systematically taped, a secret known only to a few of his closest aides. Incredibly, but in another sense predictably, Nixon, who showed so little sensibility to the right of privacy of others, had bugged himself. It was a crucial error, because if the discussions on these tapes were ever revealed, Nixon was done for, and he knew it. Hence, he embarked on a cover-up of the original cover-up, a long and bitter struggle in which he exploited to the full the doctrine of executive privilege.

While Nixon fought a rearguard action to deny anyone access to the tapes, disaster struck from another quarter. On October 10, 1973, Spiro Agnew resigned as Vice-President of the United States just before he was to face a federal judge in Baltimore. Agnew, who had made a career out of denouncing judges who were "soft on criminals," plea-bargained his way out of a likely prison term by pleading nolo contendere (no contest) to a charge of tax evasion in return for the modest penalty of a $10,000 fine and three years' probation. However, as part of the arrangement, the U.S. attorney general revealed in detail the evidence that Agnew had received some $100,000 in bribes from contractors when he was governor of Maryland, with payments continuing after he became Vice-President.

Ten days after Agnew's downfall, Nixon suffered another severe blow, which resulted from his earlier decisions to name Archibald Cox of Harvard Law School as special Watergate prosecutor and Elliot L. Richardson as his new attorney general. Nixon should have known better than to put his faith in honest men. When Cox was appointed, the White House had stated that he would have "complete independence," and the prosecutor took that pledge so seriously that when Nixon rejected requests to turn over important sections of the tapes, Cox threatened to go to court. The President retaliated by ordering Cox fired. Unfortunately for Nixon, neither Richardson nor his deputy, William D. Ruckelshaus, were toadies, and each in turn refused to carry out that order. So, on October 20, Nixon discharged Richardson and Ruckelshaus. Solicitor-General Robert H. Bork then obliged the President by getting rid of Cox. This "Saturday night massacre" made a shambles of Nixon's promise of an independent investigation, and caused many Americans for the first time to comprehend that the President was deeply implicated in the Watergate scandal.

Nixon tried to brazen it out, but to no avail. In his State of the Union message in January 1974, he declared, "One year of Watergate is enough," and urged the country to turn its attention elsewhere. He added, "I want you to know that I have no intention whatever of ever walking away from the job that the American people elected me to do." By April, however, court orders and public pressure forced him to release transcripts of some of the tapes. Though they were carefully edited to eliminate embarrassing material, they shocked the nation by showing that White House councils of state resembled gatherings of Mafiosi. On one occasion, John Ehrlichman, who on television looked, it was observed, like "a snarling prune," said of the acting FBI director Patrick Gray, "Let him twist slowly, slowly in the wind." Nor did the release of the transcripts resolve the question of the President's guilt, for it developed that some tapes contained suspicious gaps, including one of $18\frac{1}{2}$ minutes in the record of a crucial meeting. As a result, the clamor for more information grew still louder.

Events moved relentlessly to seal Nixon's doom. As one after another of his former lieutenants confessed to, or was convicted of, criminal acts, the President's house collapsed about him. (Ultimately, twenty-five members of his administration would go to prison, including his two chief factotums, Haldeman and Ehrlichman, and John Mitchell, the first time a man who had held the post of attorney general was so disgraced.) Late in July, the House Judiciary Committee voted three articles of impeachment of President Nixon for his role in the Watergate cover-up, for manipulating and misusing the Internal Revenue Service and other federal agencies, and for refusing to give Congress tapes it had subpoenaed. Even at that late hour it was conceivable that Nixon could escape removal by the Senate, since no one had yet found the "smoking pistol" — the piece of evidence that would link the President ineluctably to the Watergate affair. However, when the Supreme Court ordered him to do so, Nixon yielded additional tapes; one of these showed that Nixon had been up to his ears in the cover-up conspiracy from the very beginning, thereby providing the long-sought smoking pistol. With that, his most loyal supporters in Congress abandoned him, and three days after he released the tapes, he accepted his fate. On August 8, 1974, Richard Milhous Nixon announced that he was resigning as President of the United States.

When the curtain ran down on the main act of the Watergate drama, analysts had their first opportunity to reflect on the long-range significance of what had transpired. To some, the scandal exposed all that had been wrong with America since 1945. The conspiracy, it was remarked, revealed the cold war obsession of Alger Hiss's nemesis from the 1940's and the reckless adventurism of the Bay of Pigs in the 1960's; in fact, the burglary team had been recruited from

"All the News That's Fit to Print"

The New York Times

LATE CITY EDITION
Weather: Partly cloudy today; cool tonight. Fair, pleasant tomorrow. Temp. range: today 65-78; Thursday 64-81. Highest Temp.-Hum. Index yesterday: 75. Details on Page 96

VOL. CXXIII..No. 42,566   © 1974 The New York Times Company   NEW YORK, FRIDAY, AUGUST 9, 1974   15 CENTS

NIXON RESIGNS

HE URGES A TIME OF 'HEALING'; FORD WILL TAKE OFFICE TODAY

'Sacrifice' Is Praised; Kissinger to Remain

By ANTHONY RIPLEY
Special to The New York Times

WASHINGTON, Aug. 8—"I will pledge to you tomorrow Vice President Ford praised and in the future, my best efforts in cooperation, leadership President Nixon tonight for "one of the greatest personal sacrifices for the country and for America and good for the one of the finest personal decisions on behalf of all of us as Americans."

Mr. Ford, who will take office as the 38th President at noon tomorrow, vowed to continue Mr. Nixon's foreign policy and announced that Secretary of State Kissinger had agreed to stay on in the new Administration.

"I pledge to you tonight, as

SPECULATION RIFE ON VICE PRESIDENT

Some Ford Associates Say Selecting a Successor Could Take Weeks

By CHRISTOPHER LYDON
Special to The New York Times

WASHINGTON, Aug. 8—Potentially the most revealing first most important decision of Gerald R. Ford's Presidential debut — his choice of a successor in the Vice Presidency — was a much-discussed mystery here today.

Close friends of Mr. Ford continued to feed speculation about more than a dozen possible candidates. But none of the friends claimed to have discussed the Vice-Presidential be speaking for him on it. A number of Ford associates thought he might hold off the decision for days or even weeks.

"Everybody's on tenterhooks up here," a Senator remarked this afternoon in a telephone interview from the Republican cloakroom, "but I think they're wasting their time. It's going to be a week or two. So far he say he's a loner on this issue."

Former Defense Secretary of Melvin R. Laird, a Ford counselor in the House for more than a decade, was being quoted again today as saying he believes that Nelson A. Rockefeller—

Continued on Page 4, Column 1

Continued on Page 4, Column 1

Vice President Ford meeting with newsmen last night

President Nixon on TV as he announced his resignation

The 37th President Is First to Quit Post

By JOHN HERBERS
Special to The New York Times

WASHINGTON, Aug. 8—Richard Milhous Nixon, the 37th President of the United States, announced tonight that he had given up his long and arduous fight to remain in office and would resign, effective at noon tomorrow.

At that hour, Gerald Rudolph Ford, whom Mr. Nixon nominated for Vice President last Oct. 12, will be sworn in as the 38th President, to serve out the 895 days remaining in Mr. Nixon's second term.

Less than two years after his landslide re-election victory, Mr. Nixon, in a conciliatory address on national

Text of the address will be found on Page 2.

television, said that he was leaving not with a sense of bitterness but with a hope that his departure would start a "process of healing that is so desperately needed in America."

He spoke of regret for any "injuries" done "in the course of the events that led to this decision." He acknowledged that some of his judgments had been wrong.

The 61-year-old Mr. Nixon, appearing calm and resigned to his fate as a victim of the Watergate scandal, became the first President in the history of the Republic to resign from office. Only 10 months earlier Spiro Agnew resigned the Vice-Presidency.

Speaks of Pain at Yielding Post

Mr. Nixon, speaking from the Oval Office, where his successor will be sworn in tomorrow, may well have delivered his most effective speech since the Watergate scandals began to swamp his Administration in early 1972.

In tone and content, the 15-minute address was in sharp contrast to his frequently combative language of the past, especially his first "farewell" appearance—that of 1962, when he announced he was retiring from politics after losing the California gubernatorial race and declared that the news media would not have "Nixon to kick around" anymore.

Yet he spoke tonight of how painful it was for him to give up the office.

"I would have preferred to carry through to the finish whatever the personal agony it would have involved, and my family unanimously urged me to do so," he said.

Puts 'Interests of America First'

"I have never been a quitter," he said. "To leave office before my term is completed is opposed to every instinct in my body." But he said that he had decided to put "the interests of America first."

Conceding that he did not have the votes in Congress to escape impeachment in the House and conviction in the Senate, Mr. Nixon, said, "To continue to fight through the months ahead for my personal vindication woul- almost totally absorb the time and attention of the President and the Congress in a period when our entire focus should be on the great issues of peace abroad and prosperity without inflation at home."

"Therefore," he continued, "I shall resign the Presidency effective at noon tomorrow. Vice President Ford will take

Continued on Page 3, Column 1

POLITICAL SCENE SHARPLY ALTERED

G.O.P. Prospects Improved, Ford in Good Spot for '76 and Watergate Fades

By R. W. APPLE Jr.
Special to The New York Times

WASHINGTON, Aug. 8—President Nixon's resignation drastically altered the American political landscape.

It improved Republican prospects for the Congressional elections in November, thrust Vice President Ford into the Presidential election, ended the Watergate agony that has served to bind together the heterogeneous Democratic party and removed from the political stage the man who was the dominant Republican for the last 15 years.

In a larger sense, it seemed to presage an era of more open government, of more cooperation and less antagonism between Capitol Hill and the White House and of decline of the imperial Presidency that has marked the era since World War II.

Speaks Outside Home

Speaking without notes or a prepared text, Mr. Ford pledged to continue the Nixon foreign policy and called the Secretary of State "a very great man" whom he has known for many years.

On domestic politics, he said that he had been "very fortunate in my lifetime" to have adversaries in Congress but said that he did not think he had "a single enemy" there.

Mr. Ford said, "The net result is that I think tomorrow I can start out working with Democrats and with Republi-

Continued on Page 4, Column 2

Rise and Fall
Appraisal of Nixon Career

By ROBERT B. SEMPLE Jr.

The central question is how a man who won so much could have lost so much. How could a public figure who so well perceived the instincts of the majority of his countrymen have misused the powers and duties those same countrymen so eagerly ceded him?

The historians will be kept busy on these questions, for those who spent their time observing Mr. Nixon for the last six years the answer will well be found in a phrase he often applied to himself. "At bottom," he used to say, "I am a political man."

By his own description, this was a man of action rather than contemplation, a tactician rather than a theologian, a student of technique who seemed always impatient with such abstractions as loyalty and love, a figure whose exceptional antennae seemed incapable of self-deception but who at the end seemed incapable of seeing the extent to which he had ensnared himself and even hide what lay at the core.

To his enemies, he was both manipulative and synthetic; to his friends, a pragmatist unencumbered by inflexible principles; to those who watched him, a man who learned to be before he had learned to walk

Continued on Page 11, Column 1

and who, on reaching his destination, was not always certain what to do when he got there—except, perhaps, to keep going.

That image has only been reinforced and deepened by the transcripts of three conversations with H. R. Haldeman on June 23, 1972, six days after the Watergate break-in, which were released on Aug. 5, and the edited transcripts of White House conversations published April 30. Whatever history's judgment of those tapes, this much was clear: Faced with mounting evidence of deception and wrongdoing in his own official family, he sought not to confront the issue but to manipulate it until himself became part of the deception.

Mr. Nixon used the words "I" of those tapes, this much was but in the end they became his epitaph—a possible explanation for both his success and his failure.

For if the words implied the presence of a talent for finding opportunities for political profit

JAWORSKI ASSERTS NO DEAL WAS MADE

Says Nixon Did Not Ask for and Was Not Given a Way to Avoid Prosecution

By RICHARD D. LYONS
Special to The New York Times

WASHINGTON, Aug. 8—Leon Jaworski, the special Watergate prosecutor, said tonight after President Nixon's resignation speech that no deals had been either made or offered that would have given Mr. Nixon immunity from prosecution on any charges that might stem from the Watergate scandal.

No Immunity Sought

Mr. Nixon did not ask for any immunity assurances from Mr. Jaworski before his resignation speech, the prosecutor said, adding that none had been offered.

As Mr. Jaworski put it, "The special prosecutor's office was not asked for any such arrangement or understanding and offered none."

"Although I was informed of the President's decision this afternoon, my office did not participate in any way in the President's decision to resign," the statement concluded.

Mr. Jaworski met earlier today with Gen. Alexander M. Haig Jr., the White House chief of staff, but that meeting was said to have been only for the purpose of informing the special prosecutor of what the President would say later in the day.

The meeting did not take place in the White House, presumably because Mr. Jaworski would have been recognized there, and his visit would have excited speculation.

Earlier today, there were moves in both houses of Congress to grant Mr. Nixon immunity from prosecution, but

Continued on Page 2, Column 4

The Other Major News

Wholesale Prices Up
A new upward surge of farm prices joined a big jump in industrial prices to produce the year's largest monthly increase in the wholesale price index. The rise for July was 3.7 per cent, seasonally adjusted, and 3.9 per cent before adjustment. Page 45.

Election Bill Voted
The House approved by a vote of 355 to 48 a broad campaign-finance reform bill. The measure would set limits on political contributions, provide candidates with some strict campaigning and provide subsidies for Presidential primaries, conventions and elections. The bill now goes to a House-Senate conference committee. Page 36.

Cyprus Talks Open
The foreign ministers of Greece, Turkey and Britain met in Geneva to try to work out an effective cease-fire on Cyprus and to tackle the political problems behind the fighting there. Page 16. On Cyprus, acting President

Glafkos Clerides named a moderate Cabinet stripped of any militant proponents of union with Greece.

Mr. Clerides, who will occupy the key posts of Foreign Affairs and Interior, left for Athens on his way to Geneva for the talks on a political settlement. Page 16.

10 Police Accused
Ten New York City police sergeants were arrested for allegedly participating in a "club" that collected more than $250,000 over a decade from legitimate businesses and illegal rackets operating in Queens. Page 41.

Meskill Named Judge
Gov. Thomas J. Meskill of Connecticut was nominated by President Nixon to a seat on the Federal bench. Mr. Meskill, a Republican, stunned the state Republicans earlier this year by deciding to run for a second term amid reports that he had been offered a judgeship. Page 38.

A Tiny G.O.P. Bastion Feels Loss and Relief

By PRANAY GUPTE
Special to The New York Times

SHELTER ISLAND, L.I., Aug. 8—Six years after he put it on the line, Evans K. Griffing and his car, Evans K. Griffing was stripped off his bold, red-lettered bumper sticker today that said "NIXON."

Mr. Griffing felt a sense of unease. So did hundreds of people in this conservative community 100 miles east of New York City.

In 1968 and 1972, Suffolk County gave Richard M. Nixon the largest single election plurality of any county in the United States. Today all that changed on Shelter Island.

As the hour of the President's resignation announcement approached, many islanders expressed both a feeling of hurt at having been "betrayed" by Mr. Nixon and relief that he was leaving office.

"We tried to say by him all the very end," said Thomas J. Jernick, the Town Supervisor. "But when he disclosed on Monday that he had covered

up his role in Watergate, we couldn't support him any more. He lied to us, and for a resident of the United States to lie is inexcusable."

"We really believed in Mr. Nixon" was a phrase used again and again by dozens of islanders today.

At the same time they spoke hopefully of the Ford Administration and of moving urgently to tasks long neglected—ending the nation's political turmoil and easing its economic distress.

Shelter Island has 1,800 year-round residents, most of whom are registered Republicans.

Only last June interviews with islanders indicated that whatever else Watergate had done, it apparently had not diminished Shelter Island's faith in Mr. Nixon. People said at the time that they felt the President was being vilified by the media

Continued on Page 7, Column 4

Only Nixon Is Serene At Sad White House

By PHILIP SHABECOFF
Special to The New York Times

WASHINGTON, Aug. 8—On the momentous message his 2,027th and penultimate day he had for his audience: that as President of the United States, with his staff and family some of the first healthy, living American President to leave office before his term expired.

At 12:30 this afternoon, the White House press secretary, Ronald L. Ziegler, announced that the President would dress the nation at 9 P.M.

Mr. Ziegler did not say whether the speech would be about. He did not have to. He risked self-control even when he was struggling vainly to keep himself under control as he left the rostrum of the packed but hushed briefing room at the White House.

The young women who work in the press office would normally be brash and chattering in the motions of their jobs while doing their work, today were subdued. Some were red-eyed, tears streamed down their faces.

Mr. Nixon did not loosen his self-control even when he talked of his "regret" and his "sadness" at leaving the Presidency. His delivery, with its familiar half-smiles, did not re-

Continued on Page 2, Column 8

anti-Castro elements. Others perceived disaster for the consumer culture values of the 1950's. In *The Washington Post,* Nicholas von Hoffman, commenting that Nixon's young aides summoned before the Ervin panel were "the first full suburban generation to take all their moral nourishment from Walt Disney," asserted: "Senator Sam and his colleagues . . . have set fire to Howdy Doody land, snipped the ears off the Mouseketeers and worked an intimidating devastation on the Decade of Johnny Unitas, the cool, well-behaved, crew-cut years of precision and technique." To Charles Reich, the oracle of the counter culture, the occasion was one for rejoicing. "The system itself," he declared, "has begun to self-destruct." But this was a minority view. In Washington, many were heartened by indications that Congress might be reclaiming its authority. "Watergate is the bursting of the boil" of presidential power, Senator Fulbright maintained. Abroad, some of the most anti-American journals contrasted favorably the vigor and resiliency of American institutions that insisted on a thorough investigation — a free press, Congress, the judiciary, political parties, government agencies, an aroused and informed public opinion — with the cynicism and repression in their own lands. Italy's ultraleft *Il Manifesto* startled its readers with the headline, "Long Live the United States."

Unlike the way many other nations react when a head of state is deposed, the United States managed the transition to new leadership as though the resignation of its chief executive was an everyday occurrence. As Vice-President by appointment, Gerald Ford fell heir to the office of president. He assumed his new duties with becoming modesty. "I am acutely aware," he said, "that I have received the votes of none of you." Promising an administration of "openness and candor," he proclaimed, "Our long national nightmare is over." It was a good beginning, and the country was visibly impressed. To be sure, there was nothing remarkable about Ford. If his friends recalled that he had been a star center at the University of Michigan, his critics pointed out that he had played in the days of single-wing football, which required of a lineman neither finesse nor imagination. But the country, after the Johnson and Nixon histrionics, was not looking for anything remarkable. It wanted someone who was simple, honest, unpretentious, with no delusions of grandeur, and in his first month in office Jerry Ford of Grand Rapids seemed such a welcome relief from his predecessors that the country took him to heart.

By a single deed Ford destroyed much of this good will only four

UNCLE SAM by Bill Mauldin. Copyright 1975.
Reproduced by courtesy of Bill Mauldin.

Uncle Sam on his 200th birthday. This cartoon by Bill Mauldin of the Chicago *Sun-Times*
indicates that the America that celebrated the bicentennial of its
independence was badly bruised by Watergate and other recent tribulations.
Uncle Sam's appearance indicates that he retains the will to survive
but that the earlier ebullience is gone.

weeks after he came to power. On September 8 the new President
announced that he was granting Nixon an unconditional pardon for
all federal crimes he "committed or may have committed or taken
part in" during his tenure. Nixon and "his loved ones have suffered
enough," Ford said. "Theirs is an American tragedy in which we all
have played a part." Some condoned Ford's decision because they

thought it was motivated either by the desire to spare the country the spectacle of seeing a former president of the United States in the criminal dock, or by concern, as was rumored, that Nixon might commit suicide. To others though, this action suggested a corrupt bargain between Ford and Nixon. Whatever the assessment, it seemed manifestly unfair that the former president's subalterns should go behind bars for carrying out his instructions while the chief malefactor, whom a grand jury had named an "unindicted co-conspirator," basked in the sunshine of San Clemente.

Many of Ford's policies also served to lessen his popular following, because they were so monolithic. So good-natured was the President in his personal relations that at first he was taken to be a moderate, but in truth he was more conservative than Nixon. The liberal Americans for Democratic Action scored his voting record from his final term in Congress as zero. As President, he continued to behave like a nay-saying Opposition Congressman. Ford vetoed a wide range of important legislation — federal aid to education, health care, and control of strip mining, among others — and when he vetoed a school lunch bill, a California Congressman denounced him as "the most veto-prone Republican President in the 20th century," for that constituted his thirty-ninth negative in little more than a year, outstripping Hoover's thirty-seven in a full four-year reign. In the White House Ford proved to be just as solicitous toward business and as indifferent to civil rights as he had been as a member of Congress. He instructed the chairmen of federal regulatory agencies to do as little regulating of business as possible in the interest of "maximum freedom for private enterprise," and he was so hostile to measures like busing that the Civil Rights Commission accused his administration of accelerating a trend toward resegregation.

Ford approached the ailing economy in the same conservative mode. He had the bad luck to inherit a recession that had begun in November 1973, and his obsession with inflation at a time of rising unemployment and declining productivity made matters worse. By the spring of 1975, joblessness had climbed to 9 percent, the highest rate since 1941, and the real gross national product had fallen more sharply than at any time since 1929–32. (In one respect this slump, the most severe since the Great Depression, was even more troublesome than that of the early 'thirties, for it was accompanied by the steepest price increase in over a quarter-century.) During the recession, stock prices dropped more precipitously than they had in more than forty years, and New York City was revealed to be on the brink of bankruptcy. Throughout this period the economy was being supervised by the chairman of Ford's Council of Economic Advisers, a devotee of Ayn Rand, author of that panegyric to the primitive American capitalist, *The Fountainhead,* and by the major-domo of the Federal Reserve Board, Arthur F. Burns, who slowed recovery by driving interest rates still higher. For his part, Ford passed out WIN (Whip Inflation Now) buttons, and when Congress enacted a massive tax cut to revive the economy, he vetoed it.

However, other forces acted to push Ford toward a more centrist position, a development with significant political reverberations. Three months after he entered the White House the Democrats rolled up their biggest congressional victory in a decade in the 1974 mid-term elections. Though the reconstituted legislature was far from being the "veto-proof Congress" Ford had warned voters against in vain, it did succeed in overriding his vetoes of several pieces of social welfare legislation and in coaxing him to approve measures to stimulate the economy. In part as a consequence, the economy started to climb out of the trough in the summer of 1975. This trend had two conflicting effects. On the one hand, it improved the President's chances of winning election to a full term in 1976. But on the other hand, Ford's move toward the Center, which involved not only a turnabout on increased spending but also his choice of Nelson Rockefeller to be vice-president, engendered such deep hostility from right-wing Republicans that Ford barely succeeded in overcoming Ronald Reagan's bid to wrest the GOP nomination from him. Leader of a mutinous party, author of unpopular economic programs, President only by virtue of the fact that he was Nixon's designee, Ford seemed a sure loser. As one prominent Democrat put it, "We could run an aardvark this year and win."

To oppose Ford in 1976, the Democrats nominated not an aard-vark but almost as improbable a choice — James Earl Carter, Jr., a Georgia peanut farmer-businessman who had served one term as governor of his state but was otherwise all but obscure. When he started out on the long road to the White House, Carter had a na-tional recognition factor of only 2 percent. It seemed inconceivable that the Democrats would choose someone who held no office, who had no power base, and who came from a part of the Deep South where the most popular song was "Drop Kick Me, Jesus, Through the Goal Posts of Life." But Carter campaigned harder than anyone else, did his homework thoroughly (from "A for Abortion" through "Z for Zaire"), took ample advantage of the reforms that provided for a more open nomination procedure, and benefited from the circumstance that Democrats, having suffered through the McGovern folly in 1972, gravitated toward a candidate of the Center.

Above all, Carter recognized how Watergate had changed the public mood. The fact that he was an outsider with no connection to Washington proved an asset, and Carter campaigned on the promise that he would overhaul the "bloated unmanageable bureaucracy" in the national government. A Sunday School teacher and missionary of Billy Graham's evangelical Baptist faith, he not only won the support of other "born-again" Christians who had undergone the experience of conversion, but sewed up "the truth vote." At a time when the country thought a man's character might be more relevant than his program, Carter told voters, "I'll never tell a lie." He wanted, he said, a government "as filled with love as are the American people." Yet he was no simple-minded rural fundamentalist. He perused Dylan Thomas and Reinhold Niebuhr, had been a naval officer and a nuclear engineer, was fond of Bob Dylan and the Allman Brothers, and had hung Martin Luther King's portrait in the Georgia Capitol. In a series of primary races, Carter blew away his Democratic rivals, and when he emerged from the national convention with his party's nomination, he held what appeared to be an insurmountable lead over Gerald Ford in the contest for the Presidency.

The ensuing campaign turned out to be even more vacuous than most, and it nearly cost Carter the presidency. The struggle, said one Democratic senator, had "all the issue content of a student-council race." So shallow were Carter's speeches, and so fuzzy was the impression the Georgian conveyed, that he left himself open to Ford's charge that "he wavers, he wanders, he wiggles, and he waffles." Voters found it hard to know what to make of a man who acted as though he had invented piety but who sanctioned a *Playboy* interview in which he said "I've looked on a lot of women with lust" and used phrases like "shacks up" and "screws," and another with Norman Mailer in which he used a term for sexual intercourse that, as Mailer put it, was "a word that the *Times* has refused to print for 125 years." By the eve of the election, Carter's 33-point lead had shriveled to nothing, and it seemed that Ford, who had survived two assassination episodes in California, might win out. However, Ford could not shake off the impression that he was a bumbler. In a televised debate with Carter, this long-time cold warrior made himself appear stupid, and, incredibly, soft on communism by saying "there is no Soviet domination of Eastern Europe." Nor was he helped by his Secretary of Agriculture, Earl Butz, who had to resign after making a vile racial quip which was reported in, of all places, *Rolling Stone*, by, of all people, John Dean. Given a choice between "fear of the unknown and fear of the known," the country decided, but only narrowly, that it would take a chance on someone new.

Carter, in polling 40.8 million votes (50.1 percent) to Ford's 39.1 million (48.0 percent), edged out his opponent 297–240 in the Electoral College, the smallest advantage since 1916. Carter's victory alliance resembled, but did not precisely duplicate, the old FDR coalition. Unlike Roosevelt, Carter lost almost the entire trans-Mississippi West, and unlike Roosevelt, he owed success in the South (where he swept every state but Virginia) to the votes of blacks and of evangelical whites and to the regional conviction that it was "time we had a president without an accent." Carter benefited, too, from the appearance on the ticket of Senator Walter F. Mondale, who after abandoning his own quest for the highest office because he could not face a year of "sleeping in Holiday Inns," proved to be much more effective than Ford's running mate, Senator Robert J. Dole. The most striking feature of the 1976 election was not the outcome but the turnout, the lowest proportion of all eligible voters since 1948. Alienated from the political process by Watergate, and distrustful of both candidates, millions of Americans made their feelings known on Election Day by staying home.

Jimmy Carter understood well enough what the 1976 results conveyed, and from his first day in office, he took it upon himself to attempt to rekindle faith in the American political system by demonstrating that the "imperial presidency" was a thing of the past. At his inauguration he wore not a morning coat and top hat but a business suit, and instead of riding back to the White House in an executive limousine he and part of his family strolled the whole way, along an avenue of milling well-wishers. In the weeks that followed he staged symbolic events like wearing a simple cardigan as he addressed the nation, accepting random phone calls from ordinary citizens, and spending the night at the home of a beer distributor in a Massachusetts mill town. When *Women's Wear Daily* raised a mild threat to this strategy by publishing an account of one of Rosalynn Carter's shopping sprees, the First Lady barred the reporter from her next trip, for the indulgences of the consumer culture did not synchronize with the image-making of the Carter government.

Observers found it easier to identify Carter's style than to cate-

Jimmy Carter. As he moved from his home in Plains, Georgia, to the White House, the President-elect sought to cultivate two impressions—that he was bookish and unpretentious. As chief executive, Carter abandoned the trappings of the imperial presidency for what *Newsweek* called "corn bread-and-cardigan atmospherics."

gorize the content of his administration. Carter's insistence on fiscal
restraint at a time of obdurate unemployment led one writer to call
him "the most conservative Democratic President since Grover
Cleveland." During the campaign Senator Dole had described Carter
as "southern-fried McGovern," but in the spring of 1977 McGovern
accused the new president of being addicted to "Republican economics" and stated that it was difficult to remember which party had
won the election. Carter's choice to head the Federal Reserve Board
so resembled his predecessor that he was said to be Arthur Burns's
"clone." Others, though, emphasized the more liberal features of the
Carter regime. It seemed neither fair nor accurate to describe as "a
warmed-over Gerald Ford" a chief executive who put through the
strip-mining control bill that Ford had vetoed, who waged a series
of battles on behalf of the environment, who persuaded Congress to
create a Cabinet-level Department of Energy, who fostered a massive
public works program and the first national youth employment law,
and who pardoned Vietnam-era draft evaders. Carter selected six
women ambassadors and named two women, one of them black, to
his Cabinet, and saw to it that there were six black ambassadors
(including those to West Germany and Spain), a black ambassador to
the United Nations (one of Martin Luther King's most devoted followers, Andrew Young), a black secretary of the army, a black
solicitor general, and black U.S. attorneys and marshals from North
Carolina to California. Still, most of his appointments were traditional, and his assistant attorney general, the first black to head the
government's Civil Rights Division, hoped that, in coping with segregation, "the courts would not overreach." The commentator who
came perhaps closest to the mark was James Reston, who observed
that Carter had centered himself "in the decisive middle ground of
American politics."

Critics often complained less about Carter's ideology than about
the quality of his leadership, which was more technocratic than inspirational. "Carterism may be totally lacking in the scourgings of
a Theodore Roosevelt, the cathederal summonings of a Woodrow
Wilson, the rollicking iconoclasm of an FDR," said Eric Goldman.
"Carterism does not march and it does not sing; it is cautious, muted,
grayish, at times even crabbed." That no doubt went far toward explaining why by the summer of 1978 Carter's popularity had fallen to
a lower point than that of any of the five previous presidents at the
same stage. Yet Carter might well have responded that many of the
very people who had been railing so loudly against the imperial

presidency were now griping because he was not imperial enough. Russell Baker, who noted in December 1977 that "if the Carter Administration were a television show it would have been canceled months ago," also pointed out that Carter had, after all, fulfilled his promise "to restore the Presidency to the arid, nuts-and-bolts business of governing under republican forms. This is what he has done, and of course it is dull, terribly dull." When Carter did sound a trumpet call, few heeded. In a notable address on the energy crisis, he borrowed a phrase from William James in invoking "a moral equivalent of war" and one from Chicken Little in warning, "The sky is falling." But Congress dragged its heels on his energy program, and the country did not seem to mind, for despite Carter's efforts half of the nation refused to believe that there was any energy problem at all.

Even some of Carter's liberal critics acknowledged that the President was constrained by a shift in the public mood in a more conservative direction. Whereas in the 1960's folk movements usually derived from the left, in the post-Watergate period the most active groups were those like "right-to-life" organizations that protested against the Supreme Court's decision invalidating state laws restricting abortions. In Miami, singer Anita Bryant led a successful campaign to repeal an ordinance guaranteeing the rights of homosexuals; in a number of state capitols, women opposed to the Equal Rights Amendment impeded its ratification; and in California, a last-minute drive by fiscal conservatives won a 2–1 endorsement by that state's voters for Proposition 13, which slashed property taxes, thereby jeopardizing essential social services. Finally, in June 1978, the Supreme Court appeared to be sounding retreat on all the years of advance since the *Brown* decision when, in a complex 5–4 ruling in the *Bakke* case, it declared that the medical school of the University of California at Davis violated the rights of a white applicant by reserving a specific number of places for blacks. The Burger Court had departed from the spirit of the Warren Court in previous rulings also by sustaining a gag order on the press in a notorious murder case, holding that both federal and state governments may bar the use of public funds for abortions, and ruling that neither the paddling of high school students nor a police raid in California on the Stanford *Daily* violated constitutional liberties.

Carter also had to contend with a rebirth of nationalism that had been submerged in the Vietnam War but was awakened in 1979 by the Iranian crisis (followed shortly by the Russian invasion of

Afghanistan) that left many feeling angry, frustrated, and impotent. In honor of the hostages held captive in Teheran, Americans tied yellow ribbons around trees, flew giant-sized flags, rang church bells each noon, and played songs like "Take Your Oil and Shove It." In El Paso, a shooting range allowed customers to fire all day for free at a target of the Ayatollah, and in New York an Ayatollah doll was merchandised with the message "Available for those who want to strike back. Make him your prisoner. Shipped to you behind bars. Act now — get rope, pins, other torture equipment. Fabulous gift item." Americans seized on evidence of national prowess, like the unexpected victory of a green U.S. hockey team over the USSR in the 1980 Olympics. When the team went on to win the gold medal, the crowd sang "God Bless America" and chanted "We're No. 1."

Even more costly to Carter than resentment over internment of the hostages was the performance of the economy. In 1980, the country experienced the second consecutive year of double-digit inflation, the first time that had happened since World War I. (The Tooth Fairy found it necessary to leave three times as much under a child's pillow as a generation before.) When, with Carter's approval, the Federal Reserve Board drove interest rates up in order to curb inflation, a severe recession ensued with rising unemployment and continuing high prices. Americans who found fault with Carter for failing to gain release of the hostages also blamed him for the economic predicament.

Carter could not overcome the double handicap of the faltering economy and the Iranian captivity. In the summer of 1980, he received the lowest approval rating (21 percent) ever recorded. "He is like the Cheshire cat in Alice in Wonderland," said a prominent Democrat. "He is disappearing in the trees and there is nothing left but the smile." That summer the Republicans, confident of victory, nominated for president the archconservative Ronald Reagan, the former movie actor who had served two terms as governor of California. Carter made some headway in the fall with voters appalled by Reagan's misstatements during the campaign, but it was not enough to offset the impression that he could not lead. A week before the election, the *New York Times* acknowledged that Carter had shown courage on issues like the Panama Canal, had made excellent appointments, and could boast of successes in his energy program, which included creation of a Department of Energy. But it also said that "President Wobble," as it called him, "seemed to be all sail, no boat."

The electorate agreed. It gave Reagan 43.9 million votes (50.7 percent) to Carter's 35.5 million (41 percent) with the independent John Anderson receiving 5.7 million (6.6 percent). Carter, with a meager 49 electoral votes to Reagan's 489, carried only six states and the District of Columbia. Furthermore, Republicans gained control of the Senate for the first time in more than a quarter of a century and added 33 seats in the House—almost all of the changes involved the dislodging of liberals by conservatives. As a consequence, some

The old cowhand. Everyone in Southern California, it has been said, comes from Iowa. This is, of course, an exaggeration, but Ronald Reagan, who first received public attention as a Des Moines broadcaster, proves the rule. Here the President, accompanied by his wife, Nancy, escapes the pressures of the White House at Rancho del Cielo, his cattle spread in the Santa Ynez Mountains, 100 miles from the metropolis of the Sunbelt, Los Angeles.

Michael Evans/Sigma

saw in the election a new age of conservative Republicanism, though, in fact, the outcome signified less a right wing realignment than dissatisfaction with Carter's leadership. Reagan's victory did represent a shift of power from the Frostbelt to the Sunbelt. His face bronzed from riding horseback on his ranch near Santa Barbara, Reagan reflected the demand of the newer communities for predominance. By 1980, San Diego and San Antonio had moved into the list of the ten most populous cities, displacing Washington and Cleveland, while San Jose had more people than either St. Louis or Pittsburgh.

On January 20, 1981, two weeks before his seventieth birthday, Reagan became the oldest man ever to assume the presidency and the first authentic representative of the consumer culture to enter the White House. He had been a radio announcer, movie actor, and television pitch man. Though he had been featured in films such as *Bedtime for Bonzo*, Hollywood regarded him less as a star than as a "second banana." On hearing that Reagan might run for governor of California, the producer Jack Warner reportedly said, "No, Jimmy Stewart for governor, Ronald Reagan for best friend." (Reagan resented this retrospective typecasting—remembered as the actor who never got the girl, Reagan insisted that he had always gotten the girl.) He had made his way to political recognition by doing television commercials for General Electric that established him as a conservative ideologue, but not even his associates regarded him as a profound thinker. "You could walk through Ronald Reagan's deepest thoughts," said a California legislator, "and not get your ankles wet."

During his first months in office, the scoffers found that they had underestimated Reagan, for he made a highly favorable early impression. Two weeks after he entered the White House, a writer in the liberal *New Republic* stated, "He is not the ogre that Jimmy Carter tried to make him, nor the ignoramus that he's been called in this column." Reagan benefited from the national rejoicing when the hostages left Iran on the very day he was inaugurated, though that happy event resulted not from his efforts but from Carter's. He chalked up points, too, when at the end of March he quipped with his wife and the hospital staff after a bullet from the gun of a would-be assassin pierced his lung. His popularity did not derive merely from such fortuitous events or from his genial manner. He proved to be so skillful a legislative tactician that his relations with Congress were compared to FDR's, and he was flexible enough to name a black and a woman to his Cabinet. Most important, he identified himself with an economic theory that promised a bright future for America.

Reagan offered the country the elixir of "supply-side economics" mixed with a strong draught of military spending. He predicted that a combination of tax cuts and reduced government regulation would spur investment to such an extent that there would be a great new era of expansion. Since nothing else seemed to be working very well, Congress was willing to stifle its doubts and give this prescription a try. In short order, Reagan persuaded Congress to slash personal income taxes for three years while scaling down social expenditures. At the same time that Reagan got Congress to cut various welfare programs that derived from the New Deal and the Great Society, such as food stamps and Medicaid, he pushed through vast increases in military outlays, a process already under way in the Carter Administration. Reagan proposed to shell out $1.5 billion on defense over five years so that by the mid-1980's, one out of every three dollars appropriated by Congress would go to the Pentagon. Though liberal critics charged that Reagan was transferring resources from the poor to the military-industrial complex and conservatives feared that stepped up armament disbursements would unbalance the budget, the President claimed that his plan would benefit everyone—on a rising tide of prosperity, all boats would float.

Well before Reagan's first year in office had ended, however, it was painfully clear that his program was not working. Reagan did succeed in lowering inflation, but at an unacceptable cost. In December 1981, unemployment reached the second highest monthly rate since the beginning of World War II, and statisticians recorded the greatest number of business failures in forty years. Steep interest rates put the American dream of owning a home out of the reach of millions. The administration, which had pledged a balanced budget, reluctantly conceded that Reagan would run the biggest deficit in history. This prospect led even Wall Street financiers, once enthusiastic supporters, to call upon the President to reverse course. Reagan nonetheless insisted on plowing straight ahead. He demanded still greater cuts in social spending, including the elimination or sharp curtailment of federal aid to two million students. Instead of starting his second year in office by addressing problems of the stagnant economy, he unveiled the "New Federalism," which asked for a major shift of national responsibilities to the states—yet another rejection of the legacy of the New Deal.

In virtually every aspect of his administration, Reagan seemed

determined to return America to the 1920's era of business supremacy. In a 1980 headline, the *Washington Post* had characterized
his philosophy as "A Vision of America Frozen in Time," and after
Reagan took office, he hung a portrait of Calvin Coolidge in the
place of honor in the Cabinet room. Not only did Reagan sponsor
conservative economic policies, but he disappointed civil rights
groups by advocating a weakened Voting Rights Act. Furthermore,
his Attorney General announced that the Justice Department would
not file suits to achieve school desegregation through busing. None
of the President's subordinates, however, aroused so much dismay
as James G. Watt. By proposing policies such as phasing out controls over strip mining, the Secretary of the Interior raised an alarming threat to the environment. Yet despite all of the concessions
business received, it failed to undertake the new investment that
Reagan had been counting on. In his second year, the President saw
much of his initial popularity evaporate, for he was accused of
being savagely unfair to the poor and with plunging the country
into hard times.

Reagan also bore the onus of association with the Moral Majority,
which hailed his 1980 victory as a triumph for its attempt to impose
its values on the rest of the country, much to the consternation of
those who viewed its credo as neither moral nor Christian. When
Congress voted to deny federal funding to indigent women for
abortions that resulted from rape or incest, the Oregon Republican
Senator Robert W. Packwood commented, "There is growing in this
country a Cotton Mather mentality." Reagan disappointed the
Moral Majority, however, by concentrating on economic rather than
social issues and by naming Sandra Day O'Connor, an Arizona
judge, to the U.S. Supreme Court. The main challenge to her confirmation came not from those who thought she had too little experience or was too conservative, but from those who charged that
she was "soft" on abortion. A Republican Senator from Alabama,
calling abortion "even more fundamental than the issue of slavery,"
stated that it was "the issue of the century, or perhaps the issue of
our history." Nonetheless, she was confirmed with little difficulty,
evidence that the television preachers' claim to be speaking for a
majority was farfetched. Before long, college students were displaying buttons with the message, "The Moral Majority is Neither."

In the Ford-Carter-Reagan era it often seemed that America had
turned its back on all that had been started during the 1960's. The
former black militant Eldridge Cleaver ended a seven-year exile

because he was "tired of living under dictatorships" and thought post-Watergate America was "really fantastic, beyond my wildest dreams or hopes." Earlier, another one-time Black Panther, Bobby Seale, had discarded his gun in an airport locker, for he wanted "to build a house, grow a garden, do some canning and barbecue"; while the one-time antiwar firebrand, Rennie Davis, had become a distributor of consumer culture items like kitchen sinks and drove a Mercedes—like the girl in the Eagles' "Hotel California" whose mind was "Tiffany-twisted" and who had "the Mercedes bends." On college campuses, once wracked by violence, students concentrated on "the almighty grade point average," and Mark Rudd came

The first woman Justice. This was not the first milepost for Sandra Day O'Connor, photographed here with Chief Justice Warren Burger—nine years earlier she had been the first woman elected as Majority Leader of a U.S. state legislature. An early advocate of the Equal Rights Amendment, she saw the time limit for ERA expire in her first year on the bench.

D. Gorton, NYT Pictures

out of years of hiding only to find that students at Columbia, where he had been the ringleader of the 1968 uprising, did not know who he was. In "Hotel California," a call for wine got the response that "We haven't had that spirit here since nineteen sixty-nine," and in "Before the Deluge," Jackson Browne sang of "the resignation that living brings." If Rip Van Winkle had fallen asleep in the Eisenhower era and awakened in the Carter years, he would find that little had changed, observed Russell Baker. "The growing public absorption in the hedonism of public pleasure and private consumption — the hunt for the ideal restaurant, the perfect head of lettuce, the totally satisfying human relationship" were "the current equivalents of the Eisenhower age's passion for bigger tail fins, drier martinis, darker steak houses and cozier evenings with the family."

Though such generalizations held a large kernel of truth, they understated how much America had been transformed since the 1950's. If some whites were grousing about "reverse discrimination," blacks nonetheless continued to score gains. In the Eisenhower era, Richmond, Virginia had been the bastion of massive resistance to civil rights; in 1978, the old Confederate capital had a black mayor. The Supreme Court took pains to point out that it was the rigidity of the racial quotas to which it was objecting in the *Bakke* case, not the principle of giving special consideration to race. True, only a bare 5–4 majority held that view, but less than a week after the Bakke decision the Court indicated that it was willing to go along with the idea of "affirmative action" when it sustained a decree compelling the American Telephone and Telegraph Company to make amends for past discrimination by hiring more blacks and women.

The position of women had also changed dramatically in the past quarter of a century, and not only because of affirmative action programs. Even in the Reagan era, two of the country's four largest cities — Chicago and Houston — had women mayors. One indication both of the shift in national attitude and of the rising political power of women is that the proponents of ERA readily won the approval of well over a majority of the states, although they fell a bit short of getting the required three-quarters of the states to ratify in the stipulated period. Much more significant in its long-range implications was the altered composition of the work force. By the time of the Carter presidency a majority of married women were gainfully employed. This "revolution in the roles of women" would "have an even greater impact than the rise of Communism and the development of nuclear energy," said the Columbia University economist Eli Ginzberg. "It is the single most outstanding phenomenon of this century. . . . Its secondary and tertiary consequences are really unchartable."

Partly as a result of the liberation of women, the trend toward a greater openness about sex continued, despite the apparent triumph of conventionality in the 'seventies. Once again the Supreme Court was called upon to be an arbiter. When Jacksonville, Florida restricted drive-in theaters from showing films with nude scenes because they would be visible to passers-by, the Court struck down the ordinance as a violation of free speech. Even America's First Ladies had come a long way since Mamie Eisenhower and Bess Truman. An ardent champion of women's rights, Betty Ford said that she would not be surprised if her teenage daughter had an affair, that she thought premarital sex might lower the divorce rate, and that she was not worried that her husband would stray because she kept him too busy between the sheets. Had interviewers asked her how often she slept with the President, she said, she would have replied, "As often as possible." In June 1981, more than 200,000 homosexuals paraded down San Francisco's Market Street, and Gay Pride Week was observed in Middle-American communities like Des Moines.

Still, for all the persistence of change, America did seem to have come to some kind of way station in the eighth decade of the twentieth century. One of the main themes of the commentary during the bicentennial celebration of 1976 was that the United States must accept a sense of limits—to its resources, to its potential for economic growth, to its national power. Hegel had once written that America was "the land of the future," and Lord Bryce had said that America "sailed a summer sea." But in the 1970's and 1980's, analysts were stating that the nation must lower its expectations, and were even voicing prophecies of doom. "No matter what we do," wrote Robert Heilbroner, "within one hundred years civilization as we know it will cease."

Though a sense of limits was no doubt appropriate in some spheres of national life and though there had been tawdry episodes in recent times, the doom-watchers did not concede enough to the accomplishments made during the years of the consumer culture and the cold war. If it would be too much to say, with Macaulay, "We have heard nothing but despair and seen nothing but progress," the progress had been substantial enough to make the voices of gloom seem strident. The most poignant fears of 1945 had not been realized. The country had not only escaped a recurrence of the Great Depression but had achieved a trillion-dollar economy, a feat that a British economist called "the most momentous news-story so far in the history of the world." By 1972, more than half of American families enjoyed an annual income of over $10,000. Twice since 1945 the United States had gone to war, yet the dreaded nuclear holocaust had not eventuated. As a consequence of Supreme Court decisions, the civil rights movement, presidential leadership, and congressional action, the political structure had been markedly democratized. It may turn out, as a black leader asserted after the *Bakke* decision, that the United States has halted in its effort to expand the rights of minorities and has come to a "plateau," but, should that be so, it is nonetheless a plateau—a high elevation— that the country has reached, not a valley.

"The major advances in civilization," Alfred North Whitehead once pointed out, "are processes which all but wreck the societies in which they occur." In the United States, the disorders of the decades after World War II resulted in large part from a willingness to face up to problems too long ignored. As Eugene McCarthy said in his farewell address to his followers in Chicago in 1968, "I think we can say that we were willing to open the box and to see what America was." The travail of liberalism derived in no inconsiderable degree from its accomplishments. Each achievement awakened new expectations and made the nation more aware of unexplored shortcomings. But as Herbert von Borch wrote in *The Unfinished Society*, "American society possesses virtually inexhaustible capacities for self-redress." There could be little doubt that this capability for self-renewal would be sorely tested in the remaining years of the unfinished century.

SUGGESTED READINGS

Historians have, curiously, given more probing attention to the 1960's than to the decade and a half immediately after the war. David Burner, Robert D. Marcus, and Thomas R. West, *A Giant's Strength: America in the 1960s* (1971), is a judicious appraisal. William L. O'Neill, *Coming Apart* (1971), views the same decade disapprovingly. Ronald Berman, *America in the Sixties* (1968), is an excellent intellectual history. For essays and documents of the period, see Edward Quinn and Paul J. Dolan, eds., *The Sense of the Sixties* (1968); Herbert Mitgang, ed., *America at Random* (1970); Murray Friedman, ed., *Overcoming Middle Class Rage* (1971); Walt Anderson, ed., *The Age of Protest*

(1969); and Patrick Gleeson, ed., *America, Changing* . . . (1968). The publications of *Congressional Quarterly* and of *Facts on File* are invaluable.

There is ampler coverage of national elections in the 1960's than for any prior decade. Theodore H. White contributed *The Making of the President, 1964* (1965) and *The Making of the President, 1968* (1969). For the 1964 contest, there is also available Harold Faber, ed., *The Road to the White House* (1965), a study by the staff of *The New York Times,* and Milton C. Cummings, ed., *The National Election of 1964* (1966). Lewis Chester, Godfrey Hodgson, and Bruce Page, *An American Melodrama* (1970), is a fascinating account by a team of British journalists who covered the 1968 campaign. Richard M. Scammon and Ben J. Wattenberg, *The Real Majority* (1970), explodes some popular myths about the electorate. Samuel Lubell, *The Hidden Crisis in American Politics* (1970), should be read in conjunction with Frederick G. Dutton, *Changing Sources of Power* (1971).

As a campaign biography, James MacGregor Burns, *John Kennedy* (2nd ed., 1961), is in a class by itself. Arthur M. Schlesinger, Jr., *A Thousand Days* (1965), and Theodore C. Sorensen, *Kennedy* (1965), are accounts by members of the slain President's White House staff. Louise Fitz Simons, *The Kennedy Doctrine* (1972), is much more critical. Helen Fuller, *Years of Trial* (1962), and Hugh Sidey, *John F. Kennedy, President* (1963), offer contemporary estimates by Washington correspondents; and Tom Wicker, *Kennedy without Tears* (1964), presents another journalist's views shortly after the President's death. Aida Di Pace Donald, ed., *John F. Kennedy and the New Frontier* (1966), is a well-edited anthology. James MacGregor Burns, *The Deadlock of Democracy* (1963), attempts to explain Kennedy's difficulties with Congress. Among the rapidly appearing monographs on the Kennedy years are Grant McConnell, *Steel and the Presidency—1962* (1963), and Jim F. Heath, *John F. Kennedy and the Business Community* (1969).

Eric Goldman, *The Tragedy of Lyndon Johnson* (1969), comes from a historian who served in LBJ's administration. Most of the estimates of Johnson are by journalists; among the best are Robert Novak and Rowland Evans, *Lyndon B. Johnson, The Exercise of Power* (1966), and Hugh Sidey, *A Very Personal Presidency: Lyndon Johnson in the White House* (1968). Perceptive accounts by foreign journalists include Louis Heren, *No Hail, No Farewell* (1970), and Michael Davie, *LBJ: A Foreign Observer's Viewpoint* (1966). The purport of Marvin E. Gettleman and David Mermelstein's *The Great Society Reader* (1967) is indicated by its subtitle: "The Failure of American Liberalism." Among the extensive writings on welfare and poverty, see Chaim I. Waxman, *Poverty: Power and Politics* (1968); Richard M. Elman, *The Poorhouse State* (1966); and Ben B. Seligman, ed., *Poverty as a Public Issue* (1965). For government and politics in the Johnson years, *Congress and the Nation,* vol. 2 (1969), is very helpful.

The change in the nature of Negro protest in the 1960's is well detailed in Benjamin Muse, *The American Negro Revolution: From Nonviolence to Black Power, 1963–1967* (1969), and Allen J. Matusow, "From Civil Rights to Black Power: The Case of SNCC, 1960–1966," in Barton J. Bernstein and Matusow, eds., *Twentieth Century America: Recent Interpretations* (1969). August Meier and Elliott Rudwick, eds., *Black Protest in the Sixties* (1970), is an excellent anthology of *New York Times* materials. W. Haywood Burns, *The Voices of Negro Protest in America* (1963), ends before "Black Power" became a rallying cry; so too does Bradford Daniel, ed., *Black, White and Gray* (1964). Martin Luther King, Jr., *Why We Can't Wait* (1964), is an eloquent statement published the same year as Charles Silberman's thoughtful *Crisis in Black and White* and Howard Zinn's *SNCC: The New Abolitionists.* James W. Silver, *Mississippi: The Closed Society* (1964), and Frank E. Smith, *Congressman from Mississippi* (1964), both relate the experiences of courageous white liberals. Donald R. Matthews and James W. Prothro, *Negroes and the New Southern Politics* (1966), is an important study by political scientists. Among the many articles on the riots, see Joseph Boskin, "The Revolt of the Urban Ghettos, 1964–1967," *Annals of the American Academy* (1969). Robert Conot, *Rivers of Blood, Years of Darkness* (1968), probes the meaning of Watts. Lee Rainwater and William Yancey, *The Moynihan Report and the Politics of Controversy* (1967), deals with an issue that divided the scholarly community. Matt S. Meier and Feliciano Rivera, *The Chicanos* (1972), is a history of Mexican-Americans. Edward Simmen, ed., *The Chicano: From Caricature to Self-Portrait* (1971), and Wayne Moquin with Charles Van Doren, eds., *A Documentary History of the Mexican Americans* (1971), give multifaceted views. Stan Steiner has written on Mexican-Americans in *La Raza* (1970) as well as on *The New Indians* (1968). Oscar Lewis, *La Vida* (1966), is a classic account of Puerto Rican acculturation.

Hugh Davis Graham and Ted Robert Gurr, *The History of Violence in America* (1969), is an important study that may be supplemented by an anthology, Thomas Rose, ed., *Violence in America* (1969). Henry Fairlie, "The Distemper of America: A Minority Report on Violence in the United States," *Interplay* (1969), is skeptical of some of the orthodox views. Richard Hofstadter's sensitive, wide-ranging "Reflections on Violence in the United States," in Hofstadter and Michael Wallace, eds., *American Violence: A Documentary History* (1970), is one of the last pieces written by this exceptional historian whose brilliant career was tragically cut short. Daniel Bell and Irving Kristol, eds., *Confrontation* (1969), and Nathan Glazer, *Remembering the Answers* (1970), deal with the campus uprisings. Seymour Lipset and Sheldon Wolin, eds., *The Berkeley Student Revolt* (1965), covers the first major campus outbreak, and Jerry Avorn et al., *Up Against the Ivy Wall* (1968), chronicles the Columbia tempest a few years later.

The standard works on the counter culture are Theodore Roszak, *The Making of a Counter Culture* (1969), and Charles Reich, *The Greening of America* (1970). Samuel McCracken's review of Reich's book in *Change* (1971) is devastating. Herbert Marcuse states his case in *An Essay on Liberation* (1969). Daniel Bell, "Sensibility in the 60's," *Commentary* (1971), is penetrating, and Seymour Martin Lipset, "New Perspectives on the Counter-Culture," *Saturday Review* (1971), suggests that not everything about that phenomenon is new. Kenneth Keniston, the most astute observer of youth, has written *The Uncommitted* (1965) and *Young Radicals* (1968), as well as such essays as "To Heal Our Society's Deep Rifts," *Journal* (1970). Hazel W. Hertzberg, "The Now Culture: Some Implications for Teacher Training Programs," *Social Education* (1970), is discerning on the time perspective of the young. For the movement to Haight-Ashbury and the East Village, see Lewis Yablonsky, *The Hippie Trip* (1968), and John Robert Howard, "The Flowering of the Hippie Movement," *The Annals of the American Academy* (1969). Among the more enlightening articles on the counter culture are Marcia Cavell, "Visions of a New Religion," *Saturday Review* (1970); Daniel Seligman, "A Special Kind of Rebellion," *Fortune* (1969); Peter L. Berger and Brigitte Berger, "The Blueing of America," *New Republic* (1970); and Anthony Scaduto, " 'Won't You Listen to the Lambs, Bob Dylan?' " *The New York Times Magazine* (Nov. 28, 1971).

William H. Chafe, *The American Woman* (1972), traces the history of women from 1920 to 1970. For supplementary material, consult Robert J. Lifton, ed., *The Woman in America* (1965), and Robin Morgan, ed., *Sisterhood Is Powerful* (1970). Carl N. Degler "Revolution Without Ideology: The Changing Place of Women in America," *Daedalus* (1964), is a trenchant appraisal. Articles on more recent developments include Helen Dudar, "Women's Lib: The War on 'Sexism,' " *Newsweek* (Mar. 23, 1970); and Susan Brownmiller, " 'Sisterhood Is Powerful,' " *The New York Times Magazine* (Mar. 15, 1970).

The first writings on a recent administration are often ephemeral, but the literature on the Nixon years is of a much higher order. Garry Wills, *Nixon Agonistes* (1970), is a stimulating, although often tendentious, study. Mark Harris, *Mark the Glove Boy* (1964), deals with Nixon before he became President. Bruce Mazlish, *In Search of Nixon* (1972), is a "psychohistorical inquiry." Among the more useful contributions by journalists are Rowland Evans, Jr., and Robert D. Novak, *Nixon in the White House: The Frustration of Power* (1971); Paul Hoffman, *The New Nixon* (1970); and Mel Elfin, "The President at Midpassage," *Newsweek* (Jan. 25, 1971). The *New Republic's* columnist, John Osborne, has written *The Nixon Watch* (1970), *The Second Year of the Nixon Watch* (1971), and *The Third Year of the Nixon Watch* (1972). Allen Drury, *Courage and Hesitation: Inside the Nixon Administration* (1972), and Richard J. Whalen, *Catch the Falling Flag* (1972), are by worried conservatives. Gore Vidal, *An Evening with Richard Nixon* (1972), is occasionally amusing, more often tasteless. Leonard Silk, *Nixonomics* (1972), is a witty explanation of "How the Dismal Science of Free Enterprise Became the Black Art of Controls." Nixon's Democratic opponent in 1972 is the subject of Robert Sam Anson, *McGovern* (1972). David S. Broder, *The Party's Over* (1972), expresses distress over "The Failure of Politics in America," while a much more approving view of the state of the nation may be found in Arnold Beichman, *Nine Lies About America* (1972). For the new decade, see The Editors of The National Observer, *The Seventies* (1970), and Leonard Freedman, ed., *Issues of the Seventies* (1970).

Almost all of the literature on Nixon's downfall and the history of the post-Nixon era has come from journalists. In the huge accumulation of writings on Watergate, see especially The Staff of the Washington Post, *The Fall of a President* (1974); The New York Times, *The End of a Presidency* (1974); Jonathan Schell, *The Time of Illusion* (1976); and Theodore White, *Breach of Faith* (1975). J. F. ter Horst, *Gerald Ford and the Future of the Presidency* (1974) is by a Michigan newspaperman who won respect for his integrity when he resigned as Ford's press secretary immediately after the Nixon pardon. Richard Reeves, *A Ford not a Lincoln* (1975) is more critical. The 1976 election is treated in detail in Jules Witcover, *Marathon* (1977), Martin Schram, *Running for President 1976* (1977), and Kandy Stroud, *How Jimmy Won* (1977). All three volumes deal extensively with Jimmy Carter, but the most ambitious study of him is James Wooten, *Dasher* (1978).

Serious writing on the Reagan presidency has not yet begun, but Ellis Sandoz and Cecil V. Crabb, Jr., eds., *A Tide of Discontent* (1981) is a good starting place for assessing the significance of the 1980 election.

Significant Statistics

	1900	1920	1932	1945	1960	1970	1979
Population	76,094,000	106,466,000	124,949,000	139,928,000	180,684,000	203,185,000	220,099,000
Percentage urban	39.7	51.2	NA	58.6	69.9	73.5	NA
Percentage rural	60.3	48.8	NA	41.4	30.1	26.5	NA
Percentage non-white	12.0	10.0	10.0	10.0	11.0	11.1	11.8
Life expectancy							
White	47.6	54.9	63.2	66.8	70.6	71.7	74.0
Nonwhite	33.0	45.3	53.7	57.7	63.6	64.6	69.2
Gross national product (current dollars)							
Total (billions of dollars)	17.3	88.9	58.5	213.6	503.7	976.8	2,368.8
Per capita (dollars)	231	835	468	1,526	2,788	4,807	10,745
Defense spending (millions of dollars)[a]	332	4,329	1,688	84,311	51,334	78,013	137,600
As percentage of GNP	1.9	5.0	3.0	40.0	10.0	9.0	5.1
Military personnel on active duty	125,923	343,302	244,902	12,123,455	2,476,435	3,065,508	2,024,000
Labor union membership	791,000	5,034,000	3,226,000	14,796,000	18,117,000	20,752,000	21,784,000
Birth rate (per 1,000 live births)	32.3	27.7	19.5	20.4	23.7	18.2	15.1
Advertising expenditures (millions of dollars)	542	2,935	1,627	2,874	11,932	19,600	49,720
Motor vehicle registrations	8,000	239,161	24,391,000	31,035,420	73,869,000	108,977,000	154,412,000
Persons lynched							
White	9	8	2	0	0	0	0
Nonwhite	106	53	6	1	0	0	0
High school graduates (as percentage of all persons over 16 years old)	6.4	16.8	NA	NA	65.1	78.4	NA

[a] Includes veterans spending; excludes interest.

Index